War's Ends

War's Ends

Human Rights, International Order, and the Ethics of Peace

James G. Murphy

Georgetown University Press
Washington, DC

Library of Congress Cataloging-in-Publication Data

Murphy, James G., 1953–
  War's ends : human rights, international order, and the ethics of peace / James G. Murphy.
  pages cm
  Includes bibliographical references and index.
  ISBN 978-1-62616-027-9 (pbk. : alk. paper)
  1. Just war doctrine. 2. Security, International—Moral and ethical aspects. I. Title.
  U21.2.M876 2014
  172'.42—dc23   2013018247

∞ This book is printed on acid-free paper meeting the requirements of the American National Standard for Permanence in Paper for Printed Library Materials.

21 20 19 18 17 16 15 14   9 8 7 6 5 4 3 2
First printing

Printed in the United States of America

Contents

Acknowledgments

In the course of planning and writing this book, I received much support and encouragement from many people.

My late father, Frank Murphy, educated me long ago on the primacy of the political, and the importance of civilian control of the military. He first got me thinking about these things, so it is fitting that he be acknowledged first.

I am deeply grateful to Pat Riordan, fellow-Jesuit, friend, and colleague at Milltown Institute of Theology and Philosophy in Dublin, Ireland, for many years. He read the entire draft carefully, and his critical comments made this a much better work than it would otherwise have been. His work on the common good has also been influential in the conception of this book. My thanks go also to the anonymous reviewers for Georgetown University Press, whose helpful comments were enlightening.

The intellectual stimulus of conversations with Bob Araujo, Tom Carson, Rudi Casals, Chris Curran, George Dempsey, and Vera Price was particularly valuable. The Jesuits of Ireland and the Jesuits of Chicago supported the project financially, and my colleagues in the philosophy departments of the Milltown Institute and Loyola University Chicago provided stimulating contexts for doing serious philosophical writing. There are many others—friends, philosopher-colleagues, and Jesuits—whose personal and professional support must be acknowledged. Among these I thank Peter Bernardi, Bob Bireley, Blake Dutton, Máire Garvey, David Ingram, John Langan, Tom Layden, Micheál McGréil, Paul Moser, Marie Murphy, Donal Neary, Des O'Grady, Brian Paulson, Tom Phelan, Saythala "Lay" Phonexayphova, Vera Price, David Quinn, Tom Regan, James Smyth, Vincent Twomey SVD, Gvidas Vainorius (who sadly did not live to see this book in print), Mark Waymack, Vicki Wike, and David Yandell.

Chapter 1

War and Moral Theory

Reiterated over time, our arguments and judgments shape what I want to call *the moral reality of war*.

Michael Walzer, *Just and Unjust Wars*

[War is] the concept that makes it possible to understand the forms as well as the existence of peace and order.

Pasquino, "Political Theory of Peace and War"

The just war tradition is alive and well today. After emerging in ancient Rome and flourishing in medieval Europe, it experienced a partial decline in the early modern period, 1600–1900, but it has enjoyed a revival since World War I (1914–18).

The tradition developed under two headings: the morality of going to war (*jus ad bellum* as it was known in Latin), which concerns the state, and the morality of conducting war (*jus in bello*), which concerns mainly the army commanders. In the last twenty years, some ethicists have suggested that a third element should be added to the theory: the morality of building postwar peace (*jus post bellum*).

In the 1600–1900 period, the *jus in bello* part of the tradition flourished, focusing on the moral and legal rules for conducting war, noncombatant immunity, and duties to prisoners. By contrast, the *jus ad bellum* part was widely considered to be effectively out of date because it seemed inapplicable in a world of sovereign states with no international authority.[1] However, since World War I, there has been a growing sense that the pre-1900 tacit permission to states to make war as each sees fit, being required only to observe certain rules for its

1

conduct, is now over and that war should be outlawed. The rise of international law and international institutions and a gradual change in outlook give grounds for thinking that there is now significant room for the position that states must have serious grounds for going to war, that these grounds must include moral grounds, and that levying aggressive war is a crime for which heads of government and their agents may be tried in international tribunals.[2]

This development represents a significant step away from the early modern era when the ruler was considered to be above the law and to have a general right to go to war whenever he judged that the interests of the state required it. It is, by the same token, a significant step toward the kind of thinking that informs classical just war thought. However, there is still much less clarity about the morality of going to war than there is about the morally acceptable ways of waging war.[3] In addition, the shift in thinking just described is by no means universal, and treatments of *jus ad bellum* must take that fact into account. The challenge is to apply *jus ad bellum* criteria in a world midway between the supremacy of national raison d'état, and effective acceptance of the rule of international law in the restraint of war and armed aggression.

Main Themes

As others have done, I usually refer to just war tradition rather than just war theory, since there is no precisely worked-out theory of justice or right with respect to war. It is a broad tradition, a field with many different approaches.[4]

My goal in this book is to offer a conceptual analysis of the *jus ad bellum* criteria in order to facilitate their application to contemporary cases. The conception I develop is secular, not religious, although religious authors will sometimes be cited. Lists of the criteria vary. Robert Holmes cites the list offered by the US Catholic bishops as typical: just cause, competent authority, comparative justice, right intention, last resort, probability of success, and proportionality.[5] Brian Orend lists just cause, right intention, public declaration by proper authority, last resort, probability of success, and proportionality (Orend 2006, 32; and 2008). The list I propose is competent authority, just cause, right intention, probability of success, last resort, and proportionality. I accept the continuing relevance of most of the traditional criteria, but my interpretation of some criteria may diverge from traditional views. I explore each in turn, hoping to offer a distinctive interpretation of most of them. I also argue that there is a logical order among the criteria.

Certain topics will not be treated. First, I will not discuss moral conduct of war (*jus in bello*) for three reasons: (a) as noted, much more has been written on *jus in bello* than on *jus ad bellum*, (b) *jus ad bellum* is independent of *jus in bello*, and (c) *jus ad bellum* has some explanatory and ethical primacy over *jus in bello*.[6]

Second, I will have little to say about moral obligations arising from the ending of war (*jus post bellum*), although my discussion of right intention will touch on it (Orend 2006). Third, this book is not a historical study of the development of just war thought. Fourth, it is not an exposition of any particular theorist's views on war.

Individual chapters will be devoted to the *jus ad bellum* criteria of just cause, competent authority, right intention, reasonable probability of success, last resort, and proportionality. Apart from just cause and competent authority, relatively little has been written on many of the criteria. Yet the concepts involved merit unpacking and elaboration. There will also be a chapter on the good of peace, since the just war tradition requires that peace be the goal of fighting a war, and what is involved in the notion of the good of peace tends also to go unanalyzed. Prior to that, in this chapter, I address a number of general issues, exploring some of the points summarized above.

The more important conditions are the first three. Here I shall argue for the primacy of the competent authority condition, with the just cause condition being dependent on it. My thinking here was stimulated by David Rodin's important argument that the idea of national self-defense cannot be seen as analogous to an individual person's self-defense in a way that provides justification for the state's going to war (see Rodin 2002).

My thinking has also been influenced by the natural law tradition's idea that the state is meant to promote the common good. The notion of the common good may be controversial and seen in some quarters as irredeemably religious. But such a perception is mistaken, for while some religious groups appeal to the common good, the notion itself is by no means inherently religious. I treat the common good as necessary preamble to discussion of the competent authority condition since the early modern idea of the state was neutral on the nature of the state. Today, in a globalized world, there is a strong trend of thought that differentiates between democratic law-governed states and authoritarian dictatorships or "rogue" states. The difference matters because democracies are by nature oriented to certain common goods (e.g., representation, accountability) in a way that dictatorships cannot be, and there are other common goods that democracies are more likely than dictatorships to promote. I shall argue that the difference matters with respect to what counts as legitimate or competent authority for the purposes of application of *jus ad bellum* criteria.

Why Write about the Ethics of War?

There are several reasons to write about the ethics of war. First, the subject matters: war is ethically significant. It is an understatement to say that wars impinge hugely on human life. All wars have negative consequences, while their benefits are at best infrequent and always uncertain. The twentieth century saw the development of weapons and technology with the capacity to wipe out most human life in a relatively short space of time. The potential impact of nuclear or biological war is so severe that the prevention, avoidance, and limiting of war has become ever more morally urgent. In relation to that, the task of building peace is morally pressing.

Second, war is not well understood. Even if we reject the claim that war is part of the natural order, wars still seem to be a recurrent and endemic feature of human history.[7] There is no obvious reason why this should be so, nor does the ideal of universal peace and global harmony seem inherently unrealizable. Yet it has seemed so unlikely to be realized that people have looked with skepticism and perhaps some pity at those who appeared to think they see the road to the abolition of war clear before them.

Today we have not merely the dreadful history of human wars but also the history of the "war" against war, the struggle to abolish war altogether.[8] We have only to think of the hope implicit in the "war to end war" slogan used about World War I to sense the pathos of a simplistic view of war.[9] The Enlightenment's optimism that war could be eliminated, since its causes were identifiable as rooted in some relatively simple factor (e.g., dictatorship, nationalism, dynastic ambition, colonialism, profiteering, militarism), seems naïve today. That the factors listed have been causally involved in war is undeniable. But the idea that there could be *one* determining cause of war in general that was thus the key to understanding it such that overcoming or eliminating it would virtually guarantee an end of war is not credible.

Part of the reason for the lack of understanding of war is because the label is often used to cover a wide range of armed conflicts: from all-out international conflicts such as the two world wars, through civil wars and insurrections, to humanitarian intervention involving military action.[10] Reacting against the vagueness this entails, legal theorists in the 1600–1914 era distinguished between war and other kinds of military action. Among other things, they required that war be formally declared for an armed conflict to count as a war. Sometimes political interests may be served by avoiding use of the term "war." In the 1960s, the US government's official position was that it was not formally at war with North Vietnam but merely engaged in a supportive action in South Vietnam's self-defense.

Such distinctions have only minor significance in just war thought, although that tradition offers no definition of war. Carl von Clausewitz defined war as an act of force to compel our enemy to do our will, regardless of formalities. His definition covers all those armed conflicts of interest in this book. The only condition that I impose as necessary for a conflict to count as war with respect to the different types of military action listed earlier is that it be initiated or at least continued by a competent authority. The rationale behind that criterion will be discussed in chapter 3.

It is hard to provide a neat, self-contained definition or even conceptualization of war.[11] Brian Orend offers the following: "War should be understood as an *actual, intentional* and *widespread* armed conflict between political communities. Thus, fisticuffs between individual persons do not count as a war, nor does a gang fight, nor does a feud on the order of the Hatfields versus the McCoys. War is a phenomenon which occurs *only* between political communities, defined as those entities which either are states or intend to become states (in order to allow for civil war)" (Orend 2008). I agree with his tying war to conflict between political communities.[12] But I am prepared to adopt a more permissive stance with respect to what counts as a political community in that I include insurrectionary groups and international organizations like the United Nations. Taking war as necessarily involving a political community is linked to the condition that a competent authority make the decision to go to war, and such competence is essentially political. At the same time, it has to be conceded that it is possible that an accidental outbreak of fighting between opposing armed forces might sometimes, if it became widespread, lead to a situation where the outbreak of war escaped political control.[13]

That war be intentional is also correct but vague. Taking it to mean that combatant states must intend to prosecute the war would make it trivial. Taking it to mean that the combatants must deliberately choose to go to war may make the condition too severe; even where governments stumble into war, hoping desperately to the last that they won't have to fight, it will still count as war. It is perhaps best taken as meaning that the two sides intend to fight rather than concede the demands of the other side.

Orend's requirement that there be actual fighting excludes the Cold War from the catalogue of wars. Clausewitz's definition of war as an act of force designed to make the enemy do our will seems to support that conclusion. I adopt that view. However, it should be noted that much of what is relevant to *jus ad bellum* has to do with the political rather than the military side. *Jus in bello* becomes relevant only when fighting starts. By contrast, *jus ad bellum* is relevant long before that and independently of whether any shooting actually happens. The "Cold War" was not a war, but the policies and stances of each side are evaluable by the *jus ad bellum* criteria.

I listed the fact that war has major negative impact and that war is not well understood as two reasons why the just war tradition is worth studying. A third reason for writing about it is that it is increasingly cited and discussed today by Western political leaders and policymakers, judges and lawyers, and even generals. In recent decades, American and British political leaders in particular have referred to it and more generally have felt the need to justify going to war by appealing to explicitly moral reasons and not just reasons of political necessity.

The rise in interest in the just war tradition is also significant in the area of law, as is reflected in the extensive contemporary literature on war and international law. The idea that war had to be lawful or just in some sense goes back to ancient Roman custom and thought. Stephen Neff remarks: "The most important conceptual step, or leap, occurred when war ceased to be viewed as a routine and 'natural' feature of international life, requiring no special explanation, and began instead to be seen as an exceptional and pathological state of affairs, calling for some kind of justification. In the later part of the first millennium BC, two societies—China in the east and the classical world of Greece and Rome in the west—took this step" (2005, 14). The shift had nothing to do with reflecting on how likely people, tribes, or states were to go to war, and had much to do with some view of what would be most conducive to individual and social well-being. The larger civilizations of China and Rome could envision the possibility of widespread, even worldwide, harmony and peace within which human beings could flourish. From that perspective, war was a disorder or social malfunction. The contemporary sense that war should be outlawed stands in that tradition.

This does not necessarily involve a commitment to a specifically Aristotelian or Stoic view of nature, but it does imply some view of what the international community, states, and people need in order to flourish. Any ethical theory that gives prominence to a view of human flourishing, whether that of the individual or of the group, partly closes the natural/normative or "is/ought" gap.[14] Obviously, this touches on a natural law theme. If peace is a good, it is in some sense a natural good. Thus, rejection of the underlying natural law element in the just war tradition on the grounds that it is normative may well be incoherent since it may be impossible to talk about what is most appropriate, fitting, prudent, and so on for nations or the international community without using some normative notion.

This becomes apparent when we move to the early modern rejection of the just war tradition. Thomas Hobbes saw competition, conflict, and violence as the natural order of things so that the natural law consisted essentially in the law of self-preservation whereby everybody had a right to preserve himself. The individual's right to self-preservation was absolute and was not limited by others' right to self-preservation. A person (or a state) had a natural right of preservation, even if it meant invading the land or threatening the life of another; and the other had just as good a natural right to resist that invasion in the interests of his own self-preservation. Accordingly, the *jus ad bellum* idea that war-making always involved unjust aggression by at least one party to the conflict made no sense within Hobbes's framework.

Hobbes's view did not involve a rejection of normative notions, but it certainly involved a change in the normative standards applicable to war. Where the just war tradition had some notion of the common good with respect to which the morality of particular war-making might be judged, the Hobbesian natural law identified the good with individual self-preservation understood in an unrestricted way, whether the individual in question was a particular human being or a particular state.

Neff argues that the just war tradition was undermined in the early modern period by the influence of the radically altered notion of natural law Hobbes developed, and also by a dueling or contractual view of war (2005, 132–40). Nations were sometimes in a state of peace, sometimes in a state of war, and different moral rules applied to each. When two nations went to war, it was to be thought of either as analogous to a duel or as a reversion to a prelegal state of nature. That was in contrast to the just war tradition that saw war as analogous to criminal behavior, a breach of the peace involving violence and robbery.

The horrors of the two world wars led to viewing war as evil and intolerable, and as something that the international community should seek to suppress. Between the two wars, the League of Nations represented a significant move in that direction, and the post–1945 United Nations went further still.[15] That internationalist perspective has created a space for the revival of *jus ad bellum* thought, challenging the early modern positivist view of war as a distinct state, one that is part of the natural order of human life and hence to be accepted with its own distinctive set of moral rules.

Apolitical Views of War

Application of *jus ad bellum* criteria requires some understanding of war. War is a reason-guided or rational activity grounded in political decision.[16] At least the decision to go to war is reason-guided, and that claim is central to this work. The reasons may be immoral or paranoid, but they are reasons under some description.

Various other views treat going to war as something fundamentally irrational or guided by a false consciousness. Those views are often reductionist, but adequate warrant for such reduction is rarely offered. In no particular order, I list and describe them, commenting briefly on their flaws.

First is the view that war is about profit. Marxists held this view, but they were not alone. That commercial interests have sometimes motivated governments to go to war is hardly disputable: colonial wars are an obvious case in point. But it is only too easy to identify wars where such motives play at most a minor role. The Communist states of Vietnam and Kampuchea (Cambodia) did not go to war over profit in 1979, nor did China's subsequent attack on Vietnam have anything to do with commercial concerns. Had war erupted between the United States and the USSR over Cuba in 1962, it would not have been over material resources, business interests, or profits. Even though commercial and economic factors were not irrelevant to the outbreak of the US Civil War, it would not be true to say that it was fought for profit: the Southern states fought to secede, the federal government fought to prevent them doing so and to preserve the union, and each side fought regardless of questions of economic rationality.

In cases where economic factors clearly played a significant role in the decision to invade or attack, it is often the case that other considerations also played an important role, and in such cases it may not be clear whether the economic factor alone would have been a sufficient cause to bring about war. Iraq's invasion of Kuwait in 1990 may have been motivated by economic concerns since Iraq was heavily in debt following its 1980–88 war with Iran. But it was not the only motive since Iraq had long claimed Kuwait as part of its territory and had attempted to enforce that claim in the early 1960s.

Even in cases where economic and financial motivations are among the reasons for resorting to war, such motives are not necessarily determining or overriding. While economic factors were important background factors leading up to World War I, they did not figure in the frenetic discussions and fateful decisions of the politicians and the generals in the weeks between the assassination of the Archduke Franz Ferdinand in late June and the first shots being fired in the last days of July and the first days of August. Prior to 1914, although there was a growing economic rivalry between Germany and Britain, it seems to have played little role in Britain's last-minute decision to enter the war. In a speech to the House of Commons on August 3, 1914, Britain's foreign secretary Sir Edward Grey identified Britain's interests as maintaining the independence of Belgium and the status of France as a great power; he made no reference to economic interests. If anything, we should expect that in modern industrialized countries economic motivations would tend to militate *against* going to war, owing to its expense, disruption, and uncertainty.

Second is the view that war is like children squabbling or drunken men getting into fisticuffs after the pubs have closed: something nonpolitical and emotional. Some wars in the more remote past have been like that: the most recent example was the one-hundred-hour "Soccer War" between Honduras and El Salvador in 1969 over events at soccer matches between their national teams.[17] Some pacifists appear to hold that view, and certain feminists hold a variant of it, viewing war as merely the outburst of irrational male aggressiveness.[18] As with the previous view, this view applies to some cases but won't do as a general theory of war.

The third and fourth views are identified in Henry Kissinger's memoirs, where he comments on the reductive trends in popular thought about foreign policy and by extension about the wars, military deterrence, and military intervention that might flow from it:

> Two schools of thought developed [in the United States]. The liberal approach treated foreign policy as a subdivision of psychiatry; the conservative approach considered it an aspect of theology. Liberals equated relations among states with human relations. They emphasized the virtues of trust and unilateral gestures of goodwill. Conservatives saw in foreign policy a version of the eternal struggle of good with evil, a conflict that recognized no middle ground and could only end with victory. Deterrence ran up against liberal ideology and its emotional evocation of peace in the abstract; coexistence grated on the liturgical anti-communism of the Right. (Quoted in Howard 1983, 281)

Let's take the third view as Kissinger's "liberal" approach, where relations between states are analogized to relations between individuals. Wars can sometimes arise (at least in part) from misunderstanding, and we need not deny that such elements as individual choices and interpersonal relations between rulers can play a significant role in causing or averting war. However, that concession does not entail or imply that war can be understood as inherently analogous to a breakdown in interpersonal relations.

The fourth view, war as a crusade against evil, is similarly misleading. As with the "liberal" approach, rejection of it is not to be taken as saying that such elements can never find any place in war. But war cannot be understood on its own terms or as an instrument of policy by viewing it uncritically through the crusader's interpretative grid any more than it can be grasped through the communication facilitator's interpretative grid.

The final view to consider is not reductionist, but it is still apolitical in its view of war. It is found in some Christian commentary on war, which holds explicitly to a strong, even overriding, moral presumption against war.[19] It interprets *jus ad bellum* as strictly as possible so that it converges asymptotically on pacifism, regardless of whether doing so makes its criteria virtually impossible to meet.

That position undermines the practical element in judgment oriented to action. It tends to be undiscriminating between combatant states, or implies the greater guilt necessarily lies upon the state initiating war. An apolitical moral stance in such matters neither takes politics seriously nor appreciates the moral aspect of the political decision to go to war. The *jus ad bellum* criteria can be neither credible nor applicable except as grounded in political goals and goods, whether those of a particular state or those of the international community.[20]

"Just War": Avoiding Reification

The term "just war" tends to direct attention to the state of affairs of war rather than to the action of a particular state in waging war. But classic just war theory deals with actions: decisions to go to war, and the conduct of the war.

Early modern thinkers, such as Hugo Grotius, followed by Christian von Wolff and Emer de Vattel, introduced the novel idea that war should be thought of as a distinct state of affairs and not just a set of acts.[21] This has led to a misleading reification of war. The point of doing so was to develop the idea that a different kind of law (and by implication a different kind of morality) applied to relations between individuals and between states, depending on whether they were in a state of war or in a state of peace with each other.

Within that early modern legal framework, speaking of a just war in the *jus ad bellum* sense would have been misplaced. Legally, it would be taken to mean no more than that the proper formalities of giving notice of the intention of prosecuting war and the like had been observed.[22] Discussion of moral and legal issues would have found some purchase only within the context of the conduct of the war—that is, in *jus in bello*.

Classic just war thought could not have accepted the idea that war was a distinct "state" or state of affairs in the sense that the moral norms applicable to it differed from those of peacetime. In that tradition, a ruler's justification for going to war was to restrain and punish violent criminals, to protect the weak and the oppressed, to do justice and restore order: that meant trying to squeeze out or eradicate any zone where justice, social order, and the other values and goods of peace were missing. The just war tradition implicitly rejected the idea that a different morality applied in situations of war.

At any rate, classic just war tradition would have taken the view that, as a state of affairs (as distinct from the agents and actions involved), there can be no such thing as a just war in the sense of a good war.[23] However, ambiguity on this point remains. An example can be found in Robert Holmes's objection to William O'Brien's reliance on the distinction between *jus ad bellum* and *jus in bello*: "O'Brien says repeatedly that violations of the principles of proportionality and discrimination by the allies during World War II . . . did not prevent those wars from being just. The violations were wrong. . . . It is just that they are offset by the overwhelmingly just causes for which the United States was fighting. But to say that a war can be just *overall* despite violations of *jus in bello* criteria" does not seem plausible to Holmes (1989, 173).

The problem with Holmes's remarks is that it is difficult to make sense of talk about "the war being just" or being "just overall." One could make a case for or against the claim that a particular state acted rightly or justly in going to war, just as one could make a case for or against the claim that the conduct of the war by its army was occasionally, often, or usually unjust. The two arguments would seem to be mostly independent of each other. If, hypothetically, it is determined that a state was justified in going to war against a blatant aggressor, but its troops often commit atrocities, it is hard to see how that could remove the state's justification for going to war. Similarly, the state's being justified in going to war will not excuse the atrocities. Moral evaluation of the war "itself" or the war "overall" seems impossible because the object of evaluation does not appear to be a moral object. What can be morally evaluated are the decision to go to war and the conduct of the war. There isn't some third entity, a combination of those two perhaps, that can be morally evaluated over and above those two things or as a summation of the moral status of the two. Talk of decision and conduct refers to actions, which are morally evaluable; talk of "the war itself" does not refer to action, so it lacks any morally evaluable entity to target.

If we take World War II, the war being discussed by O'Brien and Holmes, it is impossible to answer the question, was the war just? Even allowing for the obvious point that Nazi Germany was the aggressor, so that Germany's part in the war was unjust, it doesn't automatically follow that it was "a just war" for the allies. Broadly, I think it was. But the *jus ad bellum* criteria have the merit of moving us away from any reification of the war to look at the agents and their actions. It forces us to ask whether Britain and France, Britain particularly, delayed too long in going to war with Germany; whether the USSR was complicit in the outbreak of aggressive war in 1939 since it signaled its compliance with German intentions a month earlier and it too invaded Poland subsequent to the German invasion and attacked Finland not long after; and whether the USSR's intention in fighting Germany after 1941 included the annexation of territory, since it annexed territory from nine countries as a result of World War II.[24] In view of that, it is important to understand that the *jus ad bellum* and *jus in bello* criteria are constraints on the intentions and actions of various agents, not qualities or parts of some reified moral entity called "the war."

Another important reason for not focusing on war as a separate state of affairs is that it disconnects war from the political context from which it emerged and divorced from which it makes no sense. In a famous passage, Clausewitz states that, while we acknowledge that war is connected to politics, in practice we forget the connection. He is often quoted as saying that war is "politics by other means," which is often taken to mean that the political is suspended when at war. This is a misinterpretation, as the following quotation shows.

It is well known that the only source of war is politics—the intercourse of governments and peoples; but it is apt to be assumed that war suspends this intercourse and replaces it by a wholly different condition, ruled by no law but its own. We maintain, on the contrary, that war is simply a continuation of political intercourse, with the addition of other means. We deliberately use the phrase "with the addition of other means" because we also want to make it clear that war in itself does not suspend political intercourse or change it into something entirely different. . . . War cannot be divorced from political life; and whenever this occurs in our thinking about war, the many links that connect the two elements are destroyed and we are left with something pointless and devoid of sense. (Clausewitz 1976, 605)[25]

War is not an alternative to politics; it does not, for instance, necessarily exclude negotiation, and the use of or threat to use force is politically communicative. Clausewitz's remarks provide an appropriate prolegomenon to ethical evaluation of war. Just as to go to war disconnected from the political context is "pointless and devoid of sense," so too ethical evaluation of a state's decision to go to war disconnected from its political context tends in the direction of a formal, abstract (and pointless) moral condemnation of the state of war as meaningless slaughter and pointless destruction.

Statist versus Internationalist Perspectives

The impact of two world wars removed much of the glamour and romance of war and shifted legal thought away from the idea of war as a kind of duel, a formal and artificial space with moral rules different from those that apply in peacetime. The related recovery of the just war tradition's view of war as justified to protect people from massacre and despoliation has reinforced that development. Together they have helped move international law and politics toward regarding war as subject to law not just in its conduct but also in its being chosen by governments.

In recent decades, war—always a political matter—is increasingly being treated also as a legal matter. When war is analyzed in a legal context, the analysis often has similarities to that yielded by the just war tradition. Insofar as international legal institutions can give some force to legal judgments in this area, reflection in the just war tradition will be easily applicable.

But international law, the United Nations, and the international courts do not yet have the power to enforce their rulings in the way that sovereign states do. The other context, that of traditional power politics in international affairs, has by no means been superseded or become irrelevant. In today's world, the two contexts, that of international order and international law (not quite the same thing) and that of sovereign states, coexist uneasily.

Since the sovereign-state dimension of international political life is still a reality, even if pared back by the emergent dimension of international law holding that states have a duty to intervene in order to protect, any serious theoretical treatment of justice in war must not ignore that dimension. A purely formal outlay of the just war tradition, particularly of the *jus ad bellum* part, would give the impression that only the context of international order and the rule of law were relevant. Since we do not yet live in such a world, however desirable, that approach is too narrow.

The challenge then is to see whether *jus ad bellum* can be applied also in the sovereign-state context, in a quasi-Hobbesian relationship where each considers only its own interests. In dealing with the first three *jus ad bellum* criteria, I shall try to keep both contexts in view.

The internationalist perspective has grown more influential in the Western world in recent decades. In addition to the role of international bodies in dealing with actual or threatened conflict between states, recent decades have witnessed the emergence of the idea that international bodies should be prepared to intervene to protect citizens from gross human rights violations by their governments. Since the end of the Cold War, events in the former Yugoslavia and Somalia as well as Rwanda have led to new attention to the idea that the United Nations has a moral duty to intervene by force in specific cases on humanitarian grounds (see ICISS 2001). The creation of the International Court of Justice at The Hague marked another milestone in the journey toward bringing international relations in the matter of war, and national governments in the matter of gross mistreatment of their citizens, under the rule of law.[26]

Set against the new backdrop of a legal framework, the idea of a magistrate or supreme authority over nation-states (at least to judge, if not to enforce) in the matter of war and peace will draw thought about justice in war to attend more to the question of whether a country's going to war is justified (*jus ad bellum*). That idea has the possibility of giving justice and human rights greater weight than national sovereignty, and of developing the line of thought that gives primacy to the duty of the magistrate to restrain wrongdoers in the interest of the oppressed. With respect to the moral status of the state, the state's rights as sovereign will count for less, and its duties (and concomitant rights) of governance and promoting the common good as well as its being subject to the rule of international law will count for more.[27]

Philosophy and Law

As noted, the just war tradition has been influential on law relating to war, particularly toward the end of the twentieth century. However, while it continues to progress, it is far from complete, with many issues still unresolved and several questions as yet unclear. Although it is not quite the way I see the tradition, there is something to be said for the view that the tradition's central goal has been to seek the appropriate balance between two core values, peace and justice, and their related goals, keeping the peace and refusing provocation on one hand, and on the other hand promoting justice and defending the rights of the weakest and most vulnerable. Legal developments in this area reflect to some extent a widening acceptance in society of the moral goals of that tradition.

At the same time, this book is not a work in law but in philosophy. There are points on which I may take stands on what is ethically desirable or mandatory that are at variance with international law or current interpretations of international law. Besides, the law can be improved. Morality and the law are indeed distinct, but in the case of the law concerning war, the moral notions underlying the just war tradition have had a major impact on twentieth-century thought about the law on war. A strongly positivist attitude to law is misplaced here since it ignores the fact that world outrage at the ethnic cleansing, massacres, and genocide in such places as the former Yugoslavia and Rwanda was essentially moral. Developments in legal thought, particularly in the direction of seeing UN or other intervention to stop such horrors as clearly warranting the overriding of national sovereignty, have been driven to a significant extent by that moral outrage.

Notes

1. These developments are reflected in the work of such early modern authors as Alberico Gentili (1552–1608), Christian von Wolff (1679–1754), and Emer de Vattel (1714–67). For relevant citations from their works, see Reichberg, Syse, and Begby 2006, 374–75, 474, 507, and 514–15. See also Lee 2012, 58–61.

2. On the neglect of *jus ad bellum* thought, see McMahan 2010, 496; and Detter 2000, 157–58.

3. James Johnson (1975) provides an interesting thematic treatment of the abandonment of *jus ad bellum* after the early modern fracturing of the unity of medieval Europe.

4. A point also noted in Rodin 2002, 103–4.

5. This order is used in US Bishops 1983, sections 85–99, and cited in Holmes 1989, 164. For similar ordering, see Clark 1988, 34–35; and Johnson 1999, 28–30.

6. Robert Holmes views Paul Ramsey and James Turner Johnson as focusing "almost exclusively" on *jus in bello* (1989, 165–66). For a similar stance on the independence of *jus ad bellum*, see Walzer 1977, 21. As David Rodin correctly notes, they derive from very different assumptions about war and are not easily harmonized (2002, 166–67). On the radical view among some twentieth-century jurists that war, since no longer legally acceptable, could never again be morally permissible to both sides as early modern thought held, see Neff 2005, 335–40.

7. See Durant and Durant 1968, 81: only 268 of the 3,421 years prior to 1968 have been free of war. Doyle 1993, 195–96, lists 116 international conflicts between 1817 and 1980.

8. On the thinking and influence of British liberals opposed to war in the early decades of the twentieth century, see, for instance, Howard 1978.

9. H. G. Wells appears to have been the first to use the phrase, in the early months of the war; see ibid., 74.

10. See Neff 2005, particularly ch. 3, 5–7, and 10, for historical discussion of the legal distinctions between war, insurrection, self-defense, reprisals, interventions, and police actions. As will become clear, the notion of war in the just war tradition is wider than the strictly legal notion.

11. For lengthy treatment, see Vasquez 1993, ch. 1 and 2.

12. See also Bull 1977, 184: "War is organized violence carried on by political units against each other."

13. For some interesting legal sidelights on the question, see Neff 2005, 347–49.

14. See Foot 2001, ch. 2, "Natural Norms," for development of this idea.

15. For a comprehensive account of the development of legal thought concerning war, see Neff 2005.

16. In Clausewitz's view, it is reason-guided in many of its elements. However, two caveats apply. First, to be reason-guided is not the same as being rule-guided: he rejects the idea that war is like a duel, with precise rules that the duelists are obliged to follow. Second, wars vary in their limits, and unlimited or "absolute" war is not impossible. See Clausewitz 1976, Bk. VIII, ch. 2, 579–81. Absolute war loses sight of the political reasons or goals for which it was initiated: in such cases war swamps political reason.

17. Estimates of casualties vary from two thousand to six thousand dead. While the trigger causes may have been soccer games, the effective expulsion from Honduras of several thousand migrant Salvadoran workers in previous months had raised tension between the two countries.

18. René Girard developed a theory according to which all violence is based on irrational scapegoating that arises from mimetic struggle for desired goods. See Girard 1977.

19. That presumption is given much weight in US Bishops 1983, summary introduction, and also sections 70–71, 73, and 77–78. It is suspicious of claims that the criteria have been met, implying that they should be interpreted as strictly as possible, thereby converging on pacifism. As is argued in Johnson 2005a and as will be discussed later, that undermines the just war tradition's role as a tool of governance.

20. For discussion of the difference between just war theory and limited war theory, see Clark 1988. For an important contribution on the pacifist side, see Holmes 1989.

21. See Neff 2005, 30–39, 58, 96–102, 336–38, particularly 58 and 102, for incisive treatment of the distinction and the early modern shift in thinking. He attributes to Grotius the innovation of defining war as a state distinct from the acts of fighting involved. See O'Donovan 2003, 6–7, on the reification of war.

22. The early modern positivist view held that the king was answerable to nobody with respect to whether he was justified in going to war, since he, as sovereign, was above the law. Classic *jus ad bellum* thought and much recent contemporary thought hold that governments are under the law, whether the law of God or the natural law or international law.

23. The ancient Romans did have a concept of *bellum justum*, but the classical just war tradition of Augustine marks a radical break with it. See Augustine 1998, Bk. xix, ch. 7: "the wise man, they say, will wage just wars. Surely, however, if he remembers that he is a human being, he will be much readier to deplore the fact that he is under the necessity of waging even just wars. And if anyone either endures them or thinks of them without anguish of soul, his condition is still more miserable: for he thinks himself happy only because he has lost all human feeling."

24. I warn the reader at this point that I shall make frequent reference not to World War II per se but to Britain and France's decision to go to war with Germany over Poland in 1939. I think they were justified in so doing, and I am going to take this as a clear example (there are not many such, after all!) of an instance where going to war was justified, in order to see what that actual historical case implies for our understanding of the *jus ad bellum* criteria.

25. Clausewitz is concerned not with the moral evaluation of war but with the nature of war.

26. See Paulus 2010 for reflections on the challenges of international legal adjudication in the contemporary global context where international law's authority in the area of law is partly but not fully accepted.

27. See Luban 1994, ch. 7, on how the two lines of thought can collide. Luban's sympathies are more with the international order and justice side as he notes that Walzer (1977) upholds the primacy of sovereignty (Luban 1994, 342).

Chapter 2

The Goods of Peace

Peace comes dropping slow . . .

W. B. Yeats, *The Lake Isle of Innisfree*

A practical moral theory typically provides some account of required, prohibited, and permitted action. The *jus in bello* part of just war thought focuses particularly on that in its discussion of the limits of force and the treatment of enemy combatants and noncombatants.

The *jus ad bellum* part of the tradition also has much to say about moral behavior, but what may be more important is its view of the goods and values sought by going to war, without which *jus ad bellum* makes no sense. Peace is so obviously an integral part of the good sought by war that it is taken for granted, with the result that just war thought on peace is underdeveloped. This chapter discusses peace and other goods involved in decisions about going to war.

Neglect of the goods that going to war often intends may also have arisen from the fact that in the twentieth century, just war thought focused too narrowly on the issue of self-defense, assuming that moral permission to use force arises solely from the right of self-defense and that peace is self-evidently the absence of aggression between states. Taking that view undermines the moral claim that the international common good and what John Rawls calls the law of peoples has on policymaking. I argue that understanding *jus ad bellum* requires the focus to be primarily on the international common good. The right of self-defense is secondary relative to classical (and possibly future) *jus ad bellum* accounts.

Integral to the theory of the good envisioned by the just war tradition is a particular view of peace that can be summarized as follows: (1) Peace is an important good; (2) it usually, but not always, overrides other goods; (3) it is not generally reducible to the mere absence of violence; (4) as the quotation from Yeats cited earlier indicates, it is not to be taken as a given but must be

17

maintained and promoted; and (5) war may be a means of maintaining or promoting it.

The goals or goods intended by going to war can be loosely and schematically identified here as some appropriate combination of peace, justice, and order. In this chapter I particularly consider what kind of good peace is. The relationship between peace and justice is also clarified, particularly through discussion of the kind of peace that justice requires. I also look at some recent treatments of the good, including that offered in the later work of John Rawls.

Peace: Absence of Violence?

In the *City of God*, Augustine states that wars are fought for the sake of peace (Augustine 1998).[1] To some, such a statement may sound self-contradictory in the way that it would be self-contradictory to claim that fornication is done for the sake of chastity, or thefts perpetrated to promote honesty. However, the self-contradictoriness is only apparent.

Augustine's statement can be interpreted in a descriptive sense, concerning the actual reason why states or peoples fight wars, and in a normative sense, identifying the proper goal of fighting war. From a descriptive viewpoint, waging war is a goal-directed activity aimed at establishing a new order or new arrangement of territory or new government. He takes it that states or peoples fight wars in order to achieve some goal and thereafter to enjoy their gain undisturbed. They usually want their gain recognized and accepted as part of the new established order. Even an aggressive state desires to bring about a particular state of affairs so that, when it has been attained, there is nothing left to fight for, and in that sense it has the settlement or order—that is, the peace—it desired.

Such a notion of peace is minimalist: it roughly identifies peace with the cessation and absence of armed conflict. The minimalism is also reflected in the fact that such a notion of peace has no logical links to any other positive values.

Augustine's statement also raises the normative question: what is worth fighting for, or for what ought a state fight, or for what might a state be permitted to fight? If peace is that for which a just government may or ought fight, what kind of peace is meant? In the same context where Augustine remarks that some sort of peace is always the goal of war, he distinguishes between different kinds of peace: "[Pride] hates the just peace of God, and it loves its own unjust peace; but it cannot help loving peace of some kind or other. . . . He who has learnt to prefer right to wrong and the rightly ordered to the perverse, sees that, in comparison with the peace of the just, the peace of the unjust is not worthy to be called peace at all" (1998, bk. XIX, ch. 12, 936). While he does not say that an unjust or oppressive peace is not a peace, he does commit himself to the view that there are different kinds of peace, that they vary greatly in value, and that some kinds of peace are, by many standards of justice, of little value. We need not take this to mean that, in situations of serious injustice and oppression, the minimal peace of absence of armed conflict and general acquiescence in the established order has no value at all. It suffices to understand that in such cases the value of that kind of peace may be outweighed by other values or goods. There, promoting the good (not to mention merely defending existing goods) may require sacrificing that particular peace.

Some have tackled the challenge of specifying peace by taking it that the essential element of peace is the absence of armed conflict. In addition, it is sometimes tacitly assumed that peace is no more than that absence. Such a stance amounts to adopting what I call a minimal-peace position, defining peace in minimalist terms. Distinct from it is the view that peace is always an overriding value. Combining the two yields the position that minimal peace (peace as the absence of armed conflict) is an overriding value.[2]

The conjunction of the two positions supports the claim that it can never be right to go to war. The point on which such a stance is likely to be challenged is the conjunction itself: what reasons are there for thinking that the value of minimal peace or the absence of armed conflict is always overriding? The just war tradition is based on the claim that the conjunction position is mistaken and that in principle (even if not in practice) going to war could be warranted in order to promote justice and protect other goods.

Of course, many pacifists acknowledge that mere absence of violence is not enough and that building peace is an ongoing task; they may reject the claim that theirs is a minimal-peace view. But in particular instances where war is being considered, they typically argue on the basis of the presupposition that the absence of violence or minimal peace is a good such that no benefit arising from going to war could ever override it. They may not be content with a minimal peace, but they do think its value is overriding.

The conjunction position is also vulnerable to the charge that it does not always promote peace. One of its more obvious flaws is its notion that peace can be had simply by refusing to fight. This in turn depends on the assumption that the aggressor seeks to acquire territory, natural resources, or wealth but has no genocidal design on the lives of the state's people. Land or wealth can be used to buy off the invader, and one could envision circumstances in which that might be a more rational choice than armed resistance. But where the invader intends to perpetrate genocide, ethnic cleansing, or otherwise directly attack the lives of all or many of the population, it can hardly be argued that there is a minimal peace of any value to be had by not resisting.

A Wider Notion of Peace

In the passage quoted at the beginning of the previous section, Augustine implies that waging war in order to establish a certain kind of peace and order might be justified if the kind of peace and order intended is good. His position is thus not one that identifies peace with what I have called minimal peace since fighting for such peace would be self-contradictory. He suggests that the coexistence of injustice and other wrongs or evils with peace may seriously vitiate the value of that peace. The good or the value of peace is not something freestanding, independent of the wider nexus of states of affairs of which it is part. In any case, he assumes that in this sinful world peace will always be imperfect and incomplete, always capable in principle of improvement.

Echoing both Augustine and Hobbes, Kant comments: "The state of peace among men living in close proximity is not the natural state; instead, the natural state is one of war, which does not just consist in open hostilities, but also in the constant and enduring threat of them. The state of peace must therefore be *established*, for the suspension of hostilities does not provide the security of peace" (1983b, Ak. 349, 111). Peace cannot be taken for granted as a naturally occurring or easily obtainable good, such as might be had simply by governments refraining from going to war.[3] Second, the mere absence of armed conflict will not suffice to qualify as peace. A government seeking to make a choice of going to war may in fact, for practical purposes, be already at war, and its moral task under *jus ad bellum* may be to recognize that fact. However, Kant is relatively optimistic (compared to Hobbes) about the possibility of building peace.

What kind of good is Augustine's or Kant's just peace or the peace whose value would be overriding, and is it a kind of good that may be pursued or developed? Whether fighting for such a peace is warranted in individual instances would be open to consideration: at least it would not be self-contradictory to consider it. Assuming the practical possibility of a peace whose value is substantially greater than the value involved in the absence of armed conflict, could that value be such that it would warrant resorting to war, either to defend or to promote it?

For many peoples in history and more than a few philosophers war was evil in much the same sense that storms or earthquakes were evil: destructive, even calamitous, but also part of the nature of things, owing to human acquisitiveness and desire for security or domination. In such a context, peace was understood as minimal peace.

A significant shift away from the view of war as an inevitable part of the human social condition came with the gradual development of the just war tradition. Neff remarks: "One of the most momentous ideas in human history was the notion that war could and should be employed in a socially productive fashion, for the subduing of evil and the promotion of good—that it should be an instrument of law, rather than of greed or ambition. This is the just-war doctrine, stated in its broadest terms. It rests upon a key underlying idea: that the normal condition of international affairs is one of peace" (2005, 29–30). Probably the establishment of large empires (such as the Roman, Greek, or Chinese empires) was required in order to engender the idea of universal peace, where such would arise from the universal or near-universal rule of the emperor. In that perspective, imperial wars with nations or tribes outside the empire were either defensive or else aimed at spreading the benefits of the empire's peace and civilization. In either case, the empire's waging war was capable of being adjudged morally just. The fact that the empire's waging war was often aggressive is irrelevant here. What is relevant is that justification for war was seen as required, along the lines of restoring order or promoting the well-being of the people of the empire or their immediate neighbors.

Historically, the idea of empire is closely related to the idea of universal order, universal law, and universal community. In empires with any pretensions to political vision or advanced culture, they had some sense that all peoples, nations, and tribes constitute at some level a single moral community and are capable of being politically united.[4] To say that human beings form a single moral community implies that they can communicate with each other both within their own tribe, polis, or nation and across tribes and nations on matters of moral concern. Significant commonality of beliefs on what is good and what evil, and on what does and what does not conduce to human flourishing, makes such communication feasible. So even with wars being widespread or frequent, the idea of a well-ordered, peaceful world developed—even if only as an otherworldly ideal to be scorned. It provided the necessary background context for just war thought, a context of general or universal human goods that sometimes needed defending. Without such a context, just war thought made no sense.[5]

The just war tradition developed, and could only have developed, within a framework involving some notion of universal law. Such a notion would itself be grounded either on the idea of a universal empire (as found in Chinese Confucian thought) or on the idea of a common human nature (as developed by the Stoics under the Roman Empire).

The notion of a well-ordered, peaceful world was an ideal, or what Kant would call a regulative idea. Nevertheless, it was not a trivial idea since it was not a natural or self-evident idea. Nor was it universally accepted. Hobbes attacked the idea that peace was the "natural" state of affairs in any sense (Hobbes 1994, I, xiii, sec. 6–14; see also Neff 2005, 132–37). While not attacking peace as such, he did not think a state should allow considerations of the value of universal peace to weigh in the scales against its own interests. His influence tended to undermine the conceptual foundations and relevance of just war thought.

Two world wars and the threat of nuclear annihilation progressively moved twentieth-century thought away from the idea of war as a natural state of affairs. The development of the League of Nations first and the United Nations subsequently reflected a developing sense of a common human interest in peace and the avoidance of war.

Peace: Different Kinds of Good

The just war tradition is based on the idea that war ought to—and can—be used to establish a proper peace.[6] That means a peace that involves more than minimal peace. The tradition could be interpreted to involve a presumption in favor of peace since it is meant to be aimed at a peace that is more than the absence of violence. However, the tradition needs greater clarity on the kind of peace that war is meant to serve, and gaining that means identifying a range of related goods that add further content to the notion of peace.

We start with the good implied by minimal peace. It is a good for individuals and their families that they be secure from violence and the threat thereof. It is good for communities, local or national, not to be attacked, bombed, massacred, or have their crops seized or destroyed. Security of life and property is a good for human beings.

Such goods are presumably what are desired and intended by the minimal peace of the absence of violence. But even securing that much requires that there be some order-maintaining force. A basic level of security for life and property requires not just that others refrain from violent attack but that there be a public authority capable and willing to act to restrain others from violent attack. The good of peace is closely related to the good of order: it is important for the individual not just that there be no armed conflict threatening him or her but also that there be some order, some mechanism or structures for the handling and control of such conflict or its risk.[7] That involves two goods, or at least one complex good. If such order is to be effective, it must be enforced. Even if we don't at this point allow that its enforcement could justify war, we must at least concede the existence of a police force authorized to use force. Conceding this, we have moved beyond the most strict minimal-peace position.

Today the most common approach to analyzing such goods is in terms of rights. Thus, in some situations waging war may be a criminal activity since it violates individuals' rights. However, that approach is too limited since it yields only negative moral injunctions against violating such rights. There are also important human goods that cannot be easily expressed in the language of individual rights.

The good of peace benefits individuals and societies. However, there are different types of good, so it would be helpful to identify to which type peace belongs. John Haldane distinguishes between individual goods, private goods, collective goods, public goods, and common goods.[8] An individual good benefits the individual as individual, for example, pain relief. One individual's enjoyment of that good does not prevent another individual from enjoying it too. Peace, particularly minimal peace, might qualify as such a good. A private good is one that can be enjoyed by only one, for example, a dentist's appointment. Peace is not that kind of good.

Collective goods are aggregate goods, a notion that is applicable to something like wealth but not in any obvious or enlightening way to peace. Social or international peace is not an aggregate good in the sense that it could be divided and distributed quantitatively among individuals, or in the sense that it is constituted by the aggregation of (for example) the peaceful conditions of individual lives.

A public good is the opposite of a private good in that it is a good from which no one can be excluded, for example, clean air. Peace qualifies as a public good from which no one can be excluded, particularly when peace is considered as involving a reasonable and comparatively fair social order. Public goods benefit individuals, but they are not available for individual access. If a village is in a state of violent conflict arising from hostility between particular families, the good of peace is not available for members of other families not directly involved. The village's being in a state of conflict affects all to a greater or lesser extent. On the other hand, in a state of peace, even those who are unhappy with it still benefit from it in certain ways. It is not like the good of public museums or art galleries which they can choose not to enjoy.

What a reasonable social order involves will vary from one context to another. Following a war that has severely affected the civilian population or a civil war involving massacre and extensive violation of civilians' rights, any kind of social order that terminates the misery of the population will probably qualify as reasonable and at least "good enough for now."

Haldane's notion of a common good is of the kind of public good that requires joint action and cooperation between the members of the group. With a nod to Aristotle's idea that when we act, we act for a good of some sort, Haldane speaks of cooperation for common goods as "a form of group activity through which bonds of community are strengthened and by which goods may be secured for members of society that logically could not be available for them as individuals" (Haldane 2004, 141). His point is not that common goods are unavailable for individuals but that individual enjoyment of them requires cooperation from individuals as well as public bodies.[9]

There is some overlap between that notion of common goods and what David Rodin refers to as the common life of a community or nation, for which it might arguably be worth going to war. Rodin takes the common life to be a set of interconnected social structures and practices that constitute the cultural, political, social, and moral fabric of a group's or nation's life (Rodin 2002, ch. 7).[10] Since human beings are partly constituted by their social relations, the facilitation of such relations and their qualitative improvement is something that common or joint action can promote.

It is easy enough to imagine how cooperation between private individuals, civic groups, and nongovernmental organizations could go a long way toward building up peaceful relations in divided communities, healing civic division, and generally nurturing social peace in societies torn by intercommunal strife. Often such efforts are ineffective since groups desiring to keep intercommunal tension high may counteract them. But, all else being equal, such positive efforts will build up the peace, and will do so by involving ordinary people in the actual building of the peace, thereby giving them a stake in its success and constituting peace as a common good (as well as a public good or individual good) generated by cooperative peacemaking efforts.

The possibility that peace is a common good in Haldane's sense operates as another consideration that militates against accepting a minimal-peace notion. The minimal-peace notion tends to take peace as an essentially negative state of affairs—that is, one characterized by the absence of violence or use of force. While many parts of the world are peaceful in such a way that conflict is unlikely to erupt, there are other places that, while not actually at war, are characterized by the kind of international or intercommunal tension where full-scale conflict could easily erupt at any moment. In such cases, building peace requires action by both sides in the case of states or by community leaders and ordinary people in the case of communities. Here the inadequacy of the minimal-peace notion is clear, and one can see how peace is more appropriately envisaged as a common good, requiring individual initiative and social cooperation.

In his study of what he calls "international protection regimes," Bruce Cronin argues that before the League of Nations, and even going back as far as the 1648 Peace of Westphalia, states have cooperated to protect certain groups. At the Peace of Westphalia, religious minorities were the target group for protection as the peace treaties stipulated that such minorities in all countries were to be permitted freedom of worship. The Holy Alliance of post–1815 Europe undertook to protect royal dynasties throughout the continent, and after World War I the League of Nations focused on protection of national or ethnic minorities, as did the Organization of Security and Cooperation in Europe after the end of the Cold War in 1991. More generally, post–1945 organizations and agreements have sought to protect the rights of individual citizens. In each case, major wars were followed by international agreements to protect or ensure what Cronin views as a common good that is not reducible to the good or benefit of the individual member states (Cronin 2003, 4).[11] In such cases, the establishment of peace after major war was seen as requiring protection for certain groups or interests based on the belief that failing to do so could lead to the subsequent outbreak of war. This reflects the sense that what avoiding war meant was not so much never declaring war as building a certain kind of peace that was partly constituted by protection or promotion of certain goods. These goods were common in the sense that they were not private but public, and they also required concerted action by the agents concerned.

Charles Taylor describes peace as an irreducibly social good for individuals in that it concerns their relationships with others, much as language and culture are irreducibly social goods (Taylor 1995; see also Riordan 2008, 10–11). There can't be peace for individuals unless there is peace for the group. Even the village's peace is insecure if the nation is at war. Today in various parts of the world certain types of intercommunal conflict have a high degree of probability of spilling into neighboring states.

The notions of peace and the common good indicated here are somewhat vague and unspecific once we try to go beyond the level of generalities. This is inevitable, for the working out of the conditions of peace will vary according to circumstances. Accordingly, what is involved here is a heuristic or open-ended notion: an appropriate notion of the common good, or in this instance a notion of a common good of peace and order, is to be worked out in dialogue.[12] This is reflected in much of the recent literature on peacemaking, whether in conflict resolution at group level or in UN activities aimed at peacemaking and containing conflict.[13] Implicit in that literature are the claims that peace and order is a good, and that it does not keep itself but needs to be maintained and nurtured if it is to survive. The literature, particularly that produced since the end of the Cold War, also holds that peace is a good that the international community needs to promote. There is a growing awareness in Europe and North America that the good of peace can be threatened by war or anarchy in distant parts. Even on the most cynical reading of the motives behind NATO's intervention in Bosnia and Kosovo between 1990 to 2010—namely, to suppress those conflicts in order to prevent them drawing more non-European Muslim militants into Europe—peace in those places appears as a good needed by the NATO countries.

Also notable in the literature is the awareness that the maintenance and nurture of peace requires much more than merely trying to head off war when it looms. While some literature on the subject may be unrealistic in its view of what is achievable, there is a growing body of work based on UN experience of how to promote peace and order while simultaneously having a practical sense of the limits of what is possible in the short to medium term.[14]

Peace, Justice, and Human Rights

In the passage quoted earlier, Neff states that the original idea underlying just war thought was that war could be used "for the subduing of evil and the promotion of good" (Neff 2005, 29–30). Contemporary writers are more likely to speak of promoting justice (see, for instance, Caney 2005). Something needs to be said on the relationship between justice and the good.

With respect to the public or common good, justice plays a significant role. Respect for a few basic human rights (e.g., the right to life, the right not to be discriminated against) can reasonably be taken as an uncontroversial part of the good for individuals as well as a public good. Another part of the good for individuals is that the institutions governing society shall be just, both with regard to respecting basic liberties and with the distribution of burdens. Beyond that I need not go for the present.

Before proceeding, it might be helpful to refer to a background issue, although it is not a foreground concern in this work. The issue is the relationship of just war thought to contemporary global political theory. For global political theory, Simon Caney lists cosmopolitanism, realism, the "society of states" tradition, and nationalism as the four main competing approaches (2005, 3–15). Cosmopolitanism holds that individual human beings, not states or nations or ethnic groups, are the ultimate units of moral concern, that they have equal status as units of moral concern, and that they are of equal concern for everybody in a global way. Realism, touched on in the previous chapter, holds that the individual state naturally pursues its own self-interest, unmotivated by any altruistic moral concern, and sometimes also holds that the state ought not do otherwise. The "society of states" tradition sees states, not persons, as the key actors at a global level, and seeks to define international justice largely in terms of the relations between states. Nationalism's view is that people are partly defined by membership of a nation, and that their moral duties and rights are primarily oriented to fellow nationals.

The just war tradition relies on some notion of an international peace that is worth fighting for by some elementary standards of justice. While not absolutely incompatible with realism, the two fit poorly together. Nor is there much possibility of it fitting the nationalist approach to global political theory. Just war thought is essentially international and global in its orientation. It can find a place within both the cosmopolitan and the "society of states" traditions.[15]

In the context of just war thought, talk about justice quickly and understandably moves to talk about human rights.[16] In contemporary discussions of *jus ad bellum*, the concept of justice is primarily deontological, involving such matters as justified resistance to wrongful aggression, the duty to protect the victims of aggression, and (perhaps) a right of restitution for loss inflicted. It is the massive violation of human rights involved in genocide, ethnic cleansing, and the like that motivates us to think that resort to force in order to prevent or stop such violations not merely would be permitted but might even be morally required. If the good is about anything, it surely is about protecting the lives of the innocent and defending their rights. In line with Augustine's view, it can be argued that any part of the world where people's basic rights are extensively and life-threateningly violated cannot be described as in a state of peace. Respect for human rights is one of the most important elements constituting the human good.

Since it is extensively dealt with in the literature, I shall not rehearse it further. I want to draw attention to the fact that the good extends beyond what we would identify as human rights that impose duties upon us. Perhaps it can be approached initially by considering that the human good or general public well-being cannot be exhaustively described in terms of human rights. There are goods that government policy should promote even though it might be difficult to present them as meeting or vindicating a particular human right.[17]

In cases where injustice does not require an armed response, other considerations may dictate the kind of response that averts war. Improving relations between states in the interests of making peace more secure is one such type of good, and it is not obviously reducible to the goods that individual human rights represent. In general, it should be possible to study a state's foreign policy and to evaluate it not just with respect to its commitment to promote human rights internationally and to aid poorer countries, which would be clearly identifiable (and hence isolatable) parts of that policy, but also for the overall thrust of its policies in terms of their effect upon harmonious international relations.

It is appropriate here to bear in mind the limits of current progress. Cosmopolitans may speak of the international community and rejoice at the coming of international tribunals of various sorts, but the nation-state is not about to wither away, and the international community of states is not some kind of world government. This has a number of implications.

First, other states may not always be in a position to prevent massive violation of human rights occurring elsewhere. It does not follow that they have failed in justice or are acquiescent in human rights violation. The right to intervene by force of arms in such cases is far from generally accepted. The limits of what is politically feasible constrain governments.

Second, states are meant to represent the interests of their peoples. These interests cannot be cashed out in terms of human rights duties alone. They also concern matters of trade and commerce, wealth and poverty, and relative international position. In themselves, these are often not issues of justice. But they are matters where the human good is promoted, and there too it can be evaluated.

Directing attention toward values or rather virtues that promote the good, Caney comments: "It is entirely reasonable to argue that values such as compassion, forgiveness, and mercy, for example, should inform how regimes respond to external wrongs. The focus on justice is justified, however, on the grounds that it should define the environment within which people act" (2005, 191). Often a state's public policy may be oriented to promoting or providing things that are not strictly required under a deontological concept of justice but that clearly promote the well-being and flourishing of the people. It would be appropriate to think of the state's task in promoting the good as not confined to doing what a deontologically conceived notion of justice requires.

For instance, the building of peace requires the facilitation of harmonious social relations, requiring in turn a government willing to reduce severe social inequalities and to protect poorer groups from the ravages of criminal gangs. Radical failure in this area may give some justification to armed rebellion.

In general, too, governing and promoting the public good requires the consent of the governed. As NATO commanders in places like Iraq and Afghanistan quickly realized, victory in guerrilla war depends crucially on winning the support of the people among whom one fights, and that depends on being recognizably committed to the concrete goods of that people. Hence one can see the sense in which peace is a common or participative good as well as a public good.

Judgment

My treatment of a relatively maximal notion of peace has been broadly thematic, but it is unnecessary here to go into further detail. More relevant here is the range of political judgment oriented to a good that includes promoting and building that peace. Political judgments, insofar as they involve decisions about going to war, cannot be reduced to decisions solely about whether to go to war anymore than judgments about how to respond to armed criminals can be reduced to decisions about whether to use force against them. The requirement to make appropriate judgment about war can be met only within a developed framework of long-term policy.

That long-term policy should be oriented to the development of peace of the maximal kind outlined earlier. The moral judgments arising from or necessitated in the development of such policy are not fundamentally altered by the possibility of war or armed conflict. Practical moral judgments aimed at the good and the maximal peace that is part of it are not necessarily or inherently vulnerable to being overridden by judgments about whether to go to war in a given instance. Political decisions to go or not to go to war are not judgments in favor of war as such or avoidance of war as such but are choices of appropriate means to pursue the good and human well-being. Political judgments take decisions to go or not to go to war as means, not as ends.

To imagine that the mere choice or decision not to go to war could be a kind of self-contained policy goal or a moral achievement would be to reject political judgment (see O'Donovan 2003, 6–10).[18] Political judgment is oriented to policy goals, and war is an instrument of policy. Merely avoiding going to war does not constitute a policy, and removing the decision about going or not going to war from its political context is to obstruct understanding the relationship of war to peace and the good in general. Political judgments are made about the good, about those things that are the goals of public policy, and it is only within that framework that proper moral judgments can be made about war.

As will be seen, this line of thought moves us away from exclusive focus on the state's right of self-defense as well as away from the idea that only self-defense constitutes grounds for war.

O'Donovan notes that Francisco de Vitoria held that there could be only one just cause for war—namely, "wrong done." O'Donovan goes on: "In saying that the one just cause was 'wrong done,' [Vitoria] meant to establish the character of war as judgment, a reactive pronouncement upon an offence, and so wrest armed force away from the antagonistic concept of self-defense" (2003, 49).[19] He adds: "The attempt to privilege the defensive aim exclusively is a significant retreat from the spirit of the juridical proposal. It withdraws from the concept of an international community of right to the antagonistic concept of mortal combat; correspondingly, it is formally egoistic, protecting the rights of self-interest while excluding those of altruistic engagement" (55). Self-defense may form part of that public good and may well be a significant motivator even though it is not the noblest motivation. But it is not the moral center of gravity with respect to *jus ad bellum*. The moral core of *jus ad bellum* is the judgment of the good, whether international, national, or local.

Rawls's Antirealist Approach

My argument hitherto has rested upon the idea that human beings have some common interests and similar orientations with respect to peace and war. This concerns not just individual goods but also public and common goods. It has

also been noted that the just war tradition is oriented to the social achievement of the goods of peace and order that are necessary for individual human
beings to achieve their own goods or fulfillment.

Such a stance may appear to commit me to the view that the good is real, objective, and knowable. In philosophical terminology, it commits me to realism
about the good. But there are many philosophers who hold that there is no such
thing as an objective good; Hume, for example, holds that the good is nothing but what individuals or groups desire. Regarding social and political goods,
modern pluralism is often taken to require neutrality between the differing and
competing visions of the good that different groups hold in modern societies. In
consequence, pluralism requires at least neutrality between realism and antireal-
ism about the good. However, while I am sympathetic to realism, my argument
does not depend upon holding to realism about the good.

In fact, I propose little by way of a specific theory of human beings' nature
other than that they need peace to achieve their good or goods regardless of
whether these goods are understood in a realist metaphysical fashion as objective realities or understood practically as simply what individuals desire or take
to be their goods. Can the account outlined earlier be defended without the
realist metaphysics?

John Rawls's work in his book *The Law of Peoples* provides the material
for an affirmative response to the question. As in his earlier works, Rawls
acknowledges that in the modern world there is an irreducible plurality of
comprehensive doctrines about the good for human beings and human societies, each laden with metaphysical and anthropological assumptions. Some of
those doctrines are unreasonable, either in being internally incoherent or irrational or intolerant. Others are reasonable. Leaving the unreasonable positions
to one side, he seeks to address the reasonable ones: "I propose that in public
reason comprehensive doctrines of truth or right be replaced by an idea of
the politically reasonable addressed to citizens as citizens" (Rawls 1999, 132).
The reason for doing so is that reasonable adherents of specific philosophies
understand that they cannot find agreement on a common social life on the
basis of doctrines that are not shared.

In the case, for example, of the Stoic notion of a common human nature,
the metaphysical commitments it involves do not constitute an obstacle to the
nonmetaphysical, practical orientation I seek to tease out in line with Rawls's
thought. What is significant in that idea is not the Stoic doctrine of human
nature but the fact that their assumption of a common human nature (regardless of what it was) implies a kind of law common to all peoples. This ties in
neatly with Rawls's exploration of that theme in *The Law of Peoples*.

His notion of the law of peoples is an extension to the international zone
of his social contract theories of justice as fairness. The law of peoples is what

reasonable peoples would agree to as fair, assuming equality of status between different peoples. He defends the project against the charge of being utopian and therefore irrelevant.

> I believe the idea of a realistic utopia is essential. Two main ideas motivate the Law of Peoples: One is that the great evils of human history—unjust war and oppression, religious persecution and the denial of liberty of conscience, starvation and poverty, not to mention genocide and mass murder—follow from political injustice, with its own cruelties and callousness. . . . The other main idea is that, once the gravest forms of political injustice are eliminated by following just . . . social policies and establishing just . . . basic institutions, these great evils will eventually disappear. (Rawls 1999, 6–7)

That passage implies that many social evils are linked to war, that war arises in part at least from political injustice, and that just policies and institutions are required in order to eliminate war. What Rawls calls the law of peoples is concerned with some notion of the public good, however minimal or metaphysically neutral in conception. The goals to be pursued may not amount to a comprehensive concept of the good, but they do include social policies and institutions that are just or fair. Given that just social institutions cannot ignore armed violence, whether from criminals within the state or from external attack, it can be inferred that Rawls's minimalist utopia contains enough to support the argument outlined earlier in this chapter.

The metaphysical or moral realist on one side and the Kantian antirealist or Rawlsian constructivist on the other side would agree on the idea of a law of peoples (*ius gentium*). The realist holds to what Rawls would deem a "thick" concept of the good, and that concept would (provided the realist weren't an austere political individualist) involve a substantive notion of the public good, common to all human beings and distinct from the aggregate of individual goods, and entailing a social order that promoted that good. Such a view finds parallels in current communitarian thought (see, e.g., Etzioni 1995 and 2004). For antirealist constructivists like Kant and Rawls, the law of peoples is what would issue from a rational projection of a reasonable conception of justice based on fairness not just between individuals but also between peoples. This conception is the basis of the law of peoples. It includes equality between peoples and mutual respect for each people's right to autonomy and right to pursue the good as it sees fit within the constraints of fairness and the rule of law.

The details of realist or constructivist conceptions need not concern us here, for two reasons. First, it suffices that each involves a normative goal adequate to orient governments to the public good of peace and order. The constructivist view, as presented by Rawls following Kant (Rawls 1999, 10), endorses a "reasonably just constitutional democratic society" as a "realistic utopia" (Rawls 1999, 12). That will largely suffice to specify a major normative goal relevant to just war thought. The normative goals will be crucial for satisfying the right intention criterion in *jus ad bellum*. Second, a realist "thick" conception of the common good fully worked out is not necessary for our purposes.[20] Peace, human freedom, human rights, the rule of law, and representative government—no matter how minimal in content—seem to be key elements of the political good that the law of peoples would support.

The relevant point here underlying Rawls's theory on the law of peoples is apparent in the passage quoted a few paragraphs back: (a) the idea of international order based on fairness, equality of esteem between peoples, and a kind of reasonable pluralism that accepts differences requires for its realization that such evils as war be progressively eliminated; and (b) the task of eliminating war and other evils requires the removal of political injustice, a task that Rawls obviously takes to be that of existing states and peoples.

Rawls allows a right to war in self-defense. He allows it to reasonable liberal peoples and decent peoples, both categories of well-ordered peoples. He allows it also to benevolent absolutisms that, while not well-ordered in that their peoples are excluded from political participation, respect human rights.[21] By contrast, non-well-ordered peoples include outlaw states prone to going to war to advance their interests and what he calls societies burdened by unfavorable conditions (Rawls 1999, 106). The latter lack the conditions that would qualify them as subject to or guided by the law of peoples. With respect to them, Rawls remarks:

> On the assumption that there exist in the world some relatively well-ordered peoples, we ask . . . how these peoples should act towards non-well-ordered peoples. . . . Nonideal theory asks how this long-term goal might be achieved, or worked toward, usually in gradual steps. . . . So conceived, nonideal theory presupposes that ideal theory is already on hand. For until the ideal is identified, . . . nonideal theory lacks an objective, an aim, by reference to which its queries can be answered. . . . For these are questions of transition, of how to work from a world containing outlaw states and societies suffering from unfavorable conditions to a world in which all societies come to accept and follow the Law of Peoples. (Rawls 1999, 89–90)

In line with his more general theories of a liberal vision of justice as fairness, with respect for human rights and the right to political participation and to share in dialogue on reasonable laws for pluralistic societies, Rawls is doing much more than claiming that such societies may defend themselves against attack by outlaw states. He offers a view of an international order within the framework of what he calls ideal theory and asks how is it to be promoted in a world where its preconditions are missing.

Rawls is proposing a notion of an international common good as expressed in the principles of the law of peoples. In less metaphysically realist terms, he is proposing a vision of what reasonable people, able to participate politically and open to equality of esteem between peoples, would agree on as the best kind (or at least a sufficiently good kind) of international arrangement. Promoting it is related to issues of war and peace. Democracies may have to defend themselves from aggressive outlaw states, but that "is only their first and most urgent task. Their long-run aim is to bring all societies eventually to honor the Law of Peoples and to become full members in good standing of the society of well-ordered peoples. Human rights would thus be secured everywhere" (Rawls 1999, 92–93). He goes on to note that achieving this goal is a task for foreign policy.

Conclusion

My goal in this chapter has been to draw attention to the relevance of notions of the good as setting the framework within which alone the just war tradition can be understood. As is clear in Rawls's work and in most other writers on this topic, it is not a matter of organizing military crusades for democracy. Not merely would that generally not work, it would also often do more harm than good. Yet there may be occasions when the use of military force will be justifiable as promoting the goals he lists.

The just war tradition is not primarily about national self-defense, and (as I argue later) to attempt to interpret its criteria exclusively within a framework of self-defense leads to serious problems. Such an attempt ignores the idea that the good, conceived in realist or antirealist fashion, requires political action, and that pursuing or defending it may require going to war. Seeing the moral nature of war narrowly through the prism of self-defense leads to being unfaithful to our basic moral intuitions about the good and about international peace and the kind of order it requires. Without question, justification in going to war frequently involves self-defense. The point is that the right of self-defense in the context of war must be placed within a larger framework of the international good. The goal of this chapter has been to argue that case.

Notes

1. "Even when men choose to wage war, they desire nothing but victory. By means of war, therefore, they desire to achieve peace with glory. . . . Wars themselves, then, are conducted with the intention of peace. . . . Hence it is clear that peace is the desired end of war" (bk. XIX, chap. 12, 934).

2. The view expressed in the slogan "peace at any price."

3. See also Hobbes 1994, I, xiii, sect. 8: "Hereby it is manifest, that during the time men live without a common power to keep them all in awe, they are in that condition which is called war; and such a war, as is of every man against every man. For war consisteth not in battle only, or the act of fighting, but in a tract of time wherein the will to contend by battle is sufficiently known."

4. For more detail on this development, see Neff 2005, 30–34.

5. This must not be misunderstood as a justification of war in order to realize some heavenly ideal of universal peace. Neff correctly emphasizes that medieval thinkers did not present just war as "holy war" where the latter is understood as directed against people of different or no faith. Medieval Christian thinkers were clear that the mere fact that a certain tribe or nation was non-Christian gave no justification to Christians to attack it. See ibid., 54–56.

6. I assume a kind of metaphysical realism in this section: in talking about goods or the good of some sort, I intend something objective or real and not merely the value preferences of particular individuals or groups. Later in the chapter I shall consider an antirealist view.

7. From this point on, I treat order as an integral part of the good of peace. That implies a rejection of the minimal-peace notion since the absence of actual violence does not entail any kind of order. Augustine identifies peace with the peace or stability of good order. "Pax est tranquillitas ordinis": "the peace of all things lies in the tranquility of order" (1998, bk. XIX, chap.13, 938).

8. The list and examples come from Haldane 2004, 141–42; see also Riordan 2008, 9.

9. Instances can be found in situations of intercommunal conflict. Peace-building is to be distinguished from peacekeeping or peace-enforcing, which are matters of enforcement of law and order by the public authority. Peace-building depends upon improvements in relationships between members of the opposing communities, thereby easing tensions and warding off potential explosions of civil unrest. This is the kind of activity that local community leaders or activists could initiate and promote, and without which peace will not be built.

10. See particularly 142–44: "An adequate conception of the common life will see it as something whose value is separate from, and irreducible to, the value of the particular individuals that make it up, yet its worth must be seen as deriving from the value it has for them." Rodin does not think a case can be made for going to

war to defend such things since they are ill-defined and the individuals who "live in them" also belong to many other communities. I think his view of the common life of a community is too confined by notions of cultural similarity and group identification.

11. "I argue that international protection regimes are part of a class of institutions that are designed to promote the 'common good' for a collectivity of states. Unlike functional institutions that seek to provide consumable benefits to their participants, 'institutions for the common good' are concerned with the preservation and general welfare of the international order itself. Their development requires a consensus among a group of core states around a basic set of political and normative principles" (2003, 4)

12. For discussion of the heuristic nature of the notion of the common good, see Riordan 2008, chap. 2.

13. See Chesterman 2002; Doyle and Sambanis 2006; Seybolt 2007; Slaughter 2005; and Wheeler 2000, among many other works on peacekeeping and peacemaking.

14. See, for example, Cronin 2003, 208–9: "Over the past decade, the Security Council has expanded the role of the peacekeepers to include state-building, civil administration, facilitating democratization, promoting human rights, disarming militias, protecting populations from attack, caring for displaced persons, and even enforcing Security Council resolutions."

15. For an important recent contribution from the cosmopolitan stable, see Fabre 2012.

16. See Caney 2005; Seybolt 2007; Slaughter 2005; and Wheeler 2000 for works in this genre.

17. It is on this point that I find myself in some disagreement with the cosmopolitan tradition as represented, for instance, by Fabre 2012. Human rights are fundamentally individualistic in conception. That is both their strength and their weakness. The weakness can be compensated for by acceptance of the notion that there are various human goods that are not directly or immediately reducible to individual rights or the goods of individuals. Foreign policy failures for a particular state may undermine international order seriously, in the general judgment of historians, without having affected the rights or well-being of any identifiable individuals. There are important human goods here that can be captured only by a more generous social ontology than the cosmopolitans allow.

18. In an interesting Christian perspective, O'Donovan suggests that pacifism implicitly refuses to see the necessity of judging ("refusing the judicial proposal"), and thereby it "makes *survival* the final criterion of what may and may not be done." He states why he sees that as incompatible with the Christian view of the pursuit of peace and judgment: "To take survival as the bottom line is to revert to the antagonistic model of mortal combat, and so inevitably to retreat from the Gospel

proclamation of the universal rule of Christ and from the praxis of loving judgment. When self-defense . . . has the last word, paganism is restored" (2003, 9).

19. For Vitoria, see Reichberg, Syse, and Begby 2006, 314.

20. Besides, its working out is necessarily part of the communicative interactive political process, rather than an academic exercise. See Riordan 2008, 102, and chap. 7 in general.

21. See Rawls 1999, 4, 92, where the different categories of peoples or societies are distinguished.

Chapter 3

Good Authority

Till the war-drum throbb'd no longer and the battle-flags were furl'd
In the Parliament of man, the Federation of the world.
There the common sense of most shall hold a fretful realm in awe
And the kindly earth shall slumber, lapt in universal law.

Tennyson, *Locksley Hall*

The Priority Issue

In chapter 1 I listed competent authority, just cause, right intention, probability of success, last resort, and proportionality, in that order, as the *jus ad bellum* criteria—that is, the criteria to be met in order to be justified in going to war. On my view of *jus ad bellum*, competent priority is prior to just cause. I start by treating the reasons for that ordering and then move to listing and discussing the different candidates for the role of competent authority.

Usually just cause is given precedence over competent authority. Since doing so is rarely defended, it is probable that many writers assume that the order doesn't matter, so giving just cause precedence is seen as having no significance, not implying any kind of theoretical priority. But I hold that the order matters. First, as a general point, some *jus ad bellum* criteria depend logically on others. As I argue in later chapters, instances include right intention's dependence on just cause, last resort's dependence on reasonable probability of success, probability of success's dependence on right intention, and proportionality's dependence on nearly all the others.

Second, regarding just cause and competent authority, giving priority to the authority criterion makes a difference to how the just cause criterion is to be understood. If just cause is given priority, it could be understood as something that any agent, individual person, group, or state might have; if competent authority is prior, only an agent qualifying as a competent authority can have just cause within the *jus ad bellum* framework. I hold that competent authority is prior.[1] In so doing I am closer to the medieval view of just war than to the modern view, although that is not what motivates my stance. What motivates my position is that it yields an interpretation of *jus ad bellum* that is more serviceable in today's world.

I take *jus ad bellum* theory to be part not of an ethics of self-defense that could apply to individual persons as well as states but of a theory of governance. Some of the elements of that theory were elaborated in the previous chapter. It is the role of the state to promote various goods, just as it is the role of the United Nations to promote certain goods that cannot be promoted by individual states. These goods include the goods of human life and respect for the individual's right to life, and so also include appropriate structures and practices that defend individuals and groups. That role and project are not confined to defense of the individual from hostile attack.

Just Cause: Self-Defense?

I will explore just cause at greater length in the next chapter, but it is necessary to draw attention here to certain aspects of it. From the eighteenth century onward, nearly all modern thought about the justification of war took self-defense as the key element in just cause. Much contemporary thought takes it to be the only element so that a state has just cause to go to war only when self-defense requires it. International law holds self-defense to be the only permissible reason for going to war without the authorization of the United Nations (UN Charter 1945, Arts. 2 (4) and 51).[2]

Contemporary thought assumes that (a) the state has a right of self-defense; (b) the right is analogous to the individual's right of self-defense; (c) the state's self-defense can be understood either as defense of its citizens or defense of itself; and (d), accordingly, the state's right of self-defense can be justified either by inferential extension from the individual's right (so that the state's right of self-defense arises from its duty to protect its citizens and vindicate their right of self-defense) or can be justified simply by virtue of the analogy so that the state as a kind of legal person may be assumed to have the same right to self-defense that any human person has. The dominant twentieth-century thinking has been to argue that just as the individual has no right to use force except to protect himself or a vulnerable person in his care, so the state has no right to use force for any purpose other than self-defense.

Each of the four points can be challenged. David Rodin has recently made a powerful case against the idea that there is such a thing as a right of national self-defense. He argues that attempts to ground national self-defense on the individual's right of self-defense do not work. One attempt at such grounding is by claiming that the state's self-defense is simply the individual citizens collectively defending themselves, and the other is the argument that national self-defense is the state protecting its citizens from lethal attack. Neither will suffice to provide justification for anything like a modern state resorting to war, even in cases where one might intuitively feel that there was overwhelming justification for going to war (2002, 127–32). It would be impossible to argue that Britain and France went to war with Germany in 1939 in order to protect their own citizens, and it would be a gerrymandered or even question-begging argument that tried to show they did so to protect Poland's citizens. At the same time, Rodin's position is not pacifist since he holds that there could be situations in which a country would be justified in going to war. But arguments to support that claim cannot be based on the right to self-defense.[3]

If we accept Rodin's argument, we can no longer think of instances where a country has just cause to go to war as simply instances of self-defense similar to an individual's right to self-defense. If there can be just cause for a state to go to war, just cause will turn out to be something different from self-defense; exploring the range of such possibilities will be the main burden of the next chapter. Even if we were to admit that countries can and often do go to war in self-defense strictly conceived, it does not follow that in such cases self-defense would be the only kind of possible just cause.

Some of the elements in the just war tradition indirectly support Rodin's position.[4] Aquinas doesn't mention self-defense or defense of the people as providing just cause; he sees just cause as a matter of punishing wrongdoing, and restoring right order (Reichberg, Syse, and Begby 2006, 176–78). John Finnis holds that Aquinas doesn't mention self-defense because he takes it as self-evident that states have a right to defend themselves against unjust attack.[5] However, it is important to note (as Finnis does comprehensively) that such self-defense is not analogous to or logically derived from the individual's right to self-defense. Aquinas's magistrate is not like my personal bodyguard, hired via the social contract to protect me so that his or her right to use force to protect me is based upon or derived from my right to defend myself by force if necessary. The ruler or magistrate's role is to protect the social order and the public and common goods it embodies, and that role is not derived by analogy or logical inference from the individual's right to self-defense.[6] For Aquinas, the ruler or magistrate may kill where necessary in protection of the general good and public order (which includes such things as the defense of individuals unjustly assaulted, robbed, or threatened), but the individual may never intend to take life, even the life of an aggressor.[7]

Stephen Neff is incisive on this point in his outline of the just war tradition in premodern times.

It would be a great error to equate a just war, in its medieval incarnation, with a defensive war. It is true that wars of aggression were roundly and consistently denounced. . . . It is also true that, in a certain manner of speaking, all just wars were defensive in the very broad sense that they were designed to defend the world against wickedness, to prevent evil from overcoming good. . . . Just wars were, however, offensive in the sense that the enforcement action of a magistrate is offensive. . . . He actively searches out criminals and brings them to justice. It should also be appreciated that this detective action might take place at some point of time substantially *later* than the original criminal act. The magistrate's action could then be said to be a response to crime, but it could not be said to be a defense against the actual *commission* of a crime. . . . A situation of an aggressive attack by one state against another would be analyzed in terms of the presence and absence of a *justa causa* rather than of the exercise of self-defense. (2005, 59–60)

Neff's remarks bring out the implications of the idea that medieval just war thought is part of a theory of governance, not part of a theory of personal ethics or individual rights. Accordingly, the just war tradition (at least in its premodern phase) may be closer to Rodin's viewpoint than he realizes since it does not think of just cause as something derived from an individual's natural right to self-defense.[8]

The idea that having just cause to go to war is a matter of individual self-defense writ large or, extended to the state, is also implicitly rejected in the just war tradition's sharp distinction between *duelum* and *bellum*. *Duelum* is armed conflict between an individual and his enemy. The Christian tradition opposed it unequivocally and did not think that the natural right to self-defense allowed one to act in any way designed or intended to kill one's attacker. By contrast, *bellum*, or the resort to arms by the state or magistrate to repress criminal individuals or criminal states, was not merely permitted but might well be a positive duty of the ruler or magistrate.[9]

There are also reasons of a more empirical kind for rejecting the idea that just cause is essentially a matter of national self-defense. These have to do with the historical record with respect to particular wars. Even in cases where we would be inclined to think that certain countries were justified in going to war (Britain and France against Germany in 1939, the United Nations or the United States against Iraq in 1991), attempts to show that the just cause was essentially a matter of self-defense are unlikely to be successful. Far too many other considerations of a political nature, many turning on the issue of good governance, present themselves in such historical instances to allow us to ignore them.

Against the Priority of Just Cause

Taking just cause as logically prior to competent authority allows that just cause could obtain for an unrestricted range of agents. This view also allows that the same kind of just cause could apply in principle for all such possible agents: sovereign states, the United Nations, insurrectionary rebel groups, a particular community or ethnic group, and the individual citizen. Since self-defense or defense of weaker family members is the only possible "just cause" for the individual, all other instances of the justifiable use of force would have to be an instance or token of the same type—namely, self-defense.

Objections to that position include the following. First, the position assumes that the same basic moral framework of rights and duties applies to each of the agents listed in the previous paragraph. Even if the arguments from Rodin and the just war tradition summarized earlier were unsuccessful, they are sufficiently strong to raise plausible doubt about the viability, let alone the advisability, of making that assumption. In the case of the state, one ought not simply assume that the practical exigencies and the corresponding moral factors of public policy involving the use of force, whether by the army or the police, are fundamentally identical to those found in the individual's situation.

Second, the position generates a kind of theoretical straitjacket that obstructs working out a proper *jus ad bellum* theory. In the case of the state dealing with criminals, it seems contrived to claim that use of force to restrain and punish them is essentially a form of self-defense. The modern state's understanding of its role with respect to crime goes beyond defending itself and its citizens. Dealing with crime comes under the general heading of promoting the public good, including making and enforcing laws to maintain justice, equity, and social order and enforcing laws that do not defend people so much as improve their quality of life.

Most crime is not as such an attack on the state, so the issue of the state's self-defense does not generally arise with respect to its use of force to repress such crime. Some crime involves direct attack on individuals, threatening them with death, injury, or other serious loss, so the state's action in making laws against such behavior and enforcing them can be viewed as oriented to the defense of the individual. But even in such cases, the interests, rights and duties of the state are neither identical to nor even isomorphic with those of the individual, so the argument that suggests that the state is essentially defending individual citizens when acting against criminals does not work well. That such action by the state also is intended to protect individual citizens is true, but the concept upon which it is based has to do with the nature of society rather than with the rights per se of particular individuals.

In the case of the state's use of force against other states, we are not obliged to cast justification within the self-defense framework since there is also the option of basing it on the state's right to restrain and punish criminals. A further option, canvassed in the previous chapter, is to base it on the state's duty to protect certain common goods and to promote a kind of peace that is more than the mere absence of armed conflict.

Third, since the self-defense option confines the state's role to mere self-defense or defense of its population from attack, it is too constricting. In line with what was said in the last paragraph, the self-defense option does not give adequate weight to the role of the state in promoting such goods as peace and international order. It does this in part by generating the tacit assumption that the state has no right to use force that exceeds in scope or in grounds the right to use force that the individual person has. Such a position entails a problematic restriction on public policy. It also blocks the development of a full-blooded view of *jus ad bellum*, which sees certain bodies as agencies not so much as sovereign but rather as charged with responsibility for such public goods as peace and stable international order, planetary management of finite resources, respect for human rights, and protection of minorities.

The Priority of Authority

I assume that human beings as individuals have a right of self-defense. I also assume that the state as competent authority has a right and a duty to defend and promote certain goods.[10] The two rights are fundamentally different. Both may provide sufficient warrant for resort to use of force, but the grounds for warrant will be significantly different. If an aggressor's intentions toward the people of another state included mass murder (as Nazi Germany rounded up and murdered Jews in German-occupied territories during World War II), enslavement (as Nazi Germany intended in the case of Slav peoples), or mass expulsion of population, the defending state's action in resisting the aggressor could reasonably be described as defending its people. However, the grounds giving primary warrant for the state's defense of its people will be, in *jus ad bellum* thought, its governance role of promoting various goods—in this instance, the human rights of the affected individuals and the responsiveness of national and international authorities to human needs and violations of human rights.

With respect to war, in principle only a duly constituted public authority can qualify as a competent authority. That is paradigmatically the sovereign state, but it might devolve on lower-level local authorities in some circumstances. In a way that is hard to identify precisely, the United Nations can also function as a competent authority (see UN Charter 1945, ch. VII).

The possibility that bodies or groups other than the sovereign state could be competent to wage war entails that competent authority in *jus ad bellum* is not to be identified with sovereignty. Sovereignty as traditionally understood may be neither necessary nor sufficient to meet the competent authority criterion. The UN Charter says in effect that sovereignty is not sufficient to constitute the governments of individual states as competent authorities to wage war for any purpose other than immediate self-defense (Art. 51).

Insurrection and Authority

The traditional interpretation of *jus ad bellum*'s competent authority criterion effectively excludes individuals and nonstate groups from qualifying as competent authorities. Here I briefly turn to consider rebellion against injustice or an insurrection for liberation. Does my interpretation of competent authority mean that rebellion and insurrection can never be morally justified at all? Does it mean rebellion can never be justified within the *jus ad bellum* theory?

Regarding the first question, rebellion against a government intentionally and immediately threatening the lives of people could be justified by appeal to the individual's right to self-defense. With respect to the issue of authority, with which this chapter is concerned, the individual whose life is unjustly threatened by the government's agents needs no other authority to defend herself than her right to life.[11] The fact that neither she nor the other members of her family constitute a competent authority of the *jus ad bellum* kind makes no difference to the applicability of that right. Since, for the reasons mentioned, I am not concerned in this book with the right to self-defense, I say no more on this point other than to emphasize that nothing in the understanding of *jus ad bellum* that I propose undermines the individual's right to self-defense.

Turning to the second question, rebellion against the governing competent authority cannot as such be justified within *jus ad bellum* thought. A group within the population might rebel in order to defend their lives against a government intent on massacring them, but their justification arises from a right to self-defense, not a right to rebellion.

However, the government might cease to qualify as a competent authority, so the duty to obey it might lapse. A tyrannical government that monopolizes power and excludes ordinary people from participation and that permits radical social inequalities thereby undermines social peace and the goods that it involves.[12] In cases where the government's policy is demonstrably attacking various goods, and where the attack is serious and widespread in nature, there is a prima facie case in favor of the claim that such people have a right of insurrection, partly in self-defense, and partly to restore and rebuild peace, understood in a nonminimal way.[13] In such a case, the tyrannical and unrepresentative government facing a popular uprising ceases to count as a competent authority to wage war or suppress insurrection, and the leaders of the popular uprising may reasonably claim to have the necessary authority to launch a war of insurrection. This is not, unlike the right to self-defense, an individual right but a group right.

It is partly because of the foregoing considerations that I argue that *jus ad bellum*'s competent authority criterion ought not be understood as referring essentially to the sovereign state. Focusing on sovereignty tends to direct attention solely to a state's relations to other states, adverting to the fact that it is not subject to any higher external authority. Focusing on competent authority directs attention also to that authority's relation to its people.

In cases of insurrection against tyranny, the most difficult challenge to meet with respect to *jus ad bellum* is having competent authority. Private individuals and rebel groups cannot as such constitute competent authority. Meeting it depends on the insurrection's leaders being representative of the people, and depends on the nature of that representativeness being open to including some moral permission or moral right to lead an insurrection. I suspect that meeting the challenge has rarely been achieved, partly due to the difficulty of identifying precisely who has the right to lead that insurrection as representative of the people. That may be hard to determine in the absence of elections of any kind. Nevertheless, I am reluctant to relax the criterion, even though it is infrequently met, in the case of insurrections.[14] One may not launch a war on one's own authority but only on good authority, and that authority has to derive from having some recognizable capacity to take responsibility for the public good where no other institution is in a better position to do so.[15]

Accepting Rodin's argument, I conclude that the most appropriate way to understand the competent authority criterion in *jus ad bellum* is not as based on national self-defense. It is to be conceived more along the lines of the state's role in promoting the rule of law, good order, social justice, and other public goods.

The Role of the State

I have been speaking of competent authority rather than of legitimate authority. Legitimacy is a legal and moral notion. A legitimate government is representative of the popular will in some formal way, and it respects and enforces the rule of law. The notion of competence I take to be more practical and political. A competent government has effective control of the national territory. Both legitimacy and competence are matters of degree rather than all-or-nothing notions. Legitimacy and competence overlap to a substantial degree; however, I shall place the emphasis on competence. Some putative governments have either no legitimacy or no competence of any kind and effectively do not count as governments.

By contrast, sovereignty as conventionally understood from the Peace of Westphalia (1648) up to the present day is an all-or-nothing thing. The existence of a sovereign state with no legal superior and rights to autonomy and noninterference has nothing to do with the moral or political character of the state, or with the legitimacy or lack thereof of its current government, or with how it treats its citizens or subjects. If sovereignty is taken (as it has been) to be that which determines who qualifies as a competent authority, it follows that the moral and political nature of the regime is irrelevant to the criterion. That would mean that the competent authority criterion has no moral content and would involve a Thrasymachean position that might makes right, and that controlling the national territory is all that is needed to make certain people morally competent to govern.

The appropriate interpretation of competent authority takes it as a moral criterion. This has two aspects. First, to qualify as a competent authority, effective control of the national territory is necessary, albeit insufficient. Some commitment to the well-being of the people of the territory is also necessary. A group of bandits may have taken over the country and now exercise effective control of the territory and the organs of the state. They must now start to behave, at least in part, as if they were the government of the country with some responsibility for its care. They may still want to loot and rob, but they must also want to govern to some degree.

Second, competence comes in degrees.[16] Compared to a democratic government, a dictatorship practicing genocide against a section of its population is significantly lacking the appropriate moral (and political) character to be the relevant competent authority for that state. Its competence is minimal while a democratic government committed to the rule of law, to respecting the rights of the citizens, and to promoting their well-being has a maximal competence.

The view of authors such as Aquinas is that the appropriate authority for deciding matters of war is the same as that which has the right to make laws—that is, the prince who has charge of the public good and is representative in some fashion of the people.[17] His view is closer to an emerging contemporary view that a thuggish dictator is not to be considered as on a par with a democratic government than it is to the view that both are equally sovereign. In line with that, I argue for drawing distinctions between different kinds of regimes.

A nondemocratic authoritarian government will usually have little legitimacy since it is not democratic and hence presumably is not representative of the popular will. But it can still count as a competent authority. China's government is nondemocratic yet for most purposes it is the relevant competent

authority with which other agents must deal since it controls the territory of
China and there is no other government. Its legitimacy is defective yet not null
and void nor such that one could say unequivocally that it is illegitimate. After the Spanish Civil War (1936–39), when Gen. Francisco Franco abolished
the republic and established a dictatorship, one would agree, in 1940, with
those who held that his was an illegitimate regime. By the 1960s, the Franco
regime had lasted a long time by Spanish standards and could claim a kind of
low-grade legitimacy on the basis of the passive acquiescence of the Spanish
public and the passage of time. Even in 1940, however, foreign governments
would have been compelled to deal with the Franco regime as the de facto
government of Spain and, hence, the competent authority for many, though
not necessarily all, purposes.

A third case to consider is Burma (Myanmar), which has been ruled by an
unpopular military junta since the early 1960s. In 1990, the National League
for Democracy led by Daw Aung San Suu Kyi won a clear majority in relatively free elections. However, the military declared the elections void and
resumed power by force. One could argue that Aung San Suu Kyi and her
party were the legitimate government of Burma, and that the military junta
had no legitimacy. On the other hand, only the military had any effective
control of the country, and Aung San Suu Kyi's party were opposed to military
action to overthrow the regime. In those circumstances, the claim to be the
legitimate government would wear thin over many years, when there is no
effective control, no competence to do things. In that period, the governing
military regime has little or no legitimacy. Did it have any competence? One
reason for attributing competence to it is that other countries must deal with
it as the de facto government. A second is that, if Burma were attacked by one
of its neighbors intent on conquering and annexing part or all of Burma, the
military regime would count as a competent authority to order and organize
resistance. On the other hand, if Burma had been invaded (with the consent
of the democratic opposition) by the United Nations or some military alliance
intending to overthrow the military and put the National League for Democracy in power, the regime would have lacked any competence to resist.

I suggest that the minimum required to qualify as a competent authority is
(a) a substantial degree of support from or acquiescence by the population, (b)
effective control of most of the country, and (c) a minimal commitment to the
well-being of the population. In such situations, being a competent authority
will endow the government with a limited legitimacy.

As can be seen, my view of competent authority as found in the just war
tradition is fundamentally different from that developed in the early modern
age of Hobbes and the absolute monarchs of Europe, whose authority was
absolute, without superior, and in no way a matter of degree.

Having clarified issues of competence, I want to say a little more about the state, with respect to its legitimacy. In political philosophy, there is a range of views about the role of the state. At one end of the spectrum are authoritarian and totalitarian views holding the state to be a virtual end in itself, with the rights (if any) of the individual citizens subordinate to the needs of the state, regardless of how such needs might be conceived. Since this advocates a view of the state as not accountable to the citizens, its level of competence lies toward the minimal end of my scale.

At the other end of the spectrum is the libertarian or minimalist position, which sees the state as merely the guarantor of the basic rights of individual citizens, particularly liberty, and the enforcer of law and order. Precisely because the liberty of the citizens is such an important good, the state must be a minimal structure, being careful to extend its powers no further than is necessary to maintain life and liberty, regardless of how well-intentioned particular extensions might be.

Toward the middle of the spectrum are the positions that envisage a larger role for the state as not just protector of the rights of the individual citizens but also promoter of the public good. There are also communitarian positions of various kinds. The main point they have in common and that differentiates them from libertarianism is their rejection of the libertarian claim that a society or nation is nothing but a collection of individuals, and the public good nothing but the aggregate of individual goods.

Nevertheless, even if the public good is reductively defined as merely the aggregate of the goods of that society's individual members, a libertarian can accept the claim that the state protects the public good. Accordingly, both libertarians and communitarians can agree that the state's role is to promote the public good, that it must do so subject to the rule of law, and that it is accountable to and serves at the pleasure of the people. Taking the spectrum of opinion ranging from libertarian and communitarian positions but excluding authoritarian nondemocratic opinion, the kind of state described by such theories will qualify as a competent authority in the full sense.

A further element worth noting is that the state's role involves being authorized or empowered to judge not just through the judiciary but also through the legislative and executive branches of government (see O'Donovan 2003, 6, 14, 25–26; 2005). The three branches of government can be seen as expressions of different aspects of the kind of competence required of government: representative competence to make laws, judicial competence to adjudicate legal claims and determine when laws have been broken and when rights have been violated, and executive competence both to enforce the law and to make political judgments on behalf of the people. To the extent that any of these functions or branches of government have been subverted or suppressed, moral competence to govern (including to go to war) is vitiated. Identifying the scope of legitimate or competent authority regarding going to war involves not just focusing on the chief executive or head of state (the one who traditionally declares war) but more broadly acknowledging that going to war involves a practical judgment that is potentially multifaceted. In the case of the decision to go to war, it is a practical judgment in the political order; it is not within the political capacity of private groups to make such a judgment.

The Range of Competent Political Authority

Older notions of authority with respect to war largely confined it to the prince or ruler. In medieval Europe, the Holy Roman Emperor was superior to kings only in name and, with respect to international order, did not have anything like the limited authority the United Nations has had since 1948. From the sixteenth century, the fracturing by religious division of medieval Christendom undermined any remaining sense of a common polity or common normative culture. In addition, the rise of strong centralized monarchies in several countries led to an era of absolute monarchy, with the "right" religion being determined by the local ruler and legal thought moving toward the positivism of identifying law as essentially the enforced will of the sovereign.

The influence of legal positivism has been deep and enduring, even though qualified of late. First, it put the sovereign above the law since the law emanated from his will. Since particular sovereigns had their own ideas on what was good for their countries and peoples, it was idle to try to identify some kind of transnational good. This began to change in the late eighteenth century as the American and French revolutions led to greater acceptance of the idea that government had to be aimed at the good of the people. However, this idea had little or no impact with respect to the waging of war. Second, and following the previous point, legal positivism made the notions of international law or the traditional *ius gentium* problematic since, not emanating from a sovereign with the power to enforce, they could not count as law.

On this view, one could not coherently speak of an illegal war since going to war breaks the law of no sovereign. One might hope that sovereigns would behave justly in their dealings with other nations, but the political culture of the time and the legal positivism that later expressed it had no room for laws that might establish norms for the behavior of sovereigns toward each other. It is perhaps not surprising, then, that discussion of the just war tradition focused on *jus in bello*, justice in the conduct of war. For the *jus ad bellum* side, it could only be assumed that the sovereign alone had the right to decide in a given instance whether it was morally right to go to war. There could be no moral norms (other than defense of his country) to guide or restrain him, to prohibit or mandate his going to war. Not surprisingly, what would count as just causes were ultimately only the interests of the sovereign, his state, and his dynasty.

While legal positivism is still influential, developments in political and jurisprudential thought have moved us away from the worldview of an earlier legal positivism. Today we think of the sovereign or the state no longer as above the law but as limited and subject to law in various ways. These ways include national constitutions and international law. As noted earlier, international law was (and still is by some political "realists") often taken to be law only by courtesy since there is no sovereign as such behind it. Yet today most sovereign states like to stand well with international law, to abide by it (generally), and are willing to put some pressure on other sovereign states to conform to it. At the same time, let it be admitted that its effectiveness is limited and tenuous.[18] Even so, the relative political stability of the Western Hemisphere, of western Europe, and more lately of much of central and eastern Europe has created conditions favorable to the development and expansion of international law.[19]

Outside of realist circles, it is accepted that international law is effective law even though there is no one sovereign as such whose will has produced it. The United Nations is not a sovereign authority, and much international law has its origins independent of the United Nations. An interesting case is EU law, which has all the force of law to the point of being overriding with respect to the national laws of its members even though the European Union is not a sovereign state like the United States. Granting that assumption, a good prima facie case can be made for rejecting the claim of the political realist that the zone of international relations is necessarily a Hobbesian lawless jungle.[20] That wars occur, usually involving violations of international law, does not demonstrate that international law is without normative force anymore than the occurrence of crime shows that the national law is ineffective.

The step I wish to take next is to argue that the concept of competent authority in *jus ad bellum* should be refined in light of those considerations. The primary refinement is to expand the concept of legitimate or competent authority beyond the governments of nation-states.

Before going further, recall that, unlike pacifism and realism, just war thought is based upon faith in the possibility of bringing the zone of war and armed conflict under the rule of law. That tradition interprets war within the framework of law enforcement, and hence is open to the possibility that war can be a tool for the promotion of the public good. Pacifism and realism each deny the existence of such a possibility and consider the faith misplaced. However, given developments in international law in recent decades as well as the public opinion and political thought that generated such developments, I think the faith neither misplaced nor unreasonable.

Competent Authority: The United Nations

I consider a range of candidates to qualify as a competent authority with respect to going to war. The first candidate is the United Nations, the successor to the League of Nations between the two world wars. The usual objection to counting the United Nations as an authority is the fact that it is not a sovereign state and does not have an army.[21] In addition, the veto power of the permanent members of the Security Council (United States, Russia, China, France, and Britain) limits the range of acceptable UN political stances. That makes the United Nations a very restricted authority for practical purposes.

The UN Charter claims an overriding authority with respect to going to war (Arts. 2 [4] and 39). The United Nations authorized collective military action in support of South Korea against North Korea in 1950 and similar action to expel Iraq from Kuwait in 1990. It has also frequently authorized the limited military action of peacekeeping and, more rarely, that of peacemaking. But in a far larger number of cases, it has been unable to do so since the attempt to provide authorization was likely to be vetoed or actually vetoed by one of the permanent members of the Security Council. To that extent, an older balance of power dynamic was still operative after the two world wars.

Epur si muove: and yet—in Galileo's words—it moves. Flawed and limited though it may be, the United Nations still works at least some of the time. Just as importantly, global public opinion sees the United Nations as having legitimacy-conferring power. Individual states or peoples often appeal to it to take action to right some wrong or even merely to grant the political support of taking a public stand by passing a resolution in support of the plaintiff.

Sometimes the authority of the United Nations is exaggerated by public opinion. In the case of the Anglo-American invasion of Iraq in 2003, the fact that the United Nations did not authorize that resort to military action was widely seen as nullifying any moral justification for the Anglo-American military offensive against Iraq, since the United States and Britain were viewed by many as not competent authorities with respect to making such a decision.

It is unreasonable and ultimately impractical to deny national governments the status of competent authority with respect to war. In any case, with its lack of army or command structure, the idea that the United Nations could count as the sole competent authority with respect to war is not an idea that can be taken seriously.

The United Nations is recognized as a legitimate (and hence at least partly competent) authority with respect to *jus ad bellum*, despite its not being a state or sovereign and despite the UN secretary-general being merely a civil servant. That widespread view of the United Nations thus represents a move away from the idea that legitimate authority is tied to, if not inherently vested in, a person toward the idea that authority is to be linked primarily to law.

Competent Authority: The Law

The second kind of competent authority follows in part from the first. It is the law itself.[22] Cashing out this idea is complex, but it can be done. The central idea upon which it is based is the age-old ideal of the rule of law as distinct from the rule of persons. The extent to which we allow validity to that ideal is a measure of the weight we should give to the idea of law as authoritative with respect to war. Allowing that the UN could qualify as a legitimate authority for the purposes of *jus ad bellum* entails accepting that sovereignty may not be necessary for authority.

In the more remote past, the ideal of the rule of law had associations with the notion of a higher law. Since the late eighteenth century, it has found concrete expression in the idea of a constitution limiting lawmakers and government officials. Such constitutionalism also involved the modern distinction between the legislative, executive, and judicial branches of government, thereby reinforcing the idea that the law is not to be identified with the rule of an individual or party. By constitutionally limiting and regulating government's powers and distinguishing its functions in order to balance them against each other, the authority of the law is enhanced in the eyes of the public, thereby increasing its political efficaciousness and promoting its normative power. The normative force of the law is distinct from the will and decisions of the ruler, whether legislator, executive, or judge.

Sometimes, this normative force is overstated in ways that seek to eliminate the role of politics and even morality. There is a tendency, no doubt more noticeable among lawyers and legal philosophers, to consider the law's authority as the sole relevant authority with respect to war. Yoram Dinstein remarked in 2004: "It is totally irrelevant today whether or not a war is just. The sole question is: is war legal, in accordance with the Charter?" (2004, 880). But this is too cavalier a dismissal of the relevance of the moral dimensions of war, as these are expressed and negotiated within the political context in which policy is formulated and implemented.

In Lon Fuller's words, "law is the enterprise of subjecting human conduct to the governance of rules. . . . This view treats law as an activity and regards a legal system as the product of a sustained purposiveness" (1969, 106). International law is not just a set of rules but the project and process of promoting the creation, acceptance, amendment, and enforcement of such rules. It involves adding the international interaction of courts and legislatures to those of executive power.[23] In the case of war, it involves promoting the rule of law not just in the conduct of war (as in the Geneva Convention and other protocols for the treatment of prisoners) but also in the decision-making process of choosing war.

The early modern absolutist notion of the sovereign ruler, with no superior and unlimited internally by the law, made way for the idea of constitutional, democratic, and legally limited government. In parallel, the ideal of the rule of law leads to a moderating of the early modern view of sovereignty as the state's absolute independence from external rule. The idea of the sovereign confronting other sovereigns externally who could not, without ceasing to be sovereign, be under the rule of external law is giving way slowly to the rule of international law and the legitimacy that comes with it.

At present, this shift is neither universal nor irreversible nor certain to succeed. The foundation of the League of Nations in 1919 may have reflected optimism about the rule of international law, but significant setbacks occurred in the 1930s as major states repudiated international agreements, and the post–1945 Cold War era gave little grounds for hope (see Koskenniemi 2004).

However, progress in the rule of international law is not illusory.[24] Nor is it nullified by the fact that such law has been frequently violated any more than state criminal law becomes a dead letter simply because many citizens break the law. Even though international law is often not enforced and violations are sometimes not punishable, it does not follow that it has no normative or standard-setting effect—that is, that it ceases to be an authority. If that were the case, it would not be taken as seriously as it is today. A rich notion of international law derives from the long tradition of political thought going back to Grotius and Kant. In recent writing, Jürgen Habermas argues for the realization of "the Kantian project of overcoming the state of nature between states" not through the establishment of a world republic or world government but through the constitutionalization of international law (2006, xxii; also ch. 8).[25] Even if the Kantian stance is considered impractical, the same objection could be made to being law-abiding among the lawless. And in even considering justice with respect to war, we are saying that being law-abiding is the right thing to do.

The idea of the law as international authority and the acceptance of the rule of law as a normative ideal have a number of implications. In the framework of an older and cruder legal positivism, such concepts would have seemed impractical. Today, however, it is easier to distinguish between law-abiding states and criminal or lawless states. The Nuremberg trials after World War II reflect a groping toward the idea of the criminal state as distinct from criminal individuals like presidents or generals.[26] While the intention of the war's victors in setting up the Nuremberg tribunal was to try German leaders primarily for crimes against peace, specifically launching aggressive war and only secondarily for crimes against humanity, the long-term effect of Nuremberg was more significant with respect to crimes against humanity. The Nazi attack on the human rights of Jews and others was treated as a violation of law even though it had been ordered by a legally constituted government.

As David Luban's discussion shows, the Nuremberg heritage is ambivalent since the moral and political significance of each of the two sets of charges cuts in different directions. Giving primary weight to crimes against peace at Nuremberg tended to reinforce the importance of national sovereignty, even when the government is violating the rights of its citizens, whereas giving primacy to the charges of crimes against humanity tends in the direction of holding that a state's sovereignty should not outweigh the duty of other countries to stop it—by armed intervention, if necessary—from carrying out genocide.

While sovereignty and crimes against peace were given greater weight up until 1990, the current of thought has moved in the other direction since 1990. In the post–Cold War era there has been increased acceptance of the idea that it is morally right, even imperative, for the United Nations or individual states with the requisite power to intervene in order to prevent or stop genocide or similar crimes precisely because they are crimes in the eyes of international law. This development is ongoing, and its implications still debated, with the outcome still fluid.

How does the fact of this development support my claim that the law is a kind of competent authority? Granted, it is not immediately obvious. But if some international court determined that a particular state was engaged in genocide, requiring decisive action to put a stop to the events in question, such a judgment or declaration would provide moral and legal grounds for action. The action might be taken by the United Nations, individual states, or even a private volunteer group. Regardless of who stopped the genocide, the competent authority for the necessary military action would be provided by the law and the court that interpreted or elaborated the relevant law. The authority here would not be that of the United Nations, for if for some reason (e.g., a veto of action by one of the permanent members of the Security Council) the United Nations could not decide to adopt the necessary measures, it would not follow that nobody could have the authority to initiate action. It can also be added here that the establishment of such international tribunals as the International Criminal Court at The Hague to try government members or agents who commit such crimes reinforces my claim that the authority is not directly the political authority of states or the United Nations but rather legal: the authority of law or, as Francis Jacobs terms it, the sovereignty of law (see Jacobs 2007, 53–54; also ch. 1–4).

The so-called war on terror in which the United States was engaged after 2001 has generated much discussion. A major criticism of the US conduct of the war has been its resort to illegal or legally dubious methods, including torture and rendition, under the Clinton and Bush administrations. It has been cogently argued that the US administration should have sought the assistance of the legislature since, particularly after al-Qaeda's attacks on the US homeland on September 11, 2001, Congress would probably have given the administration most of what it wanted (see Wittes 2008). The war on terrorism is an instance of the kind of war better described as police action, which requires appropriate legislation.

While this war sometimes involves military action, as in Afghanistan and elsewhere, the primary focus is on a kind of international criminal, for the indiscriminate slaughter carried out by such groups cannot reasonably be seen as anything other than criminal. Wittes argues that the struggle against groups such as al-Qaeda requires more than the conventional criminal law or the laws of war; new laws are required. More than would be the case with other kinds of war, the authority to wage the "war on terror" derives from the law. Given that, as Clausewitz noted, a key dimension of war is political, the political dimension of the struggle against an inherently lawless terrorism requires that its opponents not act in similarly lawless fashion but that they use the law and make new laws in order to combat it.[27]

The idea behind the war on terror is of a war undertaken by democratic law-abiding states to deal with criminals, terrorist groups, and rogue states that oppress their own citizens and terrorize others. (I leave aside the question of whether that view was fully accurate after 2001 or a fair description of the different actors.) That is very close to the idea underlying *jus ad bellum*: that resort to war is a police action, is modeled on the legitimate state's use of all necessary means to repress and possibly punish violent crime and restore order, and is authorized not so much by the ruler's own authority as by the authority of the law that does not merely permit but commands the ruler to enforce justice. *Jus ad bellum* thought projects the idea or image of a world where the possibility of a global rule of law is within sight or imaginable, even if it is estimated that it will take a long time to accomplish.

Finally, it could be objected that one can view the law as an authority only by courtesy, since the law itself cannot make a practical judgment. But this fails to note that the courts, whether judges or prosecuting magistrates, can and increasingly do make such judgments. In 2008, the International Criminal Court indicted then-president Omar Bashir of Sudan for war crimes. The fact that (as it appears at the time of writing) he is unlikely to be arraigned is beside the point. Besides, similar opinions were once voiced about indictments of Slobodan Milosevic, former president of Yugoslavia/Serbia; Radovan

Karadzic, leader of the Bosnian Serbs; and Charles Taylor, former president of Liberia, but they all wound up before the court.

Allowing the law as authority means rejecting Kant's view that there could be no question of any kind of punishment or law enforcement by one state against another: "For punishment occurs only in the relation of a superior to those subject to him, and states do not stand in that relation to each other" (1991, 153, Ak. 347). On this view, without world government and an end to national (i.e., divided) sovereignty there can be no such thing as international law, at least as far as issues of war and peace are concerned. However, the developments in international law and public opinion suggest that Kant is too absolute in his view: "By definition war arises in the absence of an adequate formal authority to resolve a dispute. But public order abhors a vacuum. The just belligerent is supposed to venture, informally and with extraordinary means, the judgment that *would* be made by a formal court, *if* there were a competent one" (O'Donovan 2003, 23; see also Habermas 2000, 51). Not just the United Nations but also the law and the international community, typically understood as individual states oriented to a wider common good, are authorities empowered to judge.

Competent Authority: States

The third instance of competent authority is the state. Of the different kinds of cases in which the state could function as a competent authority in waging war, I start with two that are easy to identify and relatively uncontroversial. The first is when the state engages in war to protect its people against attack by some external force. The second is when it intervenes in another country in order to protect a significant section of the people of that country against lethal attack by their own government, or against life-threatening consequences (e.g., famine) of a breakdown of social order.

The first kind of case refers to wars against an attacker who wishes not merely to defeat a particular country's army or to overthrow its government but also intends to kill, enslave, or otherwise directly attack the population. Instances include the attack by Nazi Germany on Jewish and Slavic peoples, not just on the states where Jews or Slavs lived, and al-Qaeda's attacks on European and American civilians. In protecting its citizens, the state's right and duty to act is underpinned by citizens' rights.

What of cases where the attacking country does not seek to injure the civilian population? In the classical just war tradition, Aquinas and such later writers as Francisco Suarez would have taken it for granted that a state has some right to defend itself (as distinct from its population) against external attack; hence, the state is a competent authority in such cases. It might not always be justified in exercising that right (for instance, if the attack were an act of justifiable retribution for the state's previous depredations on its neighbors), but the state's right in general to resist external attack was taken for granted. This is similar to the UN Charter's allowing that self-defense does not need UN authorization.

However, even though the just war tradition might have accepted that view, a contemporary just war position might not, and neither might the kind of cosmopolitan position held by many political philosophers today. In support of state political sovereignty, Michael Walzer writes: "'The duties and rights of states are nothing more than the duties and rights of the men who compose them.' That is the view of a conventional British lawyer, for whom states are neither organic wholes nor mystical unions. And it is the correct view. When states are attacked, it is their members who are challenged, not only in their lives, but also in the sum of things they value most, including the political association they have made. . . . States' rights are simply [the] collective form of [individual rights]" (1977, 53–54). Here Walzer comes close to identifying the state with the society or the group of people it governs. He does identify the interests of the state as also those of the members or citizens of that state.

This seems too sweeping and unnuanced. Many of us would be reluctant to say that Britain and France's declaration of war on Germany in 1939 amounted to an attack on the German people, or that an invasion of Zimbabwe in 2008 by its neighbors in order to prevent the regime from starving its people would also have been an attack on those very people, so that the respective German and Zimbabwean governments would be justified in resisting in order to protect their people. Yet Walzer's position seems to lead to that conclusion.

In the case of states where the regime is dictatorial, flagrantly in violation of the rule of law and its citizens' rights, indifferent to democracy, and with no independent courts, the idea that the state's interest is identifiable with the interests or the good of the people is not credible. Outside armed intervention aimed at protecting civilians or overthrowing dictatorships, which may technically amount to an unprovoked external attack or invasion, cannot be, in the kinds of circumstances found in Kosovo or Rwanda in the 1990s, the kind that the state has the right to resist.

A dictatorial regime has doubtful legitimacy credentials. While such a state has a prima facie right to resist unprovoked invasion or external attack, that right is defeasible by an invading state's appropriate intentions oriented to the human good, primarily but not exclusively the good of the people living under the dictatorial regime. Sovereignty can no longer be understood as necessarily taking precedence over human rights. Thus, the state's right to resist attack is limited by the moral and legal nature of the particular state in question. It may have forfeited its right to qualify as a legitimate government or competent authority with respect to certain kinds of war.

Let's turn to the second kind of case, where a state intervenes in another country with a view to protecting that country's civilians. The context here is one where the people of some country are under attack by an internal force, often the state itself. In this case, the international community has an obligation to respond and perhaps intervene by force to prevent or stop such attack (see Arbour 2007).[28] Instances include the genocide in Rwanda in 1994 and the massacres and ethnic cleansing carried out in various parts of the former state of Yugoslavia, particularly in Bosnia and Kosovo in the early 1990s. In such cases, a state aiming to protect can qualify as a competent authority for the purpose of armed intervention. Often, successful intervention may not be possible, but that is irrelevant to the issue of authority.

It is important to note that, just as the notion of community has significant normative elements, so by extension does the notion of the international community.[29] While the United Nations has a good claim to be the main representative of the international community, the two are not identical for a number of reasons. I see no good reason for claiming either that any state not belonging to the United Nations is thereby excluded from the international community, or that any large group of states less in number than the membership of the United Nations can never be seen as representing and thereby having some of the moral authority of the international community. Consider the case where some state was committing atrocities against its own citizens, resulting in the deaths of millions and arousing international outrage. Assume that one of the permanent members of the UN Security Council has vetoed any UN military action against the offending country. If a significant number of other countries intervened militarily to stop the genocide, that could count as action by the international community. The fact that the United Nations can and sometimes does authorize military action does not entail that the United Nations *alone* has such authority, or that its refusal to authorize military action amounts to forbidding it.[30]

Addressing the UN General Assembly in 1999, UN Secretary-General Kofi Annan acknowledged the apparent dilemma between acting without UN authorization and failing to act in time to protect:

> To those for whom the greatest threat to the future of the international order is the use of force in the absence of a Security Council mandate, one might ask, not in the context of Kosovo but in the context of Rwanda, if . . . a coalition of states had been prepared to act in defense of the Tutsi population, but did not receive prompt Council authorization, should such a coalition have stood aside and allowed the horror to unfold? To

those for whom the Kosovo action heralded a new era when states and
groups of states can take military action outside the established mechanisms for enforcing international law, one might ask: is there not a danger
of such interventions undermining the imperfect, yet resilient, security
system created after the Second World War, and of setting dangerous
precedents for future interventions without a clear criterion to decide
who might invoke these precedents and in what circumstances? (cited in
Franck 2002, 16)

The dilemma he addresses is directly relevant to developing and moderniz-
ing the conceptual framework of *jus ad bellum*. It touches on what might be
grounds for resorting to military force (coming under the just cause criterion)
as well as on the necessary authority for resort to force. Dealing with the
second issue, the topic of this chapter, Kofi Annan's remarks allow for the
possibility that others (in this instance, states) might well act on good enough
authority even when acting without UN authorization. Dangers to peace and
human life that are sufficiently grave and urgent present moral and perhaps
legal challenges to more authorities than just the United Nations.

Holding that military intervention for humanitarian purposes may never
be undertaken without UN authorization may imply a view of war no different from that of the early modern period, when *jus ad bellum* was collapsed
into only one issue—namely, who has the authority to go to war? That ignored the purpose or grounds for going to war. On that view, the protection
of human rights, international peace and order, and the international common good are not such that they mandate any organization or government
with responsibility for international peace and order or the ability to protect
the good to take action. There is a difference between holding, as Kofi Annan
apparently did, that the promotion of peace and order and the protection of
human rights may be best served by confining the right to resort to war to
the United Nations and to UN-authorized states, and holding that only the
United Nations has the right to authorize force. The former position takes it
that the existence or competence of an institution like a state or group of states
to use force is conditional upon its being oriented to promoting international
peace and order, whereas the latter simply makes it a matter of sovereignty
with respect to war: only the United Nations has the right to go to war, regardless of the purpose or alleged good of doing so. The latter thinks of going
to war as a kind of privilege typically associated with sovereign states, now
confined to the United Nations. The former view is closer to that in the *jus ad
bellum* view of going to war as a kind of duty to protect certain international
common goods.

At the same time, I acknowledge the validity in Kofi Annan's concern that unilateral intervention may undermine what has been achieved through the United Nations: it is a serious concern and may set a dangerous precedent—although the cost to the would-be interveners is usually such that they are unlikely to intervene often.[31] That states should have to act outside the UN mechanisms in order to prevent or stop genocide ought to stand as a moral reproach to the United Nations, and in particular to states voting against intervention or vetoing UN action.[32] Where the United Nations morally ought to take action and fails to do so, it is hard to see the moral argument requiring individual states to refrain from taking the appropriate action.

Nor need the international community necessarily operate through the United Nations or its organs.[33] To think of the term "international community" as referring to the set of all recognized countries and to that alone would lead to a position where one could hardly ever say that the international community had a view about or attitude to a particular instance of genocide since complete unanimity is rare. The term should be taken more permissively, to include not just the set of all states but also substantial subsets of that set.

Thus, for instance, if some half-dozen neighbors of a certain state are particularly concerned about its policies, they could qualify as the relevant part of the international community with respect to that state. Around 2008, the states of southern Africa could qualify jointly as a competent authority for putting pressure on the Mugabe regime in Zimbabwe. The states of Southeast Asia could similarly qualify with respect to the military dictatorship of Burma (Myanmar). North Korea's neighbors, including Russia and China, have attempted (with limited success) to exercise a similar authority with respect to its desire to acquire nuclear weapons. A prima facie case can be made for holding that neighboring states would have the authority to resort to armed force, if necessary, against a "rogue" state starving its own people.[34] Whether they would be justified in doing so is not the issue: our focus here is on the nature of the requisite authority for such action.

A more obvious example of where the international community could act with good authority even without UN authorization is when it goes to the aid of a country coming under unjustified external aggression. If an individual state has the right to resist aggression, it is hard to see how other countries would not be justified in going to its assistance. To claim that, even though the aggression in question is clearly unjustified, UN authorization must be obtained before going to the injured party's assistance is tantamount to saying that no state has authority to use military force for any purpose other than to protect its own citizens.[35] That would mean that other states have no right (let alone duty) to stop genocide occurring outside their own borders.

Whatever the legal grounding (if any) for that position, it seems morally unacceptable and politically untenable given the events in Rwanda, Bosnia, and elsewhere in the last twenty years along with the evolution of attitudes in the world at large. Even if only one country were willing to aid another under unjust attack or to rescue a populace suffering genocide at the hands of its government, the intervening state has the moral authority to do so. It is a legitimate authority in such cases, an authority derived from its membership of the international community, part of a community seeking to be governed by the rule of law, which has in various international agreements committed itself to a duty to protect.[36] That duty is not to be conceived of as solely a collective duty; it can also be appropriately understood as a severally distributed duty (see Walzer 1977, 59; Rodin 2002, 174).

That state authority is not delegated or devolved from the United Nations. It is an authority vested in the government of the state by virtue of its legitimacy or competence. Nor does it seem that it could lose that authority in favor of some kind of world government. The notion of state sovereignty is not entirely irrelevant but requires some refinement in light of the growth of international law and UN authority.[37]

In addition, to attribute such authority exclusively to the United Nations is to impose on it a moral burden that it is by nature incapable of sustaining (see Koskenniemi 2002).[38] The importance and indispensability of the state is evidenced by the instances of "failed" states, of which there are quite a few at the time of writing. Somalia is currently the most notorious instance, where there has been no effective government or central authority since the early 1990s. The Democratic Republic of Congo, one of the largest countries in the world, is not far from that plight, and central authority seems to have little force in Afghanistan and a number of other countries, including the nuclear-armed Pakistan. As the historical record, particularly in Somalia, bears out, UN agencies cannot substitute for the state.

The idea of world government, while attractive in many ways, is also unattractive in others and is unlikely ever to command wide assent. In contrast, the idea of the rule of law, conceived as something intranational (within the individual state), international (between states), and transnational (international concern with states' internal affairs), has some chance of eventually gaining acceptance.

Creation of world government is not obviously necessary for working toward the goal of effective international law and governance (see Slaughter 2005). The principle of subsidiarity, important in the development of the European Union, implies that powers should be transferred to higher-level bodies or institutions only when and to the extent that they cannot be effectively wielded at lower levels. Applying that principle to intervention, it indicates that the authority to intervene can come from below and not just from on high.

The authority of the state to extend its reach beyond its borders is recognized and even encouraged in the UN Convention on Torture, which requires individual states to try cases involving events that occurred outside the state's jurisdiction. The authority to try such cases is not delegated by the United Nations, since it is assumed that the individual state (in its judicial function) has the authority to do so. A state that was not signatory to the Convention would not act illegally or ultra vires by conducting such trials. The goal of the UN Convention, far from limiting the state's powers or transferring them to the United Nations, was to get the individual state to assert, develop, and use its authority.

The objection that allowing a unilateral right to intervene is open to abuse must carry little weight since all ethical principles can be abused. A principle excluding the right to intervene could be abused to rationalize standing idly by for selfish reasons in circumstances where reasonable people would deem the case for intervention overwhelming. All that my argument needs to make it plausible is a couple of cases where our moral intuitions urge intervention.

One such case could be the early nineteenth-century British policy of having its navy intercept slave ships, confiscate their cargoes, and free the slaves. That involved using force against such ships regardless of whether any treaty existed between Britain and the state where the ship was registered. Britain argued that its action was legal since it was stopping what were in effect pirate ships, but quite a few writers have argued that such action amounted to a violation of international law as it stood at the time (see Buchanan and Golove 2002, 885; Chesterman 2002). It should be noted that similar arguments could apply to the Nuremberg trials and to NATO's intervention in Kosovo in 1999.

There are also instances more difficult to evaluate, such as Vietnam's invasion of Cambodia (Kampuchea) in 1979 and its overthrow of the genocidal Khmer Rouge regime, and Tanzania's response to attack by Uganda in 1979 that went well beyond self-defense to overthrow the dictatorial regime of Uganda's Idi Amin. Despite the vicious nature of the overthrown regimes, in neither case did the victor seek to justify its action by appeal to humanitarian grounds. Instead, they cited self-defense and internal opposition to the regime, claiming that there had been two conflicts going on at the same time: a war between the two states and a subsequent successful military rising (admittedly with foreign help). Although the victors had their own policy reasons for their action, it is noteworthy that they still did not appeal to a duty to protect the citizens of another country from its rulers' lethal policies (see Wheeler 2000). Twenty years later, the world is closer (although how much closer is hard to say) to accepting that, in international law as well as political thought, there is a duty of humanitarian intervention.

On the other hand, not every state necessarily qualifies as a competent authority along the lines I have been suggesting. The lawless or rogue state has a diminished authority, and its competence is correspondingly reduced. In such circumstances it is not qualified to act as a bona fide member of the international community. The older positivist view took sovereignty as the defining mark of the state or government so that being a competent authority was an all-or-nothing affair. That view also had a rather amoral view of the state, where its being democratic or totalitarian, peaceful or aggressive, governed by the rule of law or by terror made no difference to its authority or legitimacy. On the view I have been supporting, those qualities should and do make a difference to the state's authority.

My discussion of the law as authority prior to considering the state raises the issue of what in the state has authority: is it the executive, the legislature, or the judiciary, or some combination of these? The executive could hardly fail to have such authority; and in the case of national defense against sudden attack it seems reasonable that it should not be hindered in responding rapidly by having to assemble parliament for debate, discussion, and voting. In the other kinds of cases discussed earlier, or in those where instant response is not required, the legislatures of contemporary democracies expect to be consulted, and the executive branch is generally prohibited from conducting a secret or undeclared war. Insofar as the law requires the involvement of the legislature or the judiciary so that the competence of the executive in this matter is limited by other competences, involvement of all three branches of government enhances the moral and political authority backing a decision to go to war.

The point can also be made by looking at scenarios where these conditions are missing. In countries where the executive is not limited by the legislature or the judiciary and may with impunity go to war as it sees fit, as was the case with Germany and Russia at the beginning of both world wars, with Japan in the 1930s, and possibly with Russia in recent years, the executive's policy goals and their pursuit are largely unconstrained by the law. Such a government's legitimacy is correspondingly weakened, and even its competence is reduced. While legally it may count as a sovereign state in some respects, the moral theory of *jus ad bellum*, where the legitimate authority condition is tied to the government meeting certain standards (the modern equivalent of which has been described earlier), may mean that in certain war-related circumstances it will not qualify as a competent authority. Such circumstances are most likely to apply in cases where it is on the verge of war with a democratic state.

On the view that sees sovereignty as the decisive element, the dictator of one state is as good a competent authority as the democratic law-abiding government of another state. I reject that view. I have sought to argue that the notion of competent authority in *jus ad bellum* is not to be understood reductively as merely having effective control of the national territory. The notion of competent authority also involves a moral element, such that the authority of the dictatorship indifferent to the rule of law or human rights is significantly less or ought to be treated as significantly less than the authority of a democratic government. By contrast with the law-abiding democracy, the dictatorship is inherently much less capable of pursuing key public human goods since its very existence typically involves a violation of some of those goods.

Conclusion

In considering several candidates for the role of competent authority, I have suggested that such authority comes in degrees, and that it is not an all-or-nothing thing, as the early modern emphasis on sovereignty implied. A government that is democratic, respectful of the rule of law and human rights, and committed to cooperation with the international community for the common good qualifies as a competent authority in the full or nondeficient sense. A regime significantly lacking with respect to any of these points has limited competence at most.

For the state, sovereignty is related to legitimacy, and legitimacy varies depending on whether the state or government is democratic and representative, whether it observes and promotes the rule of law, whether it is in effective control of the territory of the state, to mention a few. I argue that such a view, where the state is accountable and where sovereignty is related to responsibility, particularly toward the governed rather than to some degree of unrestricted power, is what the just war tradition has in mind as opposed to the view of the state found in the early positivist view.

Thus, the *jus ad bellum* criterion of competent authority is to be understood as referring to a certain kind of authority. That authority is grounded in its representative nature and its legal nature since such qualities are reliable indicators that the authority in question is oriented to the public good, a notion that embraces communal, national, and international goods. Only such an authority could qualify as a competent authority for resort to war as a matter of policy. While not irrelevant, the notion of sovereignty does not capture what competent authority involves.

The range of different authorities may seem confusing, yet it is no more confusing than is the idea that the legislative, executive, and judicial branches of government each have some authority that must relate to that of the other branches. Acknowledging the diversity of authorities is also designed to address the complexity of the modern world, and to balance optimism with realism. On the one hand, I want to allow that nonstate entities (like the United Nations or the law) could count as competent authorities. There are signs of hope in the growth and progress, fragile and reversible though it may be, of the rule of international law. On the other hand, hopes that the United Nations and international law might substitute for states or that enhancing their authority might eliminate the state's competence in the area of war are unrealistic. In matters of war and peace, lack of realism may be morally blameworthy. In any case, I am unconvinced that there are good grounds for proposing the ideal of world government in the sense that implies a total loss of sovereignty by individual states. My main qualification on state sovereignty in this context has been to argue that state sovereignty and *jus ad bellum*'s competent authority ought not be identified.

Notes

1. Aquinas and Suarez also put competent authority first. See Thomas Aquinas, *Summa theologiae*, IaIIae, q. 40, cited in Reichberg, Syse, and Begby 2006, 176–78; and Francisco Suarez, *Metaphysical Disputations* XIII, sec. 1, cited in ibid., 342. Orend takes the view that just war thought applies only to the "political community" (2006, 31) and states that the "rules of *jus ad bellum* are addressed, first and foremost, to heads of state" (2008). While Johnson follows the conventional order (1999, 28–30), he treats Aquinas's ordering perceptively (ibid., 46–49). Coady puts legitimate authority first, although it is not clear that he sees the order as significant (2008, 63).

2. See Luban 1980 for interesting interpretation of those articles.

3. Steinhoff (2007) attempts to bridge the gap by adopting a permissive (and correspondingly implausible) notion of legitimate authority: every individual person counts as such. The costs of that Hobbesian position are too high, both in yielding excessively large scope for individual resort to violence and in undermining the roles of the law and the state as well as the very idea of the rule of law. A similar objection can be made to the position in Fabre: "War is one of many steps which individuals may be tempted to take in defense of their fundamental human rights. On my account of state legitimacy, individuals have the right so to act. . . . For a war to be just, then, it is not necessary that it should be fought by a legitimate authority such as a state" (2012, 115–16). She appears to mean that the individual qua individual has such a right and that he or she is a competent authority to determine when conditions are such that he or she is entitled to go to war. Given the moral gravity of war, I deem this position excessively permissive

epistemically. It also rejects the intuitively plausible norm of *nemo iudex in sua causa*.

4. He doesn't seem to realize that. See Rodin 2002, 2: "Self-defense is also one of the lynchpins of international law's intellectual progenitor, the Just War Theory"; and 120: "By locating the notion of national-defense within a framework of ideas generated in the context of personal defensive rights, the Just War Theorist hopes to show how a state's military action in defending its own sovereign power can be morally justified." Some modern just war theorists have argued along those lines. But that is not true of the tradition prior to the seventeenth century, as my next paragraphs indicate. Besides, the revival of *jus ad bellum* thought in a more internationalist age will, among other things, require precisely the move Rodin makes.

5. See Finnis 1998, 285: "Clearly, Aquinas' discussion of just war is focused upon the decision to initiate war. It goes without saying that a state actually attacked by outside forces (having itself done no wrong warranting war) can rightly defend itself; such self-defense needs no [*iusta*] *causa*."

6. The state's duty to protect its citizens is of course connected to the well-being of individuals. The point here is that the state's role is not *directly* concerned with that as an individual good but rather as a public good. Citizens' goods are not all individual goods.

7. Finnis 1998, 275–76: "The 'power of the sword,' as Aquinas understands it, is essentially the public authority of the state's rulers, and their judicial and military officers, to execute criminals and wage war. . . . Private persons in their private capacity have no right to punish even obvious malefactors."

8. Johnson and Weigel have similarly argued that recent heavy emphasis in just war thought on self-defense represents a retrograde departure from the stances taken by the tradition in earlier times. See Johnson 2005a and Weigel 2003.

9. Neff 2005, 57: "The idea of war as a law-enforcement operation was (and remains) the very essence of just-war thought."

10. An alternative term to "competent authority" might be "legitimate authority." However, it seems less confusing to speak of competent authority. A government might have little legal legitimacy, yet its having effective control of the country gives it a certain practical competence and with it a de facto legitimacy. As I argue, some governments are more legitimate or competent than others. On the state and the common good, see Riordan 1996, 2008.

11. In 1969, when intercommunal violence erupted in Northern Ireland, Catholic enclaves in the overwhelmingly Protestant city of Belfast wanted an almost moribund IRA (Irish Republican Army) to defend them against imminent attack by Protestant mobs. Eventually the IRA responded. Had it confined itself thereafter to defending the Catholic community, it would have had some moral and political warrant for doing so. Unfortunately, its political ideology mandated

different goals, and their pursuit through armed campaign over the next twenty years endangered rather than protected the Catholic community.

12. In 2008–9, the Mugabe regime ruling Zimbabwe targeted people suspected of voting against it, evicting them from their homes and (during government-caused famine) denying them access to food. Some observers described the government as waging war upon its own people.

13. For the sake of epistemic objectivity, the severity of government injustice must be "demonstrable" or apparent to the outside observer and not just to the group immediately affected. There is, of course, always the risk of abuse of the criterion, but that objection applies to all moral criteria.

14. For perceptive remarks on this point, see Caney 2005, 205–6. With respect to the position that legitimate authority has purely instrumental value so that the lack thereof creates no moral obstacle to going to war for justice and the protection of people's rights, he rejects it, and I concur.

15. Some outside power, whether the United Nations or another state, might intervene by force on their behalf, and *jus ad bellum* criteria would be applicable to such intervention, with the requisite authority being partly supplied by the intervening power.

16. See Luban 1980 and Tesón 1992 for similar views; see also Rodin 2002, 148.

17. See Aquinas, *ST, I-II*, q. 90, a.3, where he states that the making of laws is a task for the people, or for the delegate(s) or representative(s) of the people.

18. For an interesting (and somewhat pessimistic) view of international law from 1870 to 1960, see Koskenniemi 2004. See also Neff 2005. From the side of political science, Kagan 1995 also strikes a cautionary note about any claim that the rule of international law is universally accepted.

19. For an optimistic view of the rapidly increasing growth of institutional links at all levels between different states and societies, see Chayes and Chayes 1995 and Slaughter 2005. See also Smith 2008.

20. For a summary of the elements of such a case, see Buchanan and Golove 2002, 871–81.

21. Nor does the United Nations have the military accoutrements of sovereignty. Even when various countries provide troops to the United Nations, it still lacks the capacity for strategic command. See Smith 2006, 15: "The UN is an organization without a permanent military structure. It therefore has no capacity to create a strategic command, which is why it can never offer a serious option for the use of military force."

22. The idea that law has an authority of its own derives principally from the natural law tradition. See Neff 2005, 33: "This [stoic] idea of natural law did not entail any conception, even in theory, of any universal political sovereignty, as in the Chinese case. . . . The supreme ruling force in the world, in the stoic view,

was not an emperor but rather the law of nature as such, which was supreme by virtue of its own innate power. It ruled the world by the force of reason, not by the strength of swords."

23. See Slaughter 2005, ch. 2, particularly her discussion of the development of the European Court of Human Rights and the European Court of Justice. She makes a persuasive case for holding that today the modern world is characterized more by what she terms "disaggregated sovereignty" than by the older reality (or part fiction) of a unified sovereign. That sovereign states are a reality is not denied, but there is more than states involved today in providing order and governance at global levels.

24. Kennedy 2006 sees law as ubiquitous in contemporary warfare, even going so far as to adapt Clausewitz's dictum to claim that modern war is "lawfare"—that is, a legal contest conducted by means other than verbal or written argument. His view of the development is more skeptical than is that of Slaughter, but his book gives interesting insights on the extent to which law plays a central role in modern war.

25. Kant 1983a, 33: "The greatest problem for the human species . . . is to achieve a universal civil society administered in accord with the right." See also Paulus 2010 on international adjudication, where the jurist may, while still remaining within the remit of the legal system, have to be creative with respect to gaps in the law. See Franck 2002, ch. 10, on illegal but justifiable uses of force in the international arena, and the law's evolution in this area.

26. See Luban 1994, ch. 7, for elaborate discussion of this point.

27. In 2008, the US Supreme Court in *Boumediene v. Bush* held that in territory under US control the same legal rights applied as in the United States proper. So detainees at Guantánamo Bay, Cuba, could not be treated as though they were in a legal limbo, outside the law and its protection.

28. Arbour notes that "world leaders agreed [at the 2005 World Summit] that some answers can be found in an emerging doctrine known as 'the responsibility to protect' . . . all states acknowledged not only their obligation to protect their own people, but . . . that the international community has a duty to step in on behalf of civilians at risk of genocide, war crimes and ethnic cleansing whenever a government is either directly responsible for these crimes or incapable of stopping them."

29. In the kind of instance under discussion, the normative is linked to the intentional. I am referring here to the set of states oriented to certain values and related purposes.

30. It can authorize intervention only with the consent of the Security Council, so it is possible that the United Nations has failed to authorize action because of the permanent members' veto on occasions when it ought to have done so or would have done so had it not been vetoed. From a moral viewpoint, it cannot

be assumed that the UN's refusal to authorize military intervention implicitly condemns those who act without its authorization. The UN's authority (like any authority) is limited.

31. See Stewart and Knaus 2011 on whether intervention works; sometimes it does, and sometimes it makes matters worse.

32. The fact that very little public moral odium attaches to states that vote against action in such cases and whose reasons for so doing are self-interested may arise from the bias (noted elsewhere in this book) toward not going to war: this bias suggests that opting not to go to war is always praiseworthy, at least to some extent, since it is an option in favor of peace. The just war tradition does not support that stance; it does not contain a "presumption against war."

33. For further discussion, see Buchanan and Golove 2002, 924; Franck 2002.

34. Let me again make clear that I am not claiming that the neighbors of the states mentioned would be justified in going to war with Zimbabwe or North Korea. My sole concern is to explore the concept of legitimate or competent authority. I claim that if neighboring states have the moral authority to pressure or even sanction a neighboring sovereign state (for good and sufficient reason, of course), then they also have the authority to use force against it in police action. Whether they were morally justified or prudent in so doing would depend on other conditions being met.

35. Chesterman 2002 argues for the restrictive position.

36. On the "duty to protect" agreed by many states at the 2005 World Summit, see Arbour 2007: "As for . . . when the responsibility to prevent and protect is engaged, . . . the recent opinion by the International Court of Justice is helpful. In *Bosnia-Herzegovina v. Serbia*, the court held that when a state is enabled to act, by virtue of its proximity to the events, its knowledge—real or constructive—of the relevant facts and its capacity to influence the outcome, it has a 'due diligence' obligation to employ all reasonable means to avert genocide."

37. See Johnson 2005a: "The conception of sovereignty as moral responsibility in the classic just war tradition contrasts importantly with the morally sterile concept of sovereignty in the Westphalian system. . . . The classic just war conception of sovereignty as moral responsibility provides a frame within which good rule can be distinguished from bad, for encouraging the best and critically addressing the worst, with promise for a more morally robust understanding of the international order." See also Johnson 2005b, 62–63; Annan 1999.

38. See also Franck 2002 (particularly ch. 2) for a legally sophisticated acknowledgment of the United Nations' difficulties as well as a cautiously optimistic argument suggesting that the United Nations' self-understanding has evolved through its experience of decision making from the 1950s in relation to Korea (1950) and Suez (1956) to the 1990s in relation to the former Yugoslavia and Somalia.

Chapter 4

Just Cause

What the devil signifies right when your honor is concerned? Do you think Achilles, or Alexander the Great, ever inquired where the right lay? No, by my soul, they drew their broad swords, and left the lazy sons of peace to settle the justice of it.

Sir Lucius O'Trigger in Sheridan's *The Rivals*

The previous chapter argued that, with respect to *jus ad bellum*, the competent authority criterion should be treated as prior to the just cause criterion. A number of reasons supported that argument. The most important was that the analogy of individual self-defense is not integral to what is involved in *jus ad bellum*. The theory of justice with respect to war is not a theory of general self-defense but a part of a theory of statecraft and law. Accordingly, the theory of *jus ad bellum* is properly part of a theory of governance (see Ramsey 1968, 260; Weigel 2003; Johnson 1999, 46–49; Johnson 2005a).

This chapter addresses the just cause criterion. While it is often taken to be fundamentally a matter of self-defense, the claim that *jus ad bellum* is part of a theory of governance implies that just cause cannot be easily assimilated to self-defense. Good government requires the state to be proactive in repressing crime and protecting the rights of the vulnerable as well as ready to fulfill international obligations that may involve a responsibility to protect nonnationals. Just cause is not to be thought of as arising only from instances of armed aggression launched directly against the state. Nor are we to think of war as confined to formal wars such as World War II: most armed conflicts since 1945 have not conformed neatly to the model of formal declaration of war and all-out conflict between the belligerents followed by formal cessation ending in a peace-treaty.[1] The issue of just cause also arises in the range of situations where the United Nations might mandate armed intervention for peacemaking.

A better indicator of what counts as an action for which just cause is required is the use of a country's armed forces that involves putting them in the line of fire.[2] As well as war involving military engagement and combat, that indicator includes certain kinds of deterrent actions.[3] With respect to moral issues of intent and action, putting troops in harm's way counts as morally equivalent to going to war regardless of whether actual fighting ensues.[4] By contrast, imposition of sanctions, even though it may be a prelude to war (as in the case of US sanctions on Japan prior to December 1941), does not amount to going to war unless the sanctioned state has publicly stated that it will regard the imposition of sanctions as an act of war.

Following these introductory comments, in this chapter I outline the basic elements of the traditional just cause notion. I then place it in two different contexts. The first is the model of a world of international law and elements of global governance, the natural place for a notion of just cause for a legitimate competent authority resorting to armed force on behalf of justice, human rights, and international order. The second is the "realist" Hobbesian model of a world of sovereign states, where international law is weak and often ineffective, where notions of just cause can be hard to distinguish from raison d'état and yet seem at least partially applicable. The actual world today is somewhere between the two models, so practical application of *jus ad bellum* theory requires a certain flexibility concerning how just cause is to be understood and applied contextually.

What Just Cause Involves

What counts as just cause involves reasons of a moral and political nature that explain why a state might resort to armed force and provide warrant or justification for its doing so. Outlining the traditional view, and referring to positive international law, James Turner Johnson specifies that just cause is that which gives good reason for responses of "national or regional self-defense against armed attack," "retaliation for armed attack," "international response to threats to international peace." Resorting to war in response to certain events cannot be morally justified as a merely retaliatory or Pavlovian reaction to provocation. For the resort to force to be grounded in just cause, it must involve promotion or vindication of some moral value. In Johnson's words, just cause is oriented to "the protection and preservation of value," which typically involves "defense of the innocent against armed attack," "retaking persons, property, or other values wrongly taken," and "punishment of evil" (Johnson 1999, 28–30). That will serve as an interim identification of what is involved. However, it requires both explication and contextualization. I start with explication.

To claim that there exists a just cause for resort to war is to posit a relation between three variables: first, an action or structured set of actions $[a]$; second, a value or group of values $[v]$ threatened or attacked by those actions; and third, a set of possible responses $[r]$ to those actions in order to vindicate the values in question. Given a, defending v requires or permits r. Thus, the ordered set $[a,v,r]$ formally defines just cause. The rest of this chapter deals with the range of actions or policies that might give grounds for war, the two previous chapters dealt with the goods or values that the competent authority must defend and promote, and subsequent chapters will deal with morally permissible intentions in military responses to those actions.

First, there is a range of act types that generate the right kind of grounds to warrant resort to armed force. They include such things as invasion, imminent threat of armed attack, gross violation of human rights involving death on a large scale, criminal activities of certain kinds (e.g., international terrorism or piracy), and violation of international law. I will consider some of the more prominent of these in this chapter. The range is also context sensitive: certain act types might generate just cause in some contexts but not in others.

Second, such act types have political and ethical impact on human well-being and human goods. They attack or undermine certain values. Defending those values may justify going to war.[5] In many cases of war where the just cause condition has not been met, the flaw has lain in the misidentification of values: for instance, dynastic or nationalist wars aimed at territorial expansion or national aggrandizement are motivated by values that are false. Genuine values arise from concrete human goods, including basic human rights, the rule of law, equity in the distribution of material resources, democracy and representative government, and the existence of the state: only such as they suffice for just cause requirements. Classic *jus ad bellum* thought might not have used precisely that set of concepts, but it would broadly have agreed that imperialist or nationalist wars of conquest do not have just cause whereas wars aimed at protecting human life and the rule of law often do on the basis of the nature of the putative goods protected.

Third, there is a range of war-related reactions that could be morally permissible in response to action attacking important goods: political pressure of various kinds, sanctions, threats, building coalitions, mobilization of forces, rearmament, and military action.[6]

There are two fundamentally different contexts in which just cause must be analyzed. One is the context of international law, where it is assumed that the rule of law is effective to a significant degree in states' conduct of foreign relations. The second is that of political relations between sovereign states where the rule of international law is weak or nonexistent. Each represents an ideal type or pure form at opposite ends of the spectrum: the first a Kantian universal civic society characterized by the rule of law, the second a Hobbesian jungle of each state for itself and international law little more than a pious slogan.[7]

Actual states of affairs of international politics and war today are located at varying points along the spectrum between the two ideal types. Even when respect for international law is weakest, it does not become entirely irrelevant (see Cronin 2003, ch. 1). Similarly, toward the other end of the spectrum, national interests are never totally transcended when particular countries act to enforce international law against a rogue state.[8]

Any treatment of just cause that did not take this spectrum of possible states of affairs into account would be too abstract to be of use. Since the just war tradition originated in the idea of war as law enforcement, its applicability within a context where war is understood primarily as a power struggle between nations is problematic. But it is not impossible: *jus ad bellum* reasoning can still be applied in a limited way to cases of war at the Hobbesian end of the spectrum.[9]

The bulk of this chapter is divided between treating just cause within the context of an international legal order and treating it within the context of a world of sovereign states. I consider in turn each ideal type as historically operative in recent times with a view to getting some fix on an appropriately contextualized concept of just cause. The first is the context of the global rule of law as a predominant reality against which just cause is elaborated. Just cause is largely understandable as that which requires the enforcement of the law by military action. The other is the traditional context of sovereign states overshadowed by Hobbesian *bellum omnium contra omnes* (war of all against all), thus orienting just cause to the interpretative context of the state's interests. Since these are ideal types, actual instances may present elements of both. The history of the League of Nations is a sad but vivid illustration of the effect of a cultural shift from an international legal order model to a national interest model.

International Order: Enforcing the Law

The first ideal type of *jus ad bellum* derives from the context of international law and the global rule of law. Its background is the view of justice in war held by Augustine (AD 354–430), in whose time the Roman Empire's inability to defend its borders from invasion had led to collapse and chaos. The order established by the empire was de facto the global order of Europe, North Africa, and today's Middle or Near East for more than two centuries before Augustine, so the defense of the empire was, as far as Augustine or his contemporaries were concerned, the defense of social order, justice, the rule of law, and the public good. Of course the Roman Empire was far from perfectly just, but it offered the only social order available within which some peace and justice for people might be procured.

Against that background, with its modern analogy of contemporary international law and the United Nations, identifying just cause is relatively easy. Augustine's successors from Aquinas onward analogized just cause on the grounds the magistrate has for acting against criminals in the interests of public order, justice, and the protection of the vulnerable. These grounds not merely permit but also require the magistrate to act using no more and no less force than is necessary.

That view effectively became moribund in the early modern period and had limited relevance at best in medieval times. Events surrounding World Wars I and II have led to a greater awareness of the need for that view or something like it. While initially in the twentieth century (even before World War I) the overriding moral goal was taken to be that of abolishing war by outlawing it, the occurrence of mass genocide led to others feeling that, while war ought to be avoided as much as possible, it might also be needed to protect people: precisely the point of classic *jus ad bellum* thought.

After World War II, political and military leaders of the defeated powers were put on trial for levying aggressive war. Crimes against humanity were added to the charge sheet, initially as a kind of afterthought. In view of what happened at the Nuremberg trials, David Luban argues that the legacy of the trials is ambivalent (1994, ch. 7). He notes that whereas today we focus more on the crimes against humanity, those who conducted the trials saw their main focus as on crimes against peace.[10]

> The idea that Nuremberg was to be the Trial to End All Wars seems fantastic and naïve forty years (and 150 wars) later. It has also done much to vitiate the real achievements of the trial, in particular the condemnation of crimes against humanity. To end all war, the authors of the Nuremberg Charter were led to incorporate an intellectual confusion into it. The Charter criminalized aggression; and by criminalizing aggression, the Charter erected a wall around state sovereignty and committed itself to an old-European model of untouchable nation-states.
>
> But crimes against humanity are often, even characteristically, carried out by states against their own subjects. The effect, and great moral and legal achievement, of criminalizing such acts (Article 6(c)) and assigning personal liability to those who order them and carry them out (Articles 7 and 8) is to pierce the wall of sovereignty. As a result, Article 6(a) pulls in the opposite direction from Articles 6(c), 7, and 8, leaving us . . . with a legacy that is at best equivocal and at worst immoral. (Luban 1994, 336–37)

As Luban notes, the framers of the Nuremberg trials were not unaware of the tension, and opted to keep Article 6(c) subordinate to 6(a), and to adopt a strict interpretation of 6(c) (1994, 342–43). The tension can be summed up as follows. It revolves around Article 6(a), and depends on its legal aspect (not as such on its moral aspect). According to Article 6(a), it is criminal not merely to wage aggressive war (i.e., not a defensive war) but even to plan to do so. Accordingly, plans by other states to intervene by force in the affairs of a state conducting genocidal policies against its own citizens will be criminal. Yet, without military intervention by some outside power, no action can be taken to punish this crime unless the deed (i.e., actual war) follows. Any other state attempting by military intervention to punish a state for planning war (a crime under 6(a)) itself violates Article 6(a). In Luban's words, "by criminalizing any attempt to enforce itself, Article 6(a) cuts its own throat as an instrument of international peace" (1994, 358). Article 6(a) is incoherent and offers immunity from external attack to regimes that commit genocide against their own people.

From 1945 until 1990, international opinion favored giving priority to sovereignty, making the levying of international war a worse crime than genocide. A particularly stark example of this was international reaction to Vietnam's overthrow of the Khmer Rouge regime in Cambodia in 1979. However, at least in the Western world, that began to change in the early 1990s in the direction of taking crimes against humanity as morally and legally weightier.

The international law framework for understanding *jus ad bellum* fits cases where the United Nations authorizes military action, and cases where the action of the state or coalition of states is, given the circumstances, comparable to a police action. The invasion of Kuwait by Iraq in 1990 is an instance of the kind of aggression that qualifies as providing just cause.[11] It constituted just cause for Kuwait, for countries adjacent to Kuwait and threatened by the invasion such as Saudi Arabia, and for the United Nations.[12]

UN condemnation of an international military initiative (such as Iraq's invasion of Kuwait) is often a reliable indicator that one side has just cause, partly because such condemnation typically identifies the grounds for the other side to resist.[13] But even if the United Nations had declined to act or if one of the Security Council's permanent members had vetoed any resolution condemning Iraq's action, Kuwait itself and any other country going to its aid would still have had just cause.

The law enforcement analogy is also applicable to the rather misnamed "war on terror" arising from the actions of al-Qaeda and related groups of terrorists on September 11, 2001, and at other times in attacking American and other civilians with a view to killing as many as possible. Without political motive, those actions would be unquestionably criminal. In general, political motivation does not suffice to remove such types of action from the zone of the criminal. In the case of attacks such as that of September 11, I can think of no argument that could leverage political motives into providing adequate justification for military or violent actions directed against civilians with no goal other than to kill as many as possible. As a police action, the so-called war on terror passes the just cause criterion.

My last assertion may seem too quick, and the issue not as clear as I make it out to be. But the nature of the attacks on September 11 is such that no government could reasonably fail to conclude that it was under attack and that it had a duty to its citizens to do all in its power to prevent repeat occurrences. Even if, for the sake of argument, we concede that the US government's foreign policy had provoked the hatred and vengeance of those who could strike back in no other way than by targeting civilians en masse, it still would not justify such attacks. It would neither turn al-Qaeda into a competent authority nor change the fact that its campaign involved indiscriminate and intentional (and hence morally indefensible) slaughter of civilians.[14]

International Order: Substituting for the Law

A second set of cases is presented by international political developments in the 1930s. In 1919, the victorious powers of World War I along with a number of other countries established the League of Nations to maintain world peace and to provide legal means for acting against international aggression.

Despite some successes in the 1920s, the League was in decline by the early 1930s. Although US president Woodrow Wilson had advocated the League of Nations, the US Congress voted against the United States' joining. Generally, the United States retreated very soon after World War I into neutrality and isolationism. In 1933, following the League's condemnation of Japan's military action in Manchuria as a violation of international law, Japan left the League. Later that year, the new Nazi government of Germany terminated its participation in the ongoing disarmament conference and left the League. From the mid-1920s to the late 1930s, the collapse of democracy in much of Europe accompanied by a shift toward authoritarian nationalism also tended to undermine the political culture that sustained the idea of the rule of law, whether national or international, and to discredit the values that underpinned the League.

In 1935, the League declared Italy an aggressor following its invasion of Abyssinia. The League imposed economic sanctions, but the United States and Germany continued to supply Italy with oil and coal. Italy left the League in 1937. By 1939, fourteen out of fifty-eight states had left the League. At the end of 1939, the USSR was expelled for its attack on Finland.

Why should we consider these instances in a different light than we do the first group? Is Japan's invasion of Manchuria in 1931 not as clearly a breach of international law as Iraq's invasion of Kuwait in 1990? In an obvious and immediate sense, Iraq's and Japan's actions are equally illegal, and equally capable of constituting just cause for the international community to act.

However, it is also clear that the League ultimately failed. It lacked military power to enforce its rulings, or to deter or defeat aggression by a large country. The absence of the United States from the League left Britain, France, Italy, and Japan as the only permanent members. Italy and Japan were dissatisfied with their place in the post–1918 world, and the internal politics of each became less democratic and more authoritarian in the 1920s. The admission of Germany in 1926 was the admission of a country determined to undo the Treaty of Versailles and, hence, the political order represented by the League. Thus, Britain and France were the only big powers with any political will or military muscle that might be able and willing to enforce the League's rulings.

The strength of pacifism, particularly in Britain after the war, also had a negative effect. The pacifists were often (though not always) the League's strongest supporters. Pacifists and nonpacifists conflated the League's opposition to aggressive war with opposition to war per se. That led many, particularly in Britain's Liberal and Labour parties, to hold that the League should deal with international aggression only by nonviolent means; in their view, the League could not, consistent with its goal of ending war, use military force against international aggression (see Howard 1978, esp. ch. 4).

The implication of such pacifism is that force may never be used to enforce the law. But such a position undermines the law. Its widespread acceptance among League members, particularly in Britain, generates my reason for suggesting that the wars of aggression of the 1930s, though morally as reprehensible as any since, took place in a context where the putative international law enforcers were not sure that the law should be enforced. If the local sheriff thinks that using force against the local gunslingers will make him morally comparable to them and hence that he should use only persuasion and moral example in response, the chances shrink of a legal order being maintained. If the sheriff won't or can't do what needs to be done, the townspeople will conclude that the rule of law has broken down and start to arm themselves.

Such pacifism stems in part from the mistake of reifying war—that is, of thinking, speaking, and acting as though war itself is the enemy. In the case of the pre-1939 pacifists, it led them to reject rearmament and, along with nonpacifist supporters of the League, to decry balance-of-power politics as inherently immoral. It is ironic that there were so many disarmament conferences in the 1920s and even into the mid-1930s, as though the threat of war could be eliminated by outlawing weapons and armies.[15] Subsequent events illustrated the irrelevance of such agreements. The most significant effect of the disarmament movement in the 1930s was to make the democracies less ready to fight, undermining, and demoralizing them.

In addition, decrying balance-of-power politics manifested a kind of anti-politics and thereby also a lack of political realism since it allowed nothing to the limits of power and the practical exigencies faced by such states as Britain and France. Italy's invasion of Abyssinia in 1935 had no shred of justification, so Italy's status as aggressor was beyond doubt. British nonpacifist League supporters saw it as a final test of the League's effectiveness and urged the British government to forceful action against Italy. However, senior British political officials and generals were reluctant to take such action. Their reluctance did not arise from sympathy with Italy but from desire to have Italy on Britain's side, or at least neutral, in anticipated future war with Nazi Germany. This may have seemed like mere amoral realpolitik to the League supporters, but in hindsight it seems that the political officials and generals showed more prudence and awareness of British military limits than did the League's supporters. Lack of political and military realism was also evident in the French National Assembly in the winter of 1939 when, already at war with Germany, it announced its intention of aiding Finland, which was under attack by the USSR. A few months later, France proved unable to defend itself, let alone protect Poland or Finland.

The pacifism and the lack of political realism weakened the League and undermined the effectiveness of international law. It attacked the very idea of just cause—that is, that there could be something or some value that is worth fighting for.

The refusal of the United States to join the League was a significant blow to its chances of success. Its refusal not only denied the League and the international order significant political and military support, it also tacitly rejected the legitimacy of the League. Something similar could be said about the United States' 1935 Neutrality Act, which prohibited sale or delivery of armaments to any country in a state of war. Since the United States' allies in World War I, France and Britain, were known to fear that Nazi Germany's policy could lead to war, the Neutrality Act's passage implied that the United States was not willing to help the two democracies defend the Versailles settlement against the Nazi regime. It reflected a mentality that did not see the League of Nations as part of an international democratic and legal order that merited defending.[16]

In addition to failing to help stabilize the post-1918 international order, the United States' stance toward the League gave a bad example with respect to building an international order, specifically with respect to war and peace. In line with that example, but with far more sinister import, was Japan's withdrawal early in 1933, soon followed by that of Germany. These withdrawals involved the rejection of the international order represented by the League in favor of an ideology of national self-determination unlimited by the rights of other nations, and in favor of rejection of international law as restricting resort to war. In contrast to the United States, the actions of Japan and Germany were not a retreat into isolationism but a serving of notice of rejection of international law. Both countries should have counted as rogue states in the eyes of the League by 1936 since they had signaled their intention to prepare for war and to resort to war when ready in pursuit of their goals. Japan's invasion of Manchuria in 1931 and its subsequent repudiation of the League gave the League just cause. The League's failure to use decisive force against Japan doomed it, even more so because Japan was a powerful country. After that failure in 1933 and the exit of Germany and Italy, two other important members, it is not clear that the League constituted a competent authority anymore, if for no other reason than that it lacked the political determination or the military strength to impose its will. It follows that it was no longer the kind of agency that could have had just cause for going to war. Other countries drew the appropriate conclusions and abandoned the League.

It was left to France and Britain to defend, as best they might, the League's ideals. But the task was too much for them, and concern for their own interests became their primary consideration. Given their strategic position, they cannot be blamed for that; and, as subsequent events were to show, they were weaker than they realized. They went to war in 1939 to protect Poland, and by the time the war was over, Poland's future was out of their hands. From a strategic viewpoint, the first phase of the European part of World War II concerned Britain and France against Germany, with Italy standing on the sidelines, waiting to join the winning side. It began sometime between 1935 and 1937 and was clearly well advanced by the time of the crisis over Czechoslovakia in 1938, during which Britain and France suffered a major strategic defeat in the Munich agreement. It ended with their defeat in the summer of 1940 as France surrendered and Britain was forced off the mainland of Europe. With the United States neutral, the USSR allied with Germany, and Italy now joining the winning side, Britain was reduced to a courageous but solitary and impotent defiance of Germany, without prospect of victory. While Britain and France may have been on the winning side when the war ended in 1945, the strategic fruits of the victory belonged to the USSR and the United States.

Politically and militarily, the League had been too weak to achieve its goals. Accordingly, as noted earlier, it is not clear that the League constituted a competent authority by the mid-1930s. Hence, analysis of instances of just cause after 1935 should be treated not in relation to the League but in relation to individual states.

Sovereign States: Just Cause in General

The story of the League of Nations' failure and collapse brings us to the other ideal type, that of individual states pursuing their own interests, governed by no substantive notion of the community of nations or the international rule of law. That type does not necessarily imply the acceptability of a kind or "realist" amoralism in international politics. There are no grounds for drawing that inference since moral considerations are always involved in the conduct of foreign policy and waging war, even if it is only under the heading of rational considerations.

Despite its roots in the notion of law enforcement, the notion of just cause can be applicable to moral choices about war even in the Hobbesian world. The traditional notion of just cause is that it arises from unjustified armed aggression, which generates a right or even duty of self-defense, a right of retaliation against or punishment of the offender, and a right to restitution of what has been taken or destroyed by the aggression. For a particular state to have just cause in a given instance of external armed aggression is for it to have a moral and political right of self-defense, or the moral right to punish the aggressor, or the right to obtain restoration of lost property (e.g., territory).

I start with the rights to punishment and restoration since in recent times they are usually excluded quickly as lacking the potential to qualify as just cause. Both punishment and restitution are inherently legal notions. In the absence of effective international law with independent legal jurisdiction, such grounds for resort to arms would appear to have relatively little moral force, for several reasons. First, in the absence of international adjudication, one state's judgment that it has been wronged or robbed by another state, so that it has a right to initiate military action in order to punish the other state or strip it of its ill-gotten gains, is always questionable. The old legal principle of *nemo iudex in sua causa* (nobody may be judge of his own case, or the plaintiff cannot simultaneously be the judge) provides a common-sense moral ground for questioning the objectivity of such claims.

Second, even if world opinion is sympathetic to the complainant, passage of time may erode any moral right to take up arms in order to punish or restore. Following defeat in the Franco-Prussian war in 1871, France was forced to cede Alsace and Lorraine to Germany. The German government and German public opinion were indifferent to the views of the people of Alsace-Lorraine. Many, including the British moralist Henry Sidgwick, felt that France had been treated unjustly and that it would have a right to resume hostilities in order to regain the lost provinces. However, Sidgwick acknowledged that time could change matters: "We must . . . recognize that by this temporary submission of the vanquished . . . a new political order is initiated, which, though originally without a moral basis, may in time acquire such a basis, from a change in the sentiments of the inhabitants of the territories transferred. . . . When this change has taken place, the moral effect of the unjust transfer must be regarded as obliterated; so that any attempt to recover the transferred territory becomes itself an aggression" (quoted in Walzer 1977, 56). His remarks would apply also to Argentina's claim (when it launched its brief 1982 war with Britain) that the Falklands or Malvinas Islands originally belonged to it and not to Britain.

While Sidgwick's position may not appeal to all, its rejection leads us into a position that is less tenable and that usually involves parallel injustice to the living. This can be seen when his point is generalized. Given that the boundaries, even the very existence, of many states in Europe, Asia, and North America have through the centuries been fixed by conquest and not by tracing of legal title, attempting to say where the original (and, hence, true) borders of a particular country lie is often a hopeless task. Answers are likely to be arbitrary and often self-serving. The Weimar Republic felt aggrieved by Germany's substantial loss of territory under the terms of the Treaty of Versailles, and its leaders sought its recovery. It did not occur to German politicians that the terms of the ultimately abortive 1918 Treaty of Brest-Litovsk imposed by Germany on Russia had been far more severe in terms of territorial loss than those imposed on Germany by the 1919 Treaty of Versailles.

Commenting on Sidgwick's statement, Walzer remarks that the will of the people or of the majority seems the nearest thing to a fair criterion of where boundaries should lie (Walzer 1977, 55–56; see also Rodin 2002, 190). In the aftermath of World War I and the collapse of various empires, the League of Nations' goal of setting the boundaries of new European states to correspond as much as possible with the desires of the local inhabitants still seems right. It was morally superior to the goal of many of the newly independent states (such as Ireland, Poland, and Hungary) to extend their borders as far as possible, appealing to ancient historical boundaries of wide extent.

Third, the idea that the goal of regaining former territories would constitute sufficient just cause is not one that can be accepted in principle. Since difference of opinion around boundaries is not just a matter of legal uncertainty but also a notable cause of wars, such a principle would potentially legitimize a wide range of wars. The right to restitution or restoration can yield, at most, only short-lived grounds for resorting to war.

As noted earlier, in the absence of an international legal system that is at least partly effective, punishment understood in a legal sense can play no role in our understanding of just cause when that is taken against the background of a world of sovereign states. However, there could be cases in which grounds for punishment, understood in a nonlegal sense, might constitute just cause.

Having rejected the idea that, within the framework of a world of sovereign states, just cause could arise from any kind of general right to punish or restore, I turn to self-defense. The right to self-defense is generally accepted as constituting just cause. The UN Charter allows it as the one exception to the general prohibition on resorting to war: "Nothing in the present Charter shall impair the inherent right of individual or collective self-defense if an armed attack occurs against a Member of the United Nations, until the Security Council has taken measures necessary to maintain international peace and security" (Art. 51). While clear on the right to use force in self-defense prior to the Security Council's "taking measures," the Charter is ambiguous on what is permitted thereafter, just as "measures to maintain international peace and security" is also vague.

One interpretation would deny individual states the right to armed self-defense from the point at which the Security Council has taken cognizance of the situation. But since the "measures" might be confined to imposing sanctions or might even be limited to a formal resolution and protest against the attack, that interpretation seems too rigorist and lacking in political realism.

That countries have a moral right of self-defense is reasonable.[17] As noted in the first chapter, David Rodin has advanced a tightly argued case against the idea that the state's right of self-defense is derived by extension or analogy from the individual's right of self-defense. I suggest that what is involved in a country's self-defense is essentially different from what is involved in an individual's self-defense. The two would overlap in a case where the aggressor country intended, as part of its war aims, to kill or enslave the population of the country under attack. But such overlap is relatively rare. Accordingly, self-defense in the case of a country or state needs further elaboration.

Causes of Wars: The Ethicist and the Historian

Before proceeding, I draw attention to a general point that is somewhat tangential to a consideration of just cause yet is relevant to a related moral rule of not causing war. A government or other competent authority ought not go to war without just cause or adequate moral reason; similarly, governments should avoid policies that raise the probability of other countries going to war. While the just war tradition does not specify such an obligation, it seems to me that in the Hobbesian theoretical context such a norm would be closely related to the just cause requirement.

The ethicist interprets just cause as country A having good enough moral reasons for going to war against country B, typically involving wrong or injury done to A by B.[18] A contemporary ethicist will also bear in mind that the UN Charter allows a country to resort to war only in response to armed attack.

That indicates that just cause requires actual attack. At most, UN practice would tolerate a preemptive strike or anticipatory self-defense only if there were overwhelming evidence that an attack was imminent (see Franck 2002, 105–8).

Turning from the ethicist to the historian, we get a different perspective. Whereas the ethicist is concerned with reasons that might justify going to war regardless of whether war actually occurs, the historian is not interested in reasons for going to war but in specific causes of an actual war.

Yet they can overlap, for a cause of war may also provide moral grounds or justification (i.e., just cause) for one side to fight. Germany's invasion of Belgium in August 1914 caused war with Belgium (and was a cause of Britain's going to war with Germany) and gave just cause to Belgium to fight. When the ethicist allows that A had adequate grounds for going to war with B, such grounds will be directly related to the historian's assessment of the causes of the war. That which gives moral grounds for war will almost certainly figure among the historian's list of causes of the war.

It can be argued that the ethicist needs to pay attention to the historian as well as to the lawyer. The UN lawyer says nothing else and nothing less than armed attack can justify going to war. The historian says that, depending on context, a range of actions can cause or provoke or increase the probability of war. She also says that at least some of these types of action would be known to have that effect.[19] Failure to take this into account could make the ethicist's treatment of just cause too abstract and decontextualized.

Many instances where war erupted without clear acts of aggression occurring seem to involve fear of a rising power.[20] The Greek historian Thucydides considered the main cause of the Peloponnesian war (431–404 BC) to be the rise of Athens and the fear it generated in Sparta. Athenian military and naval power, its web of alliances, and its policies made Sparta fear that it would soon be vulnerable to conquest by Athens. That convinced Sparta's leaders they had good reason to go to war while they still had a chance of winning.

Similarly, the possibility in 1701 that the resources of the Spanish Empire might come under the control of Louis XIV's France, already the most powerful country in Europe with an expansionary foreign policy, greatly alarmed Britain, the Netherlands, and Austria and had much to do with the outbreak of the War of the Spanish Succession (1702–13). The rather erratic aggressiveness of Germany in the 1890–1910 period gradually caused rivals Britain, France, and Russia to settle their disagreements in order to form a common front against Germany, setting the stage for World War I. In recent years, around 2010–13, fear that Iran might acquire nuclear weapons for politically aggressive purposes caused widespread alarm to many states and led to talk of a preventive strike by the United States or Israel. Similarly, China's neighbors have become concerned at its military rise and apparently aggressive behavior, and have moved to coordinate a common defensive response.

Do countries alarmed by the rise of a neighboring great power have just cause to go to war with the rising power? Presumably not: being alarmed or concerned about increased probability of future war does not give grounds for resorting to war. A change in the balance of military power does not as such constitute a threat of war. On the other hand, such situations are not without ethical import, if for no other reason than that they may make war more probable. An ethical foreign policy is not simply a matter of a state's refraining from going to war with its neighbors; it is also one in which it is sensitive to the impact on its neighbors of significant changes in its foreign policy, particularly if such changes are accompanied by expansion of its armed forces. A state may want a larger role in world affairs, as Germany did in 1900 and China and Iran do in 2010, without necessarily wanting war. It may desire that there be significant change in the international balance of power. To secure either of these without engaging in war, it must take account of the fears and sensitivities of its neighbors.

The just cause criterion in *jus ad bellum* says that no country should go to war without just cause. The historian's perspective suggests that this moral norm may need to be expanded to say that a state should not, without good reason, behave in a way that makes war more probable. The moral norm should be understood to prohibit provoking war, intimidating one's neighbors, and generally trying to change the international balance of power in a way that does not take cognizance of the security needs of one's neighbors. We should be wary of assuming that ethical issues pertaining to war become relevant only when a decision has to be made about whether to go to war. The historian's perspective suggests that they typically become relevant well before that point.

Sovereign States: Aggression and Self-Defense

In the Hobbesian framework focusing on the sovereign state's moral entitlements, there are several types of cases where just cause may be given. The first is the traditional case where one state launches aggressive war against another so that the latter is likely to have just cause for using force in response.

The historical record gives numerous instances of war resulting from a state suffering unprovoked aggression. Germany's invasion of Belgium in 1914 constituted unjust aggression against Belgium, as was acknowledged at the time by Theobald von Bethmann-Hollweg, the German chancellor. The same can be said of the German and Russian invasions of Poland in September 1939 as well as the subsequent German invasions of Denmark, Norway, and the

Benelux states, and Russia's forcible annexation of the Baltic republics and its war on Finland. Japan's invasions of China, the Philippines, and other Asian countries during its attempt to create an empire also qualify as aggression. Prussia's unprovoked invasion and seizure of Silesia from Austria initiated the War of the Austrian Succession (1740–48). The forceful partition of Poland by its neighbors in the late eighteenth century was aggression. Regardless of which ideal type is used as background context, those cases are clear instances of armed aggression that generated just cause for the victims.

Armed aggression need not involve actual violence. A country might decide to surrender without resistance, as Denmark more or less did when invaded by Germany in April 1940. There was little armed resistance to the forceful partition of Poland between 1772 and 1796. The USSR's demand in 1939 for Finnish territory adjacent to Leningrad with the offer of compensating territory further north may have been made in good faith and was not mere pretext for outright conquest, as was the case with Adolf Hitler's demands on Czechoslovakia and Poland. Some Finnish leaders, including Marshal Carl Mannerheim, reportedly favored giving the USSR what it wanted in order to avoid a war they knew they would lose. Even so, the general verdict is that Finland was within its legal and moral rights in refusing to accommodate the USSR. The occurrence of armed conflict depends on whether the attacked country decides to resist, as Clausewitz remarks.[21] But the moral culpability of the aggressor is not determined by whether the victim's response leads to actual conflict.[22]

Sovereign States: Unilateral Intervention

A second type of case involving war between individual states is one where there are humanitarian issues but these are not a direct cause of conflict. The fact that it is the state's own interests that are involved here, rather than humanitarian concerns or international law, distinguishes this topic from that treated earlier in this chapter, where the issue was whether individual states or others could act for humanitarian reasons or to vindicate international law or to preserve some degree of international order. Admittedly, there is overlap, but the difference of perspective, whether international order or sovereign state's rights, distinguishes between them.

Three brief wars occurred in the 1970s that are relevant here: (1) the armed intervention by India in East Pakistan in 1971, as a result of which East Pakistan was successful in seceding from Pakistan and became the independent state of Bangladesh; (2) the war of 1978–79 between Vietnam and Cambodia (Kampuchea) followed by the overthrow of the Kampuchea's Khmer Rouge government and its replacement by a government backed by Vietnamese troops; and (3) the war between Uganda and Tanzania of 1978–79 leading to the overthrow of the Ugandan dictator Idi Amin.

The political crisis and resulting internal conflict in East Pakistan led to some 10 million refugees flooding into India, putting severe strain on India's resources. When India sent troops into East Pakistan, its primary justification was not based on claiming attack by Pakistan or by invoking humanitarian need. Instead, it argued that the strain imposed by a flood of millions of refugees constituted a crime of "refugee aggression" (see Wheeler 2000, 61). Only as a secondary ground for intervention did it cite the humanitarian value of protecting human rights (Wheeler 2000, 62, 64, 74). However, there was no support at the Security Council for the claim that humanitarian concern could justify military intervention.[23]

Up to the 1990s, the international community gave the preservation of national sovereignty priority over the prevention of mass slaughter. Under the Khmer Rouge regime that ruled Cambodia from 1975 to 1979, it is estimated that 1 million to 2 million Cambodians died as a result of malnutrition and disease in labor camps, and about 300,000 were liquidated for political reasons. Demands by the Khmer Rouge regime for transfer of Vietnamese territory, along with border clashes and China's threats to intervene on Cambodia's side, led to Vietnam's decision to overthrow the regime by full invasion. Shortly after the invasion in December 1978, the regime collapsed and Vietnam installed a new government.

Vietnam's UN representative claimed that there had been two distinct wars in 1978–79: Vietnam's limited defensive war to repel Khmer aggression and a separate war of insurrection by Cambodians, with some support from Vietnam, against a tyrannical regime. This was hardly credible since there were still more than one hundred thousand Vietnamese troops in Cambodia propping up the new regime and fighting a Khmer Rouge guerrilla remnant. In any case, Vietnam made little or no use of the argument that its overthrow of the Khmer Rouge was justifiable on humanitarian grounds.

The UN debate on the issue became enmeshed in international power politics, with the United States and its allies, China, and ASEAN rejecting the new regime and continuing to recognize the Khmer Rouge government, and with the Soviet Union and its allies on the other side backing Vietnam. In 1978, US president Jimmy Carter had denounced the Khmer Rouge regime as the worst violator of human rights in the world. But following Vietnam's invasion of Cambodia, Carter's UN ambassador, while stating that governmental mass violation of citizens' human rights constituted good reason for the world to put pressure on the regime, took the position that such humanitarian concern could not justify "breaching the rules of non-intervention, territorial integrity, and non-use of force" (Wheeler 2000, 91; also 78). Substantial sanctions were imposed on Vietnam for its action.

Uganda's attack on Tanzania in October 1978 was followed by a coun-
terinvasion by Tanzania that led to the overthrow of Idi Amin as leader of
Uganda and his replacement by Milton Obote, previously in exile in Tanzania.
Despite Amin's reign of terror since 1971 with some three hundred thousand
murders to his credit, other African leaders (with the exception of President
Julius Nyerere of Tanzania) had kept silent, on the principle of noninterference. However, following Tanzania's removal of Amin, the United Nations
did not (in contrast to the Bangladesh and Cambodia instances) discuss the
issue since other African states did not support the ousted regime. There was
some criticism of Tanzania at the Organization of African Unity Summit in
Monrovia later in 1979, but for the most part Tanzania was treated differently
from Vietnam and did not earn international opprobrium.

Can the actions of India, Vietnam, and Tanzania be justified within the
Hobbesian framework where national sovereignty is the primary and overriding value? Vietnam and Tanzania could each claim that the other side had
attacked first so that their war had at least started as a war of self-defense. Each
could have argued further that the nature of the enemy regime was such that
it was unlikely to accept defeat but might very well launch a second attack at a
later time; hence, they were justified in overthrowing it. This would have been
acceptable reasoning prior to the twentieth century.

India could not plead that it had been attacked by Pakistan, so it had to
argue that the collapse of civil order in a next-door neighbor involving widespread violence and slaughter along with large numbers of refugees fleeing to
India was such that it constituted a security threat to India. That too would
have passed muster in earlier times.

It might be argued that the actions of India, Tanzania, and Vietnam violated international law. But international law is not obviously relevant when
the issue of just cause is being addressed within the older, early modern framework of national sovereignty. An appeal to international law may serve also to
admit reasons why certain regimes ought to be overthrown, even if they never
attack neighboring countries.

Accordingly, I incline to the view that Tanzania and Vietnam had just
cause since they were attacked, and that the nature of the enemy regime gave
grounds for seeking its overthrow. Even if the motives of Tanzania and Vietnam were primarily self-interested, and liberating the people of the other
country from an oppressor was a distant second, it still would not mean they
did not have just cause. The cause of justice is sometimes promoted by those
who have no great interest in doing so but whose self-interested actions have
precisely that effect.

Besides, it should be noted that such an objection might apply just as easily
to a state intervening on foot of a UN mandate. The United Nations' motives

may be pure (let us assume) in a given instance, but the United Nations has no troops of its own and is dependent on the good will and material support of militarily powerful countries who may be promoting their own national interests in implementing the UN mandate.[24]

In the case of India, it is harder to see that it had just cause to invade East Pakistan. One could, however, generalize from it and argue that within the national sovereignty framework a state could plausibly be viewed as having just cause to intervene militarily in a neighboring state if the disorder in that state is having serious spill-over effects on the first state, threatening a possible collapse of law and order. While we would not describe such an action as amounting to launching war on the chaotic neighboring state, it would be open to interpretation as an act of war and a violation of sovereignty by armed invasion.

The international law model and the sovereignty model need not be altogether at variance with each other. One might be skeptical of the viability of an effective international order and emphasize the practical importance of nation-state sovereignty and yet allow that perhaps sovereignty ought to be reinterpreted in an age where democracy and the rule of law are widely viewed as normative for sovereign states. Johnson remarks: "The conception of sovereignty as moral responsibility in the classic just war tradition contrasts importantly with the morally sterile concept of sovereignty in the Westphalian system. (Three centuries of experience with international relations stemming from the 1648 Peace of Westphalia have demonstrated that the principles of national sovereignty, territorial integrity, and noninterference in domestic affairs can, if interpreted in strictly procedural terms, conduce to protect tyrants while they oppress, rob, torture, and kill the citizens of their nations.)" (Johnson 2005a). Whether the classic just war tradition had a notion of sovereignty in the modern sense could be questioned. But it is the case that the classic tradition saw the ruler as one who had moral responsibility for the public good and could rightfully be overthrown if his governance were radically at variance with that good.

Although far from universally accepted, the recent shift in thinking moves in the direction of holding states accountable for how they treat their citizens. That means reducing the scope of national sovereignty. Sovereignty's value should be viewed as deriving from its role as promoter of the good, understood not just as the individual good of the citizens (for instance, in security of life and property) but also as the public good and the common good aimed at by a civically active and politically empowered citizenry, discussed in chapter 2.

Michael Walzer rates national sovereignty more highly than does David Luban. Luban notes that Walzer's response to the issue is to set a certain level of criminal behavior by a government toward its own people, which, if exceeded, effectively allows an exception to that state's right to sovereignty. Walzer argues that the crimes in question would need to be gross and involve a very large number of people (see Walzer 1977, 107). Luban would go further, proposing that unjust wars be redefined as "war that violates human rights" instead of "war that violates state sovereignty" (Luban 1994, 344n21). While sympathetic to that view, I shall not follow it further here or take sides between Luban and Walzer. It suffices to state that there are adequate grounds for a concept of limited state sovereignty. Even if one is skeptical about the effectiveness of international law and international institutions, one can still accept a modified notion of state sovereignty, one that relativizes it to the nature of the state and its conduct with respect to the good of its citizens, in particular with regard to democracy, human rights, and the rule of law.[25]

All of this has implications for the concept of just cause. Serious social disorder in one country caused by government oppression may be such that it negatively affects neighboring states' well-being. In such cases, the affected neighboring state might have just cause to intervene, the more so as the nature of the oppressive regime reduces the rights inherent in normal sovereignty. It is conceivable that a plausible argument could be mounted to the effect that if country A's becoming a military dictatorship has a very high probability of undermining democracy in country B, country B may in consequence have just cause to go to war with A. However, arguing this has to be left for another time.

Conclusion

The bare bones of the just cause notion are easily laid out. But decontextualized, it is hard to apply in any useful way. The major contextual choice is conceptual: a world of international law or a world of competing sovereign states. Just cause fits best in the context of a law enforcement model of the morality of war, as has been noted in a previous chapter. However, as the historical record indicates, the world is unfortunately not yet at the level of integration and harmony where that model alone is needed. We also need to be able to apply *jus ad bellum* theory in a context where sovereign states are threatened and insecure, or ambitious and overreaching.

A secondary context is more empirical: the historical record. Countries go to war for reasons, and what we count as just cause must have some relation to such reasons. Though never infallible, sometimes our moral intuitions strongly favor the position that a certain country had just cause or good enough reason to go to war, Britain and France going to war with Nazi Germany in 1939 being a case in point. In such cases, ethical reflection would be enriched and just cause be better understood by the ethicist's engagement with the historian's findings.

Notes

1. For more on this point, see Smith 2006.

2. Where a particular peacekeeping mission involves only lightly armed UN troops and does not extend to peacemaking, it does not in my view count as resorting to war or to the threat of war.

3. In *jus ad bellum* theory, I see no significant moral difference between an act and the threat to act.

4. These include Britain's deterring Iraq from invading Kuwait in 1961 by sending troops to Kuwait, and Italy's forcing Germany in 1934 to abandon the attempted Nazi putsch in Austria by massing troops near the Austrian border. The 1948–91 cold war between the US-led NATO alliance and the USSR-led Warsaw Pact alliance has points of similarity.

5. Values can be taken in realist or antirealist fashion, as discussed in chapter 2.

6. The earlier items on the list are understood as lesser steps that, if ineffective, will be followed by resort to war.

7. See Plato 1970, 626a, for an early expression of the Hobbesian view; and Hobbes 1994, 87–91.

8. It may be unreasonable to expect that states should always act only for altruistic motives in such cases.

9. It has been argued that the ideas relating to *jus ad bellum* and those relating to *jus in bello* are in some ways at odds since *jus ad bellum* assumes that choosing to go war is always immoral on one side, whereas *jus in bello* makes no such assumptions. Thus, in the 1600–1914 era, war was taken for granted as part of the natural order of things and even as a distinct legal institution; see Neff 2005, 4. Following legal interest, ethical analysis tended to focus heavily on the conduct of war, ignoring justifying reasons for going to war; see Rodin 2002, 166–67; and Rodin 2006.

10. The Charter of the International Military Tribunal at Nuremberg includes: Article 6(a): *Crimes against Peace*: namely, planning, preparation, initiation or waging of a war of aggression . . . ; Article 6(c): *Crimes against Humanity*: namely, murder, extermination, enslavement, deportation, and other inhumane acts committed against any civilian population, before or during the war, or persecutions on political, racial, or religious grounds in execution of or in connection with any crime within the jurisdiction of the Tribunal, whether or not in violation of domestic law of the country where perpetrated. Article 7: The official position of defendants, whether as Heads of State or responsible officials in Government departments, shall not be considered as freeing them from responsibility or mitigating punishment. Article 8: The fact that the defendant acted pursuant to order of his Government or of a superior shall not free him from responsibility, but may be considered in mitigation of punishment if the Tribunal determines that justice so requires.

11. The same applies to North Korea's invasion of South Korea in 1950, which was followed by UN condemnation and authorization of military action.

12. Note that the United Nations' just cause was not the same as Kuwait's just cause. The latter was grounded in the right to self-defense. Even if one argues that the United Nations or any country going to its aid has just cause by extension, it is also the case that the United Nations' just cause primarily has to do with the good of international order. If Kuwait had decided to acquiesce passively in its own conquest, it would not follow that the United Nations could no longer have just cause to respond militarily to Iraq's invasion and conquest of Kuwait.

13. UN condemnation of some military action does not create just cause for military response. In addition, the idea that military response is rendered moral (or immoral) merely by the United Nations' endorsing (or not endorsing) it undermines the moral objectivity upon which the concept of *jus ad bellum* depends.

14. Rodin (2006) suggests that fairness is a value in the just war tradition, and that it allows greater moral latitude to al-Qaeda-type groups that resort to nonconventional warfare since they are weaker than powerful states. I disagree on both points. Fairness is relevant only to a formal duel. The *jus ad bellum* tradition rejected dueling as immoral, along with any claim of analogy between war and a duel. The "fair fight" notion is irrelevant to the clash between magistrate and criminal.

15. The 1928 Kellogg-Briand Pact (the initiative of US secretary of state Frank Kellogg and French foreign minister Aristide Briand) banned war as a means of settling international disputes. By 1929, it had been signed by fifty-four states, including Germany.

16. See Kennan 1951 on US political attitudes in the interwar period.

17. I use the term "country" to denote the amalgam of government and people. I am concerned with the political community—that is, the people—not just as an aggregate of individuals but also as a civil society organized as a political community.

18. For discussion of harm, see Feinberg 1984.

19. See Walzer 1977 for extensive use of historical examples by a philosopher.

20. See Walt 1987 for interesting analysis of the origin of military alliances.

21. Clausewitz 1976, 370: "War serves the purpose of the defense more than that of the aggressor. It is only aggression that calls forth defense, and war along with it. The aggressor is always peace-loving; he would prefer to take over your country unopposed. To prevent his doing so one must be willing to make war and be prepared for it."

22. Here is one point on which the concepts of national self-defense and individual self-defense diverge. Without physical attack or immediate threat, the individual can have no right to use force against the aggressor. That limit does not apply to a state suffering aggression.

23. See also Walzer 1977, 105–7. Walzer's book predates the Cambodian and Ugandan cases.

24. This need not be sinister. Democratic governments have to take account of a shifting public opinion, which supports altruistic humanitarian intervention at one point but, when its soldiers start being killed, will suddenly demand to know why they should be put at risk to sort out the problems of others or what national interest is being served by so doing.

25. This connects to what I proposed in chapter 3 concerning the state's authority and the appropriate degree of respect to be accorded it, where I suggested that it should be conceived not as a constant but as a variable in relation to whether it was democratic, whether it respected human rights, and whether it supported the rule of law.

Chapter 5

Intention

No one starts a war—or rather, no one in his senses ought to do so—without first being clear in his mind what he intends to achieve by that war and how he intends to conduct it.

Clausewitz, *On War*

In the just war tradition, following competent authority and just cause, having a right intention is the third of the three most important conditions for being justified in going to war. Relatively little has been written on it. While superficially it may seem clear, appearances are deceptive. The concept requires a fair deal of clarification.

Aquinas and the Tradition

Following Augustine, Aquinas states that to have a right intention in going to war is to "intend the advancement of good or the avoidance of evil," and adds that "those who wage war justly aim at peace, and so they are not opposed to peace, except to . . . evil peace." He cites Augustine: "We go to war that we may have peace. True religion looks upon as peaceful those wars that are waged not for motives of aggrandizement or cruelty but with the object of securing peace, of punishing evil-doers, and of uplifting the good" (Aquinas, *ST* II–II, q.40, in Aquinas 1988, 221–22). This was discussed in chapter 2.

Aquinas's remarks suggest a few general points about intention. First, they express the schematic point that war must be waged for a good purpose or end. At this general level, it doesn't matter whether the end is defined positively (as something to be achieved) or negatively (as something to be prevented or removed). A minimal-peace notion is tacitly excluded as what is to be intended, so more than the mere absence of conflict is meant here. Accordingly, while an intention to avoid war in particular circumstances may be morally correct, a general policy based on an overriding intention of avoiding war in all circumstances is morally questionable because the intention of such a policy is misguided in the *jus ad bellum* view.

Second, the just war tradition rests upon the assumption that there are public goods to secure so that it might be permissible and in some cases mandatory for a government to resort to armed force. The just war tradition takes it that peace of a certain kind is the goal to be intended and pursued. Alternatively, one could put it that peace is one of the key ingredients of the public good that right intention pursues. That suggests that the nature of a context-appropriate peace must be worked out theoretically as a goal of public policy. Between the end of promoting the public good and the means of fighting comes a chain of means–end connections that have to be elaborated in detail for individual cases.[1]

Third, the passage from Augustine quoted by Aquinas includes both motives and goals under the general heading of intention. I argue later that motives should be distinguished from intentions, and that something important is lost if intention in the just war tradition is taken to be a matter of motive. For Aquinas, morally acceptable motives must not be vindictive or driven by desire of conquest. In line with that, we can reasonably infer that motivation must be directly related to a general good that includes the good of the country against which the legitimate authority proposes to wage war. Even if a government is motivated primarily by concern for its people or its own political position, that motivation is not morally objectionable provided there is no intention to violate the rights, well-being, and general good of the aggressor state's population.

Fighting for Justice?

In some views of intention, the good tends to be identified with justice. On this reading, a right intention aims at restoring peace with justice. Justice seems more concrete, more specific than the more vague- or abstract-sounding good.

There are pros and cons to this approach. That justice is part of the good can be taken for granted. Military intervention aimed at stopping genocide or ethnic cleansing, removing the government or other forces responsible for such crimes, or punishing those responsible would clearly reflect the intention to do justice to the people suffering gross violation of their human rights, and would also qualify as a promotion of their good. Such cases show governments intent on doing justice, thereby manifesting right intention in resorting to force.

Consider the case of Britain and France declaring war on Germany in 1939. Our moral intuitions are that they were justified in going to war, but it is less clear how their doing so could be seen as aimed at securing justice. Being morally justified in performing a particular action or adopting a particular policy logically entails that some good was to be attained or some evil prevented by so doing. But it does not follow that the good or the evil in question can be fully translated into the language of justice. If we take doing justice or acting justly in a deontological sense of giving people what they are owed, morally or legally, or of vindicating their rights (as something owed them), it is not clear that the good or the evil-prevention in the case of Britain and France going to war with Germany in 1939 can be spelled out in terms of doing justice to some group or nation. Identifying justice as that ingredient to which right intention is tied may be too theoretically restrictive.

There are a number of reasons for thinking thus. One is that talk about justice must refer to justice for specific people, whereas promoting the good or preventing evil can be more general in scope. In 1939, Britain and France doubtless thought that Germany's attack on Poland was unjust. Yet it is probably inaccurate to say that their intention in going to war over it can be specified as seeking to do justice to Poland. Surely they had considered Hitler's invasion of Czechoslovakia in March 1939 as unjust to the Czechs and a violation of the Munich agreement of 1938, although they had not gone to war over it. When they guaranteed Poland's security after March 1939, effectively promising to go to war to protect Poland, their intention probably had more to do with maintaining a certain kind of peace and balance of power, involving no further expansion of German power, than with doing justice to aggrieved peoples. The historical record suggests that their conception of the political good they wished to preserve or attain involved in some respects less than, and in other respects more than, doing justice to injured parties.

The consideration of justice, not as a deontological giving others their due but as a virtue we would wish to find in individuals and governments, quickly leads to the realization that there are other virtues required of the ruler, such as practical wisdom, foresightedness, moderation, courage, and endurance.[2] A government cannot successfully pursue the good without those virtues. Foresightedness may warn against armed intervention even when aimed at securing justice. Pursuit of justice, regardless of other considerations including consequences, might reflect a mindset of "Let justice be done though the heavens fall" (*Fiat justitia, ruant coeli*). It is not clear that such a sentiment expresses a politically and morally responsible stance to take in the matter of war; nor, in any case, is it a moral principle. Thus, in 1956, the United States and its NATO allies protested the USSR's crushing of the Hungarian uprising but refrained from armed intervention lest it lead to world war with probable use of nuclear weapons. Intending justice may possibly not suffice for an intention to qualify as right intention.[3]

On the other hand, foresightedness or prudence or practical good sense may indicate the advisability of intervention prior to injustice occurring. The British government's action in dispatching troops to protect Kuwait in 1961 against anticipated aggression by Iraq was foresighted. No doubt, on the assumption that it was unjust on the part of Iraq to threaten to invade Kuwait, the British government's action showed some concern for justice, but what is more notable is the practical good sense. The exercise of that virtue promoted the good of peace, stability, and social order. Here an intention to promote justice may not be strictly necessary for right intention to be present.

These cases indicate the challenges involved in spelling out right intention. I summarize some provisional conclusions. First, the just war tradition takes the public good, both national and international, as the proper goal of right intention. Second, the good of international order involves peace with justice but is not reducible to it. It involves other things as well. Third, the attaining of the good, as distinct from the good as goal or regulative ideal, depends on intending more than peace and justice, and may depend on practicing other virtues than justice. Each of these factors has to be understood in a way that can be integrated into a wider understanding of the general good.

Conflating Cause and Intention

The fact that little has been written on right intention in *jus ad bellum* may arise from a tendency to conflate right intention with just cause, and a tendency to conflate intention with motive. I deal with each in turn.

The conflation of just cause with right intention appears in the US bishops' 1983 document, where right intention is specified as: "War can be legitimately intended only for the reasons set forth above as a just cause." These reasons are "to protect innocent life, to preserve conditions necessary for decent human existence, and to secure basic human rights" (quoted in Holmes 1989, 164).[4] Here cause and intention are conflated in the notion of reason.

Brian Orend similarly appears to confuse cause, reason, and intention. On just cause, he states: "A state may launch a war only for the right reason. The just causes most frequently mentioned include: self-defence from external attack." Further on, speaking of right intention, he adds: "A state must intend to fight the war only for the sake of its just cause" (Orend 2008). Thus, for both the bishops and Orend, just cause and right intention are not merely symmetric but virtually identical. The implication is that once just cause has been found and identified, the appropriate right intention becomes self-evident. That means right intention is determined by just cause so that, given just cause appropriately and precisely specified, there is one and only one corresponding right intention that the relevant government can adopt.

That position misses a number of important distinctions. It also ignores the point that intention is typically oriented to some kind of policy or action. It is one thing for a state to have just cause to go to war; it is quite another for it to have worked out a contextually appropriate response, involving a well-crafted intention. The state or competent authority usually has little control or responsibility with respect to just cause since it will usually arise primarily from the actions of others. By contrast, the state is responsible for having a morally appropriate or right intention since it may have a range of choices in the matter. For that reason alone, it seems unlikely that right intention can simply be read off from just cause.

Let's consider the relationship between cause and reason. Causes in the human sciences are closely allied to reasons. Still, they are distinct concepts. Consider the following simplified version of one aspect of World War I. Assume Britain had just cause to go to war with Germany in 1914 on the basis of Germany's unprovoked invasion of Belgium and despite British warnings to Germany of its likely reaction to invasion of Belgium. Having just cause in that sense would mean having adequate moral reason (and, presumably, political reason) that would justify war with Germany. Add the not unreasonable assumption that while a disinterested desire to vindicate Belgium's rights was one of the reasons why Britain went to war, it was not the determining or crucial reason. That reason was its desire and intention to ensure that Germany did not get control of the channel ports from northern France to the Netherlands since such a development would seriously threaten Britain's own security. Had Britain and Germany succeeded in reaching an accommodation in the 1890s, or had Germany been able in July 1914 to give credible assurance to Britain that it would evacuate Belgium after the looming war, Britain might not have gone to war over Belgium in August 1914. But since neither of these possibilities was realized, Britain went to war to protect what it perceived as its interests—namely, Belgium's independence and France's position as a great power. Here Britain's reason had primarily to do with protecting its own interests and only secondarily involved Belgium's rights.

On the assumptions outlined, could one still say Britain had just cause to go to war with Germany? I think the answer is yes. The moral grounds justifying going to war with Germany are not nullified merely by virtue of the fact that the determining reason for Britain's action was its own self-interest. Had Britain intended to occupy Belgium after defeating Germany, its reason in the sense of intention would have been incompatible with vindicating Belgium's rights to independence and territorial integrity.[5] But since this was not the case, I see no difficulty in claiming that Britain had reason (in the sense of just cause or justifying ground) to go to war with Germany over its invasion of Belgium even though that was not the crucial or deciding reason or motive that made Britain decide to go to war. A further reason for making this distinction is that just cause refers primarily to the country or people attacked, whereas intention in responding must refer primarily to the state responding to the attack. (Note that the state responding to the attack need not be the state or country under attack. The fact that in many cases the two countries or states will be one and the same does not undermine the validity of the distinction.) The just cause generated by Germany's attack on Belgium applied to any state, and particularly to the states that had guaranteed Belgium's neutrality in the 1830s. But intentions in going to war must always be referred to the country going to war.

A further general consideration to bear in mind is that a government might clearly have just cause and yet decide not to go to war. If right intention is tightly tied to just cause so that having a right intention is no more and no less than intending to rectify the injustice, a decision not to go to war in such instances would seem to indicate a lack of right intention and hence possibly be morally wrong. Yet such a conclusion seems to lack adequate warrant since the way in which it is arrived at necessarily involves ignoring important contextual factors that a government considering war must bear in mind.

The foregoing suggests that right intention is not necessarily or at least not precisely a matter of intending to rectify an injustice or injustices as presented in what counts as just cause. Admittedly, right intention can't be disconnected from the evil, attack on the good, or injustice involved in just cause. Having a right intention does require that the proposed policy to be adopted shall, at a minimum, not ignore or accentuate the injustice involved in just cause and shall be such that it will foreseeably rectify the injustice to the extent feasible even if that is not directly aimed at or if it is only an indirect result.

Ideally, right intention in going to war would be directly aimed at rectifying the injustice done and establishing peace on the basis of that rectification. In the case of the Gulf War of 1990–91, the intent of the United States and its allies, mandated by the United Nations, was to evict Iraq from Kuwait and restore its independence. The greater the extent to which the intention can be a symmetric response to the evil or injustice involved in the cause, much as law enforcement is a symmetric response to a crime, the better. However, historical analysis of the intention expressed in a policy involving resort to war in response to undeniable aggression may show that the intention is not precisely to reverse the injustice.

Let me give a rather elementary example. The United States's intention in going to war in 1991 was to liberate Kuwait by driving out the Iraqi army. It could not achieve that goal, however, without also inflicting a heavy defeat upon or even destroying the Iraqi army. Since the time of Frederick the Great of Prussia and of Napoleon, it has been well known that defeating an enemy is not a matter of occupying territory but of defeating the enemy army so that the enemy is compelled to come to terms. Right intention in that case had to include defeating the Iraqi army, even though defeating the Iraqi army did not in itself constitute part of what it meant to liberate and do justice to Kuwait. Thus, right intention might involve a cluster or group of intentions: the intention of freeing Kuwait, and the intention of defeating Iraq, either by means of the military defeat of its army and consequent political defeat or by means of a political defeat alone, represented a humiliating climb-down by Iraq. It might also involve the intention (particularly on the part of the United States, the main agent of Iraq's defeat) of being prepared to impose and maintain a postwar political settlement or at least to ensure that Kuwait was not reinvaded when the UN-mandated forces went home.

While related to the intention of doing right by Kuwait and liberating it, these intentions cannot be subsumed under that intention without losing important theoretical insights. They also reflect the fact that right intention, as part of *jus ad bellum*, is part of a nexus of political factors and considerations. We can neither ignore nor prescind from these factors in analyzing right intention.

In the US bishops' letter and Orend's article, the conflation arises in part from the ambiguous word "reasons." Reason could be taken in the sense of cause ("The reason why she fell was that the robber pushed her"), or of motive ("The reason the robber pushed her was that he wanted to get her purse"), or of intention ("The reason the robber pushed her was to make her fall and thereby immobilize her"). The bishops and Orend conflate the idea of reason as a cause (in this instance, just cause) with reason as intention. For the reasons given earlier, the conflation is misleading and obscures what is involved in right intention.

Conflating Motive and Intention

A second important distinction relevant to understanding intention is the distinction between motive and intention. Motive concerns the driving forces behind an action or policy, typically focusing on its psychological origins. It is what is sought in asking why one is doing something, where the "why" is analogous to an efficient cause. By contrast, intention has to do with what one is trying to do or accomplish. It too can be the object of a "why" question, where a teleological or final cause is sought.

In much of the just war literature, however, the distinction is missed.[6] Somewhat like Aquinas, Orend conflates motive and intention in the following passage:

Having the right reason for launching a war is not enough: the actual motivation behind the resort to war must also be morally appropriate. Ulterior motives, such as a power or land grab, or irrational motives, such as revenge or ethnic hatred, are ruled out. The only right intention allowed is to see the just cause for resorting to war secured and consolidated. If another intention crowds in, moral corruption sets in. International law does not include this rule, probably because of the evidentiary difficulties involved in determining a state's intent. (Orend 2008; see also Orend 2006, 46–47)

As with the cause/intention conflation, the motive/intention conflation leads to missing important nuances.

Modern psychology has taught us that actions frequently have many motives. A man might marry a woman out of love, prudent self-interest (since she has various character traits he thinks necessary in a wife), greed (since she is well-off), and desire to show off a trophy wife to his colleagues. The question as to which is the determining motive could be difficult to answer. Motives tend to be somewhat hidden and are often hard for others to divine. Some motives may be subconscious and unknown even to the agent.

By contrast, intention is closely related to action in a kind of one-to-one relation. Intention is what can be read off from the action or attempted action. While motive answers the question "Why are you doing X?," intention answers the question "What are you doing or trying to do?" Both motive and intention have psychological dimensions, whereas intention but not motive is action-dependent in the sense that it cannot be identified except as action-related. Merely having a motive does not mean that an intention has been formed. One has an intention only when one has either chosen a goal to pursue or chosen a goal and a means to it as well. Intention is always intention to act or to adopt a policy involving a coherent series of actions.

The link between intention and action can also be seen from the action side. Action is distinguished from mere behavior by the fact that action is inherently intentional. It is identified or specified by the intention it embodies. A might kill B and C might kill D in similar and equally deliberate manner; the respective intentions of A and C are virtually identical—namely, to kill somebody. Yet their respective motives for doing so can obviously be different. In law there is no such thing as a criminal motive, whereas there is such a thing as criminal intent. That A and E might have had motives for wanting B's death does not make them criminals or provide any evidence that either of them intended to kill B.

In general, **motive plays no role in *jus ad bellum* theory**: it does not feature in *jus ad bellum* in the way that intention does. That doesn't mean we have no moral interest in a government's motives for going to war, or that its motives can never be identified or evaluated. Sometimes they can, and moral evaluation may deem them admirable, laudable, reasonable, understandable, opportunistic, rapacious, irresponsible, or evil. But such evaluation casts little light and certainly finds nothing determinative with respect to right intention or just cause. If a government's intention is morally wrong, that may give prima facie grounds for questioning either the probity or the prudence of its motives. But that's as far as we can go, for the fact that its motives might be morally dubious will usually indicate little about the moral character of its intention.

It's not hard to think of scenarios where agents do the wrong thing out of good motives, or do the right thing out of selfish, even vicious motives. A man who rescues somebody from drowning may do so out of humanitarian or altruistic motives. Another might do it from a selfish motive of seeking reward since he knows that the endangered person is wealthy and likely to express gratitude in monetary terms. Nevertheless, the same act type is instanced in the two cases, informed by the same type of intention—namely, that of saving the drowning person. In each case the action is morally right: it is always right to save someone from drowning regardless of one's motives for doing so.

As my example suggests, intention can be discerned with some reliability. An observer could easily see what each man is trying to do and probably also make out from their preparatory moves what each intended to do. As I argue, development of the concept of intention in *jus ad bellum* shows that discernment of the intentions of the other side is relevant to having right intention. Neville Chamberlain and Édouard Daladier wanted to discern Hitler's intentions in the late 1930s, the great powers of Europe had significant anxieties about each other's intentions in the summer of 1914, the United States was concerned about Iraqi dictator Saddam Hussein's intentions from the end of the first Gulf War in 1991 to the onset of the second war in 2003, and at the time of writing, Israel and other countries are uncertain and fearful about the intentions of an Iran that hurls incendiary rhetoric at Israel and seeks to acquire nuclear capacity. Intentions can often be identified, and a major part of international diplomacy is concerned with seeking to divine the intentions of other states.

By contrast, motives are much harder to discern since they are not clearly reflected in action. Motives are relevant to the assessment of the moral quality of the agent (or the government, in the case of going to war). But *jus ad bellum* has no need to deal with motives, nor could it do so without introducing confusing elements.[7] In the case of the two Gulf wars in 1990–91 and 2003, it was alleged that the United States and its allies were motivated by a desire to secure the Middle East's oil and, hence, that they could not be justified in going to war. Whether they were so motivated or not can be debated. But it is irrelevant to the justification of their going to war if the *jus ad bellum* approach is followed. It is their intention, not their motivation, that is relevant here.

A final reason why motive cannot play a role in *jus ad bellum* is that introducing it could make the conditions for being justified in going to war impossible to fulfill. To demand that governments be motivated only by disinterested or even altruistic motives is to ask the impossible. As Michael Walzer remarks: "An absolutely singular motivation, a pure will, is a political illusion. The case is similar in domestic society, where we take it for granted that parties and movements fighting for civil rights or welfare reform do so because their members have certain values *and also* because they have certain ambitions—for power and office" (quoted in Decosse 1992, 11). In some cases in recent decades, such as armed intervention to prevent genocide or civil anarchy producing famine, it is probable that intervention by the United States and other countries has been motivated largely by altruistic or humanitarian concerns. However, a decision to commit a country's armed forces to action will normally depend also on motives related to the national interest. Indeed, when altruistic action leads to casualties, citizens are likely to start demanding to know what national interest is being served by putting their sons and daughters in harm's way.[8]

Motives are relevant to *jus ad bellum* only to the extent they cast light upon conditions such as right intention or just cause. They are relevant only sometimes and always indirectly, never directly.

Intention and War's End

In recent years, there has been discussion of *jus post bellum* (justice after war) to complement *jus ad bellum* and *jus in bello*. While the discussion raises interesting and important issues, it still needs a lot of thinking through. In particular, it does not seem to be appreciated that some of what allegedly comes under the heading of *jus post bellum* actually belongs to the theme of intention. A case in point is illustrated by Orend's tendency to take *jus ad bellum*, *jus in bello*, and *jus post bellum* as referring to justice at three different times: the period before going to war, the period during war, and the period of the termination of the war.[9] In dealing with *jus post bellum*, he discusses the ends of war, starting off with: "The first step is to answer the question: what may a participant rightly aim at with regard to a just war? What are the goals to be achieved by the settlement of the conflict?" (Orend 2006, 162).

But the right aim in waging war is not something that becomes relevant only in the "termination phase" of the war, when the war's end is in sight. To assume that it is relevant only then is to verge on making going to war senseless since one of the most important moral concerns (perhaps the most important) for any state in going to war is: what does it hope to achieve, what is it aiming to do, what are its goals, what will count as winning? Those are not *jus post bellum* issues, but *jus ad bellum* issues. They are relevant from the very moment that war is contemplated. They are central to the notion of right intention. For any government going to war or resorting to armed force, it is doing so in order to achieve certain goals, and since the achievement of those goals will mark the intended termination of the war, that government is already thinking about the end of the war in deciding whether to go to war.

Various moral issues do become relevant at the end of a war. Orend lists the following conditions for *jus post bellum*: (a) proportionality in the peace settlement, avoiding vindictiveness; (b) vindication of the rights whose violation caused the war; (c) punishment of rights-violators in the leadership of the defeated country and punishment of human rights violations by the troops of all sides; (d) discrimination between combatants and civilians in imposition of sanctions or penalties; (e) compensation to be levied, within reason, from the defeated country for those wronged by its actions in war; and (f) reformation of the political, legal, and military structures of the defeated country, for example, in human rights training, reform of police, judiciary, and so on, with a view to its rehabilitation in the international community. Orend adds: "The terms of a just peace should satisfy all these requirements. There needs, in short, to be an ethical 'exit strategy' from war" (2008).

These criteria or conditions are certainly consistent with the spirit of just war thought. However, if they are morally required for a just termination of the war, they must figure in some way in a government's intention in going to war. The *jus post bellum* line of thought implies that in order to qualify as having a right intention in going to war, the government would have a moral obligation to aim at achieving a state of affairs such that these criteria would be met.

But only item (a) can be taken as definitely required in any peace settlement. As for the other conditions, the kind of peace that the unjust aggressor's opponent or opponents may settle for could well be such that it would not go so far as to vindicate the rights of all those whose rights were violated by the aggressor, let alone punish the aggressor's leaders or exact compensation from the aggressor state. It is not to be assumed in a priori fashion that to settle for such a peace must necessarily be wrong. The conditions Orend lists appear to fit only cases where the victor is a large and wealthy power (such as the United States) and where the opponent has been defeated to the point of having to surrender unconditionally and submit to a possible reform of its internal political and security structures at the hands of the victor. Such cases occur: the surrender of Germany and Japan in 1945 and the conquest of Iraq in 2003 are obvious instances. But these are by no means the only kinds of cases that the just war tradition has to consider. Wars can end in a variety of ways. They include limited wars, where the intentions of the side with just cause fall well short of requiring the unconditional surrender of the aggressor state, or of achieving a settlement that can achieve the goods or goals listed by Orend as required by *jus post bellum*.

In addition, while it is not an overriding moral factor, the desirability of fighting no more war than is necessary points in the direction of fighting a limited war, rather than always demanding the conquest of the aggressor, which is the direction in which Orend's *jus ad bellum* conditions tend. The limited war fought by the United Nations and the United States against Iraq in 1991 is a case in point since they did not remove the Iraqi dictator or insist on the kinds of reforms required by Orend's list. Yet it would be hard to argue that the United Nations and United States acted wrongly by not insisting on such reforms and punishments. The issue of whether those conditions come into play at all must depend on the *jus ad bellum* intention or intentions of the side with just cause. The question to be answered before addressing treatment of the defeated is that of what to aim at in fighting war. The range of morally acceptable intentions must be identified first.

The *jus post bellum* conditions that Orend lists are only partly relevant to the legitimate authority's intention in going to war. Insofar as they are not relevant, concerning only the aftermath of the war, they have to do with re-forming the defeated country and reestablishing a proper social order. In some cases that task may not be one for the victor, but for the United Nations or others. It is mistaken to assume that country A acquires certain moral responsibilities toward country B simply by virtue of having defeated B. There are certain general norms that country A must follow, such as not oppressing the defeated country, but these moral norms apply regardless of whether we have a *jus post bellum* theory in which to frame them.

Insofar as Orend's conditions are relevant to right intention, they are better understood within the framework of *jus ad bellum* since a lack of the proper or right intention would entail the wrongness of going to war in the first place. With regard to right intention, I reject the claim that the conditions he lists must determine right intention in going to war. At most, they indicate certain parameters of a negative kind—that is, certain prohibitions to be observed insofar as circumstances arise in which they might be relevant.

A number of objections to Orend's position can be briefly listed. First, there is no straightforward connection between country A's being justified in going to war with country B and what A may rightly intend in deciding to go to war or what it may intend at various significant moments in the war.

Second, it is possible that A might be justified in fighting, for example, in self-defense (as Poland would have been against Germany in 1939), yet be in no position at the end of the war to sort out *B*'s internal affairs. I see no adequate grounds for holding that such an outcome must cast doubt on the moral quality of *A*'s initial decision to go to war. Nor do I see grounds for holding that Poland should, in its decision to resist Germany, have intended the kind of things in Orend's list. If Poland's intention was to do no more than to successfully fight off its aggressor's attack, I cannot see how it could be faulted for not intending the items on Orend's list of *jus post bellum* criteria.

Third, with respect to condition (b), vindicating the rights violated by the defeated country's aggression may no longer be possible, and regarding (c) and (e), attempting to punish or extract compensation may do more harm than good to the long-term cause of peace.

Fourth, in a case where the defeated country's government has collapsed, it may be the case that, precisely because *A* has defeated *B*, *A* is politically unable (e.g., due to being politically unacceptable to *B*) to restore or rebuild a basic internal order in *B*. In such cases the UN or some other countries or agencies may be in a better position to do so. Where this applies, *A* is not morally obligated to meet condition (f), reforming the political structures of *B*.

For these reasons, it seems excessive to claim, as Orend does, that all these conditions must be met in order to have a just peace. Extrapolating from that, intending to fulfill the conditions cannot be assumed to be required in order for a state to have a right intention in waging war. They might, in a particular instance, turn out to be relevant to having a right intention, but they cannot be taken to be in principle required for having a right intention.

The correct moral intuition underlying the notion of *jus post bellum* is the idea that rebuilding peace after war is a morally and politically significant matter, and that failure to do so may sow the seeds for future war. Victors may have to take some responsibility in this matter, particularly in the interest of reconciliation between victor and vanquished. However, it goes too far to try to make doing so into a strict deontological moral duty to be imposed on the victor, for the reasons listed. Besides, making it a duty for the victor, as though the victor *A* owes it in justice to the vanquished *B*, suggests that merely by virtue of defeating *B*, *A* has somehow done *B* an injustice. Such a stance, however implicit, undermines the very notion that *A* might have been justified in going to war.

Intention: First Pass

Up to this point, I have dealt with what right intention is not: it is not the same as motive, it is not in one-to-one direct correspondence to just cause, and, while it concerns the desired outcome of the war, recent discussions of *jus post bellum* do not capture it. That it is oriented to peace of a certain kind can be taken for granted, but I have not gone further than that. Whether the peace in question is simply peace with justice is open to question. I have shown that intention should not be confused with cause or motive. Such confusion occurs in some recent literature, arising in part from ambivalent and imprecise use of the term "reason" and from failing to distinguish between reason as ground for action, reason as motive, and reason as goal-oriented intention.

As a first pass at identifying right intention, I list the following elements. First, intention is action-oriented: it is always an intention to do something, whether that something be a particular action, a series of coordinated actions such as making war, or a policy oriented to a particular end or nexus of ends. Second, intention is outcome-oriented. That applies particularly in the case of political action since it is aimed at averting or bringing about a certain type of state of affairs. Third, under *jus ad bellum*, the ultimate end of waging war is a certain kind of political order and stable peace in that order. War is a means to a political end, not an end in itself. Fourth, to aim at a particular political order is to take it as good, even if not the ideal.

In chapter 2 I discussed the idea that good public policy aims at peace, respect for human rights, the rule of law, and mutual parity of esteem between nations. How precisely that cluster of values or political desiderata can be the object of *jus ad bellum*'s right intention remains to be seen, for it is too abstract, too historically decontextualized to say that right intention is purely and simply a matter of promoting those values. At this point let it suffice to draw attention to the fact that societies lacking or violating those values are precisely those most likely to refuse mutually respectful relations with their neighbors and most prone to war. The states that do not respect their own people's rights or care about their good are unlikely to respect the rights of other societies; those where the rule of law is despised will have the same attitude to international law.

The foregoing indicates in broad terms what right intention generally aims at. It aims at the good, here specified as the sociopolitical good. In a world characterized by a plurality of conceptions of the good, it is desirable to regard the task of elaborating the good as dialogic, requiring input from as broad a range of conceptions of the good as possible. There are limits to that pluralism, however. A conception of the good that did not embrace all human beings equally (as, for instance, in Hitler's conception) would lie beyond the scope of reasonable and acceptable conceptions of the good. The sociopolitical good is thus a general public good. That good is not (or at least not merely) the aggregate of individual goods. The common sociopolitical good includes peace, order, the rule of law, and some minimal respect for personal dignity.

Those appear to be an absolute minimum. Right intention in *jus ad bellum* is aimed at restoring or establishing that good or order, and in a given case where war is contemplated, specifics of that good will have to be identified.

With that in mind, it is significant that democracies tend not to go to war with each other.[10] There is something to be said for the claim that governments with high levels of democratic legitimacy and committed to human rights and the rule of law are less likely to have aggressive intentions. That could be parlayed into a soft presumption of right intention on the part of such governments when deciding on war, with a corresponding withholding of presumption of right intention in the case of governments lacking such qualifications.

Right Intention: Mandatory and Permissible

In particular contexts, right intention will have to be specific. The good sought might include stable peace involving mutual security, restoration of fairness in relations between the belligerents, vindication of the rights and well-being of certain groups (e.g., minority ethnic groups), punishment of criminal governments, or establishment of democracy and the rule of law, some of which are on Orend's list for *jus post bellum*.

However, the word "might" is deliberately chosen. The good aimed at by right intention has mandatory or required elements as well as merely permissible elements. The mandatory side of right intention concerns the negative injunctions arising from the concept of right intention. It concerns what the aggrieved party is prohibited from intending. An unjustly attacked state may not intend to conquer the aggressor or annex some of its territory or in general use the aggression of the other as an excuse to violate the rights of the aggressor state or its people. Insofar as its intent is punitive, it may not intend to make war in order to directly or intentionally punish the civilian population.

On the side of positive injunctions, right intention by a government going to war to defend itself against aggression by a dictatorship might involve no more than the intention of repelling or defeating the aggressor, or it might also include the intention to overthrow the dictatorship and support the establishment of a democratic regime. At this prima facie level of analysis, it is not apparent that a particular state suffering unjust aggression is in general required to do either of those: to confine itself to self-defense or to turn its neighbor into a democracy. Considerable scope has to be allowed to context-sensitive consideration of what is prudentially feasible in specific cases.

That is why identifying right intention's goal as peace with justice is mistaken because it is likely to tie right intention to a relatively inflexible set of demands. The demands of justice tend to be pretty absolute. To require that the United Nations or a country with just cause intend to rectify all injustices having any causal connection to the outbreak of war (and, hence, presumably be morally accountable for doing so) is to demand too much since it may demand what is not achievable.

In general, demanding that right intention aim at nothing less than lasting peace or peace with justice on pain of ceasing to qualify as right intention is to fall victim to a kind of hubris. It would be like requiring that right intention aim at fighting a "war to end war," an achievement that is not within human power.

When taken at a general abstract level, justice tends to be seen as involving such things as undoing injury or wrong; restoration, presumably of the *status quo ante* (the state of affairs prior to the unjust behavior); or giving people what they are owed. The third is too general to be of much help here, but the other two are more promising. So, applied to something like Germany's treatment of Czechoslovakia or Poland in the late 1930s, this suggests that right intention for the League of Nations or any other great state with the power and the political will to tackle Germany would have been to make Germany evacuate Czechoslovakia and Poland and perhaps pay reparations to both countries. That such an intention would be morally acceptable and in that sense "right" seems clear. But would it be morally required? Had Britain and France had other intentions, could they qualify as right intentions? I shall suggest that some of them could. If I am correct in that, it follows that we cannot limit right intention to the doing of justice conceived of as described at the beginning of this paragraph.

It is also possible that circumstances may change dramatically during war since war upends many of the previous arrangements and landmarks. Whatever Britain and France's intentions in going to war in 1939, restoring Poland's and Czechoslovakia's independence and territorial integrity was beyond their power after their strategic defeat in 1940. Britain's intention metamorphosed into defeating Germany and terminating the Nazi regime regardless of what would happen to Poland and Czechoslovakia thereafter. Assuming their initial intention in 1939 qualified as a right intention, did their later intention also qualify? It seems hard to say that it didn't or couldn't so qualify. To this I return in the next section.

Let's turn to what right intention involves with respect to the aggressor state, particularly with respect to its people. Assume a case where the United Nations or a great power defeats a dictatorial regime arising from circumstances where it is generally agreed that the regime was to blame for the outbreak of war so that the United Nations or the great power had just cause. Assume that defeat leads to the collapse of the dictatorship and of basic social order so that the country spirals into violence, anarchy, and nascent civil war. Is the United

Nations or the great power morally responsible or culpable, by virtue of having caused the dictatorship's overthrow, for the outbreak of anarchy? It seems wrong to say that it is since this assigns moral responsibility for the suffering caused by the breakdown of social order to the victor rather than to the dictatorial regime responsible for causing the war.

In my hypothetical case, it seems right that the United Nations or great power should carry some responsibility to maintain social order and protect the civilian population. But it is not responsible in the sense of culpable for the sufferings of that population. Accordingly, its responsibility arises from the general humanitarian duty to bring aid to the extent that is feasible, not from some kind of guilt for bringing about social chaos or from some kind of duty to make reparations. Where the United Nations went to war not because of aggression launched by the dictatorship but solely to remove a dictatorial and unusually oppressive regime, it has a much greater responsibility to ensure that what replaces the dictatorship is, even if not democracy, at least a considerable improvement from the perspective of the civilian population in terms of its respect for their rights and care for their well-being.

The next step is to apply that to the issue of right intention. In going to war, a state necessarily intends or aims at the military defeat of its opponent so the United Nations or great power intends the military defeat of the dictatorship. Depending on the particular situation, the United Nations or great power may also decide that nothing less than unconditional surrender and removal of the regime will ensure that war does not start again at a later date. That was the attitude that Britain, the USSR, and the United States took toward Germany and Japan in World War II. If it does so decide, its strategy for conducting war will intend that outcome. Assuming that it is justified in refusing to accept less than unconditional surrender and regime change, is it responsible for the resultant anarchy? Is it obliged, if it reasonably foresees severe suffering by the civilian population under the resultant anarchy, to refrain from adopting that intention? Again, I think the answer is "no" in both cases. Right intention need not include, for the reasons given in the previous paragraphs, taking steps to prevent social collapse in such a way that would preclude seeking regime change. It was wrong for Allied bombing strategy to target German cities since in so doing they directly attacked civilians. It was not wrong for them to seek to overthrow the Nazi regime, even though doing so would indirectly cost many lives since, far from seeking to spare the civilian population once it was clear that the war was lost, the regime was prepared to fight to the bitter end.

Right intention is primarily negative with respect to duties to the civilian population on the other side, concerned with what one may not inflict on it. Postwar occupying powers may acquire duties toward the population—not because they went to war but simply because they are the occupying powers. Justice, then, does not accurately capture what is involved in the pursuit of the good that is the object or goal of right intention since it is likely to cast it in terms of incurred obligations to particular groups.

In the case of a small country successfully resisting a larger country (again assuming just cause), it is even more difficult to envisage that it could be morally constrained with respect to right intention by positive duties of justice toward the population of the larger country. Consider North Vietnam's strategic defeat of the United States in the struggle lasting from the early 1960s until 1975. For the sake of argument, allow that it had just cause on its side. It is hard to see how its having a right intention would have required it to consider whether going to war with the United States would have seriously destabilizing social effects on the US population to such an extent as to restrain it morally from fighting the United States. Indeed, North Vietnam gradually became aware that American public opinion was a crucial center of gravity from a strategic point of view, particularly after its heavy defeat in the 1968 Tet offensive turned into a propaganda coup and a political victory as US public opinion was shocked by the scale of the fighting and a demoralized President Johnson announced his intention not to seek reelection (see Gray 1999, 96). Serious social unrest in the United States would have significantly helped North Vietnam, and it is hard to see how encouraging or provoking it would have involved a wrong or unjust intention on North Vietnam's part.

Intending too Little

Britain and France went to war with Germany in 1939 to protect Poland. Their strategic defeat in 1940 meant that postwar Poland's political future would be largely determined by Germany or the USSR, or both, with little scope for other powers to alter that fact. Admittedly, Britain refused to make peace with Germany after its expulsion from the mainland of Europe and continued to fight. However, its strategic intention at this later stage was primarily to defeat Germany and end the Nazi regime even if that meant that Poland might fall under the domination of Britain's ally after 1941, the USSR. This doesn't mean that Britain's intention necessarily involved injustice to Poland or that it neglected Poland's rights. It does mean that Britain took the destruction of the Nazi regime and its empire as the most important good to be achieved in the international political situation of the 1940s. As argued earlier, it seems awkward or forced to take this as a matter of promoting justice since it is hard to argue plausibly that when Britain decided in the summer of 1940 to continue the war, its intention in so doing was to defend the rights of the Polish people or, indeed, those of any specific group for whom justice was being sought by going to war. It is preferable, because it is theoretically less constricting, to see it as a matter of promoting the good.[11]

The broader notion of right intention as pursuing the common good allows flexibility in other ways. It may be that the side with just cause to go to war has to settle for less than would be morally desirable or even—all things being equal—morally required. While it is morally wrong to go beyond what the range of right intention will permit, it is not self-evidently wrong or a violation of right intention to do less than might be warranted. If it is wrong, that has to be argued.

Let us suppose that Britain and France had defeated Germany in 1940, and Germany had sued for peace, offering concessions but not unconditional surrender. If Britain and France had treated on that basis with the Nazi government and contented themselves with requiring Germany to evacuate Poland but without obliging it to surrender Bohemia and Moravia, this would (in hindsight) have been a disappointing outcome. As an intention of fighting the war, this would have been modest indeed. Yet this intention would have done justice to Poland, ensuring that the specific act of aggression that had caused the war was undone, and would have involved far less killing than insistence on unconditional surrender and removal of the Nazi regime would have required.

Would such a limited intention have been morally wrong on the grounds that it did not seek or pursue sufficient change? At first glance, it seems not. If one takes the line that right intention should be restricted to the remedying of the injustice or disorder that caused the war, one would probably have to approve the intention not merely as good in itself but also as rightly limited. But if one takes right intention in a wider or more permissive sense, one might allow that more expansive intentions could also qualify as right and possibly even hold that the narrower intention was wrong because it was too limited. One could argue on the basis of a political analysis that the Nazi regime was too dangerous to world peace to be allowed to survive. In 1939, vindicating Poland's independence was one thing; restoring good or half-decent political order and stability to Europe involved a much larger project.

Could a wrong intention include not merely doing too much but also not doing enough—that is, failing to restore good order and justice or perhaps restoring only a limited amount? The implications of the question are revealing. If one says "no," this suggests that there is no objective standard or ideal relative to dealing with aggressively evil regimes, particularly those that are also powerful enough to constitute a serious danger to the world at large, such as the Nazi regime. That effectively would negate the idea of good international order as relevant, and also suggests that the United Nations or the great powers have no duties with respect to maintaining international order and peace, other than the duty of not attacking it. Yet the history of the League of Nations seems to provide an object lesson of the consequences of well-intentioned great powers being overly reluctant to go to war to protect the international order. Great powers can attack peace and undermine international order by being aggressively conquest-minded; perhaps they can also subvert them by failing to stand up to rogue states.

Accordingly, I think the answer is "yes." A state or the United Nations does not necessarily fail the right intention criterion by not fully reversing the injustice or attack on the common good involved in the act of aggression, but it is possible that it could fail the criterion. A state could fail to have a right intention by adopting an overly minimalist intention with respect to the aggressor state, or by adopting an intention that focused narrowly on its own interests in a context where the rights of other countries were at risk of violation. I suggest that Britain and France would be open to the charge of failing the right intention criterion in going to war with Nazi Germany in 1939 if their intention was to do no more than protect Poland's territorial integrity. The inability to achieve the goals indicated by a right intention and the military and human cost of doing so being prohibitive are the only morally acceptable excuses for failure in this area. *Jus ad bellum* is a theory of governance, and in the abstract it assumes an outcome where the government (or coalition of governments) can dictate and impose a just settlement. They may not be able to do so, or the human and military cost may be prohibitive or severely disproportionate. In such cases, it suffices that the intention or aim inherent in their policy and military strategy tends to the good, even if they have to settle for less.

This issue is connected to others. If the right intention condition may be violated by failure to do enough (when a state could do more) to restore order and justice, it could also be violated by a powerful state or the United Nations not having the intention to respond firmly to aggression or threatened aggression by outlaw states.

At this point it may be objected that right intention is a condition in *jus ad bellum* and hence has no relevance outside of that context. The objection claims that in deciding not to go to war to defend another nation under unjust attack or in deciding to follow a policy of strict neutrality, a government is not deciding to choose war, so the criteria listed in the just war tradition cannot apply to those decisions. Even if that state's policy could reasonably be termed selfish, cowardly, lacking in international solidarity, or imprudent, it still has nothing to do with lacking a right intention in the sense relevant to *jus ad bellum*.

I disagree. That line of thought treats war as a state of affairs or activity outside of the zone of the political and hence having no relevance to the task of promoting the good. Of course, war is always a tragedy for humanity, as religious leaders and others rightly claim, but it can also serve the good. The very idea that war might ever be justifiable implies as much, most of all in the right intention condition. It was good that the Nazi regime was overthrown; it would have been better if it had been overthrown earlier. The fact that it was overthrown by war does not nullify that good. Given the nature of that regime, it can be plausibly argued that only war could have ended it. Right intention is precisely the condition in *jus ad bellum* where the good to be promoted is identified and practical means found and chosen to pursue it.

In general, these considerations indicate the difficulties that arise from identifying just cause with self-defense. One can't argue that Britain and France went to war with Nazi Germany in self-defense without deploying a contrived and, hence, unconvincing argument. To extend what counts as self-defense to defense of others may not be as contrived, but it may be unnecessarily or counterintuitively restrictive, as the examples illustrate. Taking just cause and right intention as better framed in the context of defending or promoting the international good turns out to be a more viable strategy since it offers a more contextually sensitive and flexible notion of what may be rightly intended.

Right Intention Is Political

Right intention in the context of *jus ad bellum* is, first and foremost, a political and strategic matter. It concerns the government's strategic goals. Precisely because right intention is a political matter, it is not something confined to the zone of war or to discussions bearing on war. War is not proposed first and right intention for it then sought. It is, or ought to be, the other way around. Right political intentions on the part of governments or the United Nations may, precisely because they are right, bring up the possibility of resorting to force in order to realize them.

All of this leads to the conclusion that right intention cannot be identified with removing or undoing the injustice or aggression that has been a key element in creating just cause. In some cases, it will involve doing just that, but not always and not necessarily. It may sometimes amount to much more, sometimes to less, than removing or reversing the injustice.

In any case, the identification of right intention is a political task. First, it is political not just in the sense that it is carried out by a politically competent or legitimate authority but also in that it is worked out within a political context embracing the aggressor's action and the possible responses to it. Second, the political task is conditioned by practical factors having to do with what is possible for the competent authority in question.

Third, depending on the context, there will often be a range of morally acceptable right intentions that could be embodied in policies for action.

This point has some relevance to the last resort condition, which is discussed later. The earlier that a government or the United Nations faces the prospect that it may have to go to war, the wider its range of options and, hence (in principle), the wider the range of possible right intentions with respect to going to war. '

Fourth, there is no principled boundary between right intention in peace and right intention in war. The government's intentions are political in nature—that is, oriented to reasonable political goals, intending the good. The issue of right intention does not suddenly arise when war is contemplated.

Fifth, a decision not to go to war in a situation where there are some grounds for doing so must also pass the test of whether the intention embodied in the decision not to go to war is morally correct. In the same way that refraining from acting is sometimes the moral equivalent of an act, so choosing not to go to war or intervene militarily is an intentional action that can be morally evaluated.

It is sometimes thought that, even where there are admittedly some grounds for going to war, a decision not to go to war always has some moral goodness since it amounts to choosing peace. Since peace is a good, choosing peace must necessarily be morally right or have the presumption of being morally right. On this view, even in a situation where there was significant justification for choosing war, one could still never say that a decision not to go to war was immoral or an attack on the good.

But that line of thought ignores the role of practical reasonableness in the political zone. At the practical level of judgment and decision with which we are concerned, such thinking must be excluded since it is essentially antipolitical. It may even be destructive if it cuts across or derails attempts at political discernment of what a prudent and reasonable authority ought to do.

To cite the obvious case, Neville Chamberlain's conviction that, in the Munich agreement that he, Édouard Daladier, and Benito Mussolini had made with Hitler, he had preserved "peace in our time" and thereby acted rightly strikes us today as illusory. His desire for peace and intention of doing all he could to preserve it were morally laudable, but his refusal to discern that the time had come to go to war exhibited impractical and, hence, morally flawed judgment. Doubtless, the fact that he did not succeed in appeasing Hitler permanently and that war ensued a year later is the strongest reinforcement in the popular mind of his being imprudent and misguided. But even had Hitler been satisfied and had not proceeded to attack Poland, Chamberlain's action would still have been wrong. The remarks of Clement Attlee, leader of the British Labour party, in the House of Commons regarding the Munich agreement highlight its moral, political, and even military significance:

The events of the last few days constitute one of the greatest diplomatic defeats that this country and France have ever sustained. There can be no doubt that it is a tremendous victory for Herr Hitler. Without firing a shot, by the mere display of military force, he has achieved a dominating position in Europe which Germany failed to win after four years of war. He has destroyed the last fortress of democracy in eastern Europe that stood in the way of his ambition. He has opened the way to the food, the oil and the resources that he requires in order to consolidate his military power, and he has successfully defeated and reduced to impotence the forces that might have stood against the rule of violence. (Quoted in Craig 1978, 707)

The military language of victory and defeat used in each of the five sentences quoted reflects their speaker's grasp of the fact that Chamberlain's concessions to Hitler, aimed primarily at keeping the peace and preventing war, gave victory to Hitler and inflicted defeat on Britain, France, Czechoslovakia, and democracy in eastern Europe in general. Chamberlain presumably thought that notions of victory and defeat applied only to war and hence were inapplicable since war had been avoided. Attlee understood that victory and defeat were ultimately political, like war itself, as Clausewitz argued, and saw that Hitler had won a "tremendous victory," the more so because he had got the victory without having to undertake the risky business of actual fighting. Attlee's remarks reflect clearly the point that the zone of the political spans both war and peace. Furthermore, political defeats have military consequences. In the *jus ad bellum* framework, one does not necessarily avoid military defeat simply by refusing to go to war.

Sixth, **right intention of the kind required for going to war is also required for policies of military deterrence.** The Cold War between NATO and the Warsaw Pact from the late 1940s until the end of the 1980s offers a good example of the way in which a policy of sustained military deterrence involves decisions and actions closely analogous to those involved in fighting a "hot" war. The fact that the Cold War sometimes found expression in localized "hot" wars is irrelevant. All that matters here is that the policy of deterrence was not a bluff but expressed an intention to open fire under certain conditions. It is another illustration of the key point of this section—namely, that right intention transcends formal dividing lines between the "state of peace" and the "state of war" since NATO and the Warsaw Pact were technically at peace yet heavily armed and ready to fight with each other at short notice. Right intention does not become relevant only when the competent authority must decide whether to fight a "hot" war.

Intention in Neutrality

In view of the political nature of right intention, the intention informing neutrality is open to question. On examination, the stance of principled neutrality turns out to be morally problematic. It is one thing for a state to decide, with respect to a particular war, to remain neutral. There could be morally acceptable reasons for doing so.[12] But neutrality with respect to all international conflicts, a principled neutrality maintained in abstraction from any context where aggression, genocide, or tyranny challenge the international community, seems morally wrong, perhaps seriously so. It violates the right intention condition since it amounts to saying that the state will never use force in the international arena to defend justice, human rights, peace, or other important international goods and, hence, it rejects the intention to defend or pursue these things, whether alone or in concert with other states.

In the just war tradition, neutrality is unacceptable as a principle of action or a standard or norm of international behavior. Neff explains why:

> The law-enforcement model of war left no room for neutrality for third states. For one thing, since there was really no such thing as a state of war in just-war thought, so there could hardly be a distinct status of neutrality either. The rights and duties of third states simply remained as they always were, since war involved no suspension of natural law. This logical point was reinforced by a moral one: that third states could no more be "neutral" during a war than ordinary citizens could be "neutral" with regard to the capturing of an accused criminal by a magistrate. In fact, neutrality in such a situation would fall dangerously near to being a wrongful act in itself. (Neff 2005, 59)

The law enforcement model of war is, of course, central to the just war tradition. It is central to the twin moral intuitions that war for aggressive and exploitative purposes is wrong, and that the public authority should protect the weak against violence and injustice. The state is meant to promote the public good, as are such international organizations as the United Nations. The UN Charter itself assigns the United Nations the right to use force in order to deal with international aggression. Neutrality in that scenario is standing by inactively, knowing that injustice is taking place and refusing to help in stopping it.

That a particular state might be unable in a given instance to help, or might stay neutral in a particular instance for reasons peculiar to that instance, might be morally acceptable. But principled neutrality is not morally acceptable, for it reflects an intention not to stop aggression, prevent genocide, or promote international order in cases where force is required in order to do so.[13] The political intention manifested by principled neutrality is incompatible with the right intention presented in *jus ad bellum*. As argued earlier, right intention is not something that becomes relevant only when war is proposed, or only when a state decides to go to war. The intentions of nonbelligerents and neutrals are also subject to the same moral evaluation.

Levels of Intention

So far in this chapter I have discussed issues to which right intention is irrelevant as well as some issues where it is relevant. At this point we can go deeper in analysis of intention. With respect to war, there are several levels at which one can discern intention.

1. Intention at the most general level, where the ultimate goal of public policy is the common good of all human beings, limited goods of a particular community, or a kind of amoral self-interest.
2. Intention at the ethical and political level of international political relations and interaction.
3. The intention or intentions involved in the decision to go to war.
4. The intentions involved in specific campaigns that are part of war-fighting, both at the strategic level of choice of where and how to fight and whether to fight on the offensive or the defensive, and at the operational or tactical level of how precisely to fight in particular instances.
5. The intentions of the officers and soldiers relating to fighting well, dealing with the enemy, and various other issues.

The intentions concerned in items 1–3 are those of governments, the United Nations, and any other competent authorities. Item 4, insofar as it concerns war-fighting strategy, is the business of both political rulers and the general staff, so their intentions are its focus. Item 5 concerns that part of the just war tradition concerned with *jus in bello*. To a large extent, intention at the operational and tactical levels in item 4 also has more to do with *jus in bello* than with *jus ad bellum*. Since *jus in bello* is outside the scope of this book, I won't deal with 4 or 5.

The opening section of this chapter dealt with item 1. What I hope I have shown at this point is that fleshing out what right intention in *jus ad bellum* involves requires treating 2 and 3. That right intention involves promoting or seeking the good, peace, and justice is easily said and readily conceded. But governments thinking of going to war are not thinking of those goods in such general terms. Their intentions relate to more concrete goals. The issue then is to evaluate the actual intentions of governments in order to see how ethical value is realized in policy decisions and strategic choices.

The Scope of Ethics

Application of ethical analysis to the issue of the government's or the competent authority's intention has been relatively rare. When ethical analysis is associated with war, it usually is taken to concern the conduct of the war and the behavior of commanders and soldiers.

This arises in part from the bias in much modern ethics toward treating ethics as concerned solely with the Right—that is, with norms and rules of behavior, thereby neglecting the Good—that is, the values or goals to be discerned, desired, and pursued. In Colin Gray's comprehensive treatment of modern strategy, this bias is noticeable in the few pages he devotes to ethics. While in sympathy with his Clausewitzian commitments, I find his views on ethics confused. His remarks are nonetheless suggestive, as the following extract reflects:

> Ethics are important. . . . People care about right conduct. In principle, political action is subject to ethical assay, whereas ethically driven action should not be subject to authoritative political judgment. In the practical world of strategic effect, however, a consequentialist logic rules. The justice of behavior is weighed in the light of its intended, anticipated, and actual effect. . . . In practice, it is hard to locate many unambiguous historical cases wherein prudential strategic logic was challenged from within the relevant defense community by people wielding explicitly ethical principles. The elastic realm of military and strategic necessity, even mere prudence, has a powerful ethic of its own. Ethics functions as the dog that does not bark and sound a moral alarm in strategic decision-making. (Gray 1999, 72–73, 74)

In this quote, a number of strands of thought are entangled. Gray seems to see ethics as being about rules for action or behavior and apparently expects them to be prohibitive. This is reflected in the remark that "ethically driven action should not be subject to political judgment," in the comment that "prudential strategic logic" is rarely "challenged . . . by . . . explicitly ethical principles," and in the final observation that ethics fails to "sound a moral alarm in strategic decision-making." A number of points can be made in response.

First, ethics includes not just rules for action but also some vision of the goods worth pursuing that embody values worth promoting, and toward which action should be oriented. The rules-for-action aspect tends to be more significant in the conduct of the war than at the level of political decision to go to war with certain goals. However, moral vision is possible at the strategic level. The political and strategic goals of Nazi Germany's wars were evil since they were aimed at conquest of eastern Europe and virtual enslavement of the Slav population. Prussia's seizure of Silesia from the Austrian empire in 1740, precipitating the War of the Austrian Succession, was nothing but an immoral land grab. The same could be said of Mussolini's attack on Abyssinia in 1935 as of many of the colonial conquests of Britain, France, and Portugal. NATO's armed intervention in the former Yugoslavia to stop Serbian atrocities directed against Bosnians and Kosovans seems ethically acceptable, even laudable. Nor was ethical concern absent from NATO's public statements at the time of the intervention. The German strategic war plan in 1914 failed the ethical test by requiring the invasion of Belgium, as was more or less acknowledged by the German chancellor at the time. Thus, it is not true that ethics never has anything to say about policies and decisions involving war, or that it invariably fails to "sound a moral alarm in strategic decision-making."

Second, Gray's rather Kantian view of ethics (particularly of right action) leads him to distinguish it sharply from rationality and practical reasonableness. He assumes that ethical imperatives are always categorical and never hypothetical, so they hold always and regardless of circumstances. He seems to think of ethics as the application of universal moral rules in an immediate or unmediated way to particular cases and typically only as setting limits. One might apply a moral rule forbidding direct or intentional attack on noncombatants to Britain's policy of carpet-bombing German cities during World War II, and then conclude that the carpet-bombing was morally wrong. Concerns about prudence or practicality may in such a case be either irrelevant or yield no overriding considerations. But for strategic issues, what is moral to do may be partly such precisely because it is rational or prudent to do. It was rational and prudent for Britain to dispatch a small number of troops to Kuwait in the early 1960s when intelligence reports indicated that Iraq was considering invasion of Kuwait, just as it was rational and prudent of the United States' President Clinton to react rapidly to Iraq's mobilizing its forces near the Kuwaiti border in 1993. In both cases the actions were morally correct because the goal (protecting the independence of Kuwait against threatened military aggression) was good.

Thus, "prudential strategic logic" is not something alien to ethical judgment. If anything, it is indispensable to implementing the "explicitly ethical principles," at least as far as the application of *jus ad bellum* is concerned.[14] Ethical principles in this area, where they are oriented to the general good of humanity in the international field, cannot be effective without paying attention to strategic logic.

To hold that "ethically driven action should not be subject to political judgment" risks making ethics unreasonable. When the USSR was suppressing the 1956 Hungarian uprising, there was a moral case for military intervention by NATO in order to protect the Hungarians and vindicate their right to self-determination. But the possibility that such intervention would unleash all-out war between NATO and the Warsaw Pact had to be weighed against that. That consideration is not just prudential; it is also moral. In fact, in this instance it is moral because it is prudential.

Gray appears to think that in the world of strategy only a "consequentialist logic" is used for ethical reasoning, and this he takes not to be a genuine ethic at all. I agree with him that consequentialism is a dubious ethical theory, but weighing outcomes, effects, and consequences does not make one a consequentialist. After all, no serious normative ethical theory can be indifferent to consequences. Consequentialism is the doctrine that consequences alone determine the moral rightness or wrongness of action, and actual, not intended, consequences at that. The political and military strategist is not forced into holding that doctrine merely by virtue of being required to take consequences seriously. One can avoid consequentialism simply by accepting that there are some constraints on the range of what is permitted, even when the consequences are good.

Intention in International Relations

Wars and the risk of war arise from the interplay of international politics as well as from developments in the internal politics of a nation leading it in the direction of insurrection, civil war, or breakdown of social order. Good governance requires that political leaders pursue the good in such a way as to avoid or reduce the probability of war occurring, the destructiveness of war, and the politically negative consequences of war. Achieving that goal requires flexible and imaginative use of means. Depending on the context, achieving the goal might require adopting policies ranging from the conciliatory to the vigorously deterrent, ranging from noninterventionist refusal to be provoked to launching a preemptive attack.

The last sentence allows a wide range of options to the competent authority involved. The question arises: how can such a diverse, even contrasting range of strategies be integrated into a theory of right intention? How could one assume that in one context preemptive war could manifest right intention and in another context conciliation and compromise would show right intention?

A first step is to distinguish between proximate and remote intentions. In the context of *jus ad bellum*, proximate intentions concern situations where the possibility of having to go to war with a particular country has a significant possibility of materializing within the next two years. Concern that country *A* possibly intends to attack country *B* arising from the current political situation between them would be oriented to trying to make out the proximate intention of *A*. For country *B* to qualify later, in the event of attack, as having right intention under *jus ad bellum* would require that it be preparing now, whether by improving its defenses, making alliances, seeking international support, negotiating to resolve differences, or some other means, to deal with the threat of war. Even if *B* is later the indisputable victim of aggression at the hands of *A*, so that it then has a right intention simply by virtue of its intention to resist, it can also have a right intention in its prudent preparation against the threat of attack.

Remote political intentions concern long-term goals with respect to other countries. So, one might analyze a state's strategic goals with respect to its neighbors, and its goals with respect to its wider position in the world. This would involve taking into account both what it says it desires to achieve as well as what it actually does, for example, its alliances of various kinds—political, military, economic, and so forth. Intentions here are best identified as aimed not at such goals as universal peace and justice but at national self-interest and, where the state aspires to a world leadership role, at certain goods that go beyond its own self-interest narrowly conceived. However, what is particularly interesting to other countries is whether a state identifies its national self-interest as including the maintenance of international peace and order, and the managing of conflict by negotiation. In the case of a state whose remote intentions include significant change to the international order, other states have reason to study its policies with a view to seeing if its desired changes are consistent with international peace and, if they are not, to seek to contain if not remove the remote threat. The containment policy of the United States and NATO toward the USSR from 1948 to 1990 is a possible example of a right intention oriented to countering remote or nonspecific risks of war.

Remote intentions with respect to policy issues where war is involved or likely to be involved are not in principle indiscernible. It is possible to make out the remote intentions or long-term strategy of the United States with respect to its war in Afghanistan from 2001; its anxiety about Pakistan, a nuclear-armed country with very shaky governmental institutions; and its desire to promote India as a counterbalance to China. Evaluating each policy with respect to the goodness of its goals can be done. It is regularly done by policy analysts as well as by journalists.

My concern with such policies has to do with their promoting peace and justice or making war more likely. That puts it vaguely, but examples may make it clear. In the late 1930s, Hitler desired and intended to go to war with the USSR. He did not desire war with Britain and possibly not with France either, but he intended to fight them if they obstructed his plans for central and eastern Europe. The overall thrust of his policies was oriented to war, not to promoting peace or justice.

Germany's foreign policy between the fall of Bismarck in 1890 and 1914 increased tensions with its neighbors and thereby made war more likely, even if neither Kaiser Wilhelm II nor his successive chancellors intended to go to war in the way that Hitler intended later. Germany had no proximate intention of going to war with any of its neighbors. But its policies indicated a remote intention of doing so. Wilhelmine Germany felt that its place in the world was less elevated than it should be, and it sought by rather truculent behavior to make its neighbors treat it with more respect. Its leaders failed to realize that their behavior might be interpreted as threatening, and as expressing aggressive intentions. Perhaps the most notable example of that was its construction of a navy around 1900 in an attempt to rival the British fleet while simultaneously rejecting Britain's offer of an alliance. The German government did so, convinced that British interests were so deeply at variance with those of France and Russia that no rapprochement between them was possible, and so there was no risk that Britain would join the camp of Germany's enemies. By 1909, that conviction had been proved wrong. After 1910, a rather desperate Germany, acutely aware of its isolation, hardly knew anymore how to avoid war.

The fact that historians may differ on how to interpret such historical developments itself points to the object of attention here: the intentions of governments and how to evaluate them. The evaluation may not be explicitly moral, in the sense of self-consciously using ethical terms. It suffices that, for instance, the inferences Britain drew from German policy in the late 1890s induced the belief that Germany anticipated and half-intended war with Britain, leading it to the conclusion that it should conduct its own foreign policy accordingly. Possibly Germany didn't intend anything of the kind; if so, its tragedy was that it failed to grasp that its actions were threatening Britain. Such failure on the part of a government is culpable; it represents a failure of political realism, possibly a failure to show proper respect to the other state, and certainly a failure of prudence and failure to promote peace.

Wars often arise in part from misjudgments and misinterpretation. Occasionally there is no misunderstanding leading up to war's outbreak. In both types of scenarios, the intentions of the belligerents and the interpretations of those intentions are directly relevant to understanding why war broke out.[15]

While the actual outbreak of conflict, for example, in Germany's invasion of Poland or the USSR in World War II, or in the border clash between the USSR and China on the Ussuri River in 1969, naturally features most prominently in the context of discussion of cause, what is crucial for the formation of right intention is correct reading of the intention of the potential aggressor. In 1941, Stalin refused for several days to believe that the intention behind Hitler's attack was the complete conquest of the USSR. In the 1969 Sino-Soviet border clash, each side was uncertain and fearful of the other's intentions.

We are here concerned with what precedes and underlies the clash of arms—namely, the play of intentions on both sides. The intuition I am trying to tease out here is that when we go beyond the general philosophical level to the political and strategic level, fulfilling the criterion of right intention in *jus ad bellum* requires divining the intention of the other side so that one's own intentional response can be shaped appropriately.[16] To reiterate a point already raised, to imagine that the right intention criterion becomes applicable only when an attack has begun or has been explicitly threatened is to sell the just war tradition short, or indeed any serious ethical theory with respect to war. Good government requires not just pacific intentions but also practical reasonableness or prudence: good governments must discern the aggressive intention of the other state in advance, seek to deter it as credibly as possible, and be prudent in discerning the most favorable time for responding to it militarily.

Walzer refers to the War of the Spanish Succession (1701–14), which arose from the anxiety of England, Austria, and other countries over the apparently imminent and potentially vast augmentation of the power of France's Louis XIV through the accession of his grandson to the vacant Spanish throne (1977, 78–80). Certain other actions by Louis XIV at the same time seemed to confirm the English view that his intentions were aggressive. In the early 1960s, the USSR became confused as to the intentions of the United States with respect to Cuba, arising from the United States' first providing substantial support for the abortive Bay of Pigs invasion by Cuban exiles and then allowing it to fail by not using its own military forces when the invading force was pinned down on the beaches. This apparent weakness and indecisiveness on the part of the United States led the USSR at the time of the Cuba crisis in 1962 to underestimate US political determination.

Prior to the Anglo-American invasion of Iraq to overthrow the Saddam regime in 2003, there was much debate as to whether Iraq had nuclear weapons or other weapons of mass destruction. UN inspectors had previously reported that there was much weapons material unaccounted for, but they had been expelled some time previously by Iraq. Under threat of imminent war, Iraq allowed their return. However, cooperation was grudging and hard to obtain.

While no weapons of mass destruction were found, it was hard to be sure that none existed.

Focusing on the weapons could never have decided the issue. If the UN inspectors had found no weapons of mass destruction, doves would have said that it proved Iraq didn't have them, and hawks that it showed how well they were hidden. But if weapons had been found, doves would claim that it meant Iraq was now safely disarmed, and hawks that it proved how determined Saddam was to get such weapons. Judgment on this issue was misled by focusing on the weapons rather than on Saddam's intentions in trying to acquire them. In itself, abstracted from political context, the possession of nuclear weapons has no clear political significance. It is the political intention underlying the goal of acquiring them, and the intended political impact of having or using them that is significant. Given the numerous wars that Saddam Hussein had initiated and his threat to reinvade Kuwait in 1994, a few years after the Gulf War, the United States and its allies had reason for thinking that he would attack again at a time of his choosing and might well deploy nuclear weapons in doing so.[17]

At the time of writing, the United States and various European states are actively pressing Iran not to acquire nuclear weapons, mainly out of concern that the Iranian government intends to provoke a conflict with Israel, and that Iran's having them would terrify certain Arab countries into seeking to acquire their own nuclear weapons. It is not the possession of nuclear weapons as such that arouses concern but the possibility that they will be used aggressively, even if only to make destabilizing threats.

Let me try to pull together a number of elements that bear upon right intention at the political level. Right intention excludes preparing to attack one's neighbors or developing armaments in a way that is likely to threaten or intimidate them, or is likely to make them think that one is preparing to attack them. It also excludes military action, whether it be rearmament or disarmament, that alters or threatens to alter the political balance in such a way that other states' anxiety or aggressiveness rises significantly.

It is a condition of having or acquiring a right intention that its political grounding be understood. It must be accepted that other countries have interests, that they have a certain right to pursue those interests, and that such pursuit may cut across one's own country's interests. Right intention involves being proactive in dealing with potential conflict and finding ways to avoid war.

Right intention involves a certain political realism. It accepts, as just noted, that conflict and tension may arise. Right intention is not to be confused with "meaning no harm." Just as right intention will lead a state to avoid the dangers of bluff, misreading of intentions, aggressiveness, and paranoia, so too it also requires avoiding the dangers of a naïve and apolitical idealism. Even the assumption that countries and states are naturally peace-loving and that peace is the natural state of affairs can be dangerous under some circumstances and may obstruct having a right intention.

Right intention requires that the individual state conduct its affairs so as to promote global peace and justice. Thus, disarmament may in some political contexts not make the world more peaceful and orderly since it may encourage tyrannical states and make weaker states feel dangerously vulnerable. While this appears to involve speaking of right intention as though it were disconnected from the context of war, it is all too easy to find examples of continuity. The development of a situation where war is imminent may show that a state's previously aggressive behavior has led other states to refuse to tolerate it any longer, and a way out cannot now be easily found. Its military weakness in the 1930s undermined Britain's ability to develop a right intention in dealing with Hitler.

Talk about being unable to have a right intention may be puzzling. However, recall that intention is not the same as motive. To have an intention is to have an intention to act, and a government cannot intend to do that which it has no means to do. Intention is what is embodied or can be embodied in action. The United Nations might on some occasions be incapable of having a right intention with respect to some situation where massive military intervention is needed owing to lack of political will among various countries to provide the necessary troops and, hence, its own incapacity to deliberate on actions designed to embody an appropriate or right intention oriented to military action.

Intention in Action

The idea of divining the intent of the other side may be dismissed on the grounds that it is very difficult if not impossible to read the other's mind. But one can observe the actions, omissions, words, and silences of others, and one can draw inferences from them. If I threaten somebody with an apparently loaded pistol, the fact that it is unloaded does not mean that I have not threatened that person. Actions, like meanings, are public and have a kind of public meaning.

Behavior is communicative because the meaning of words and actions is public. Dr. John Spooner may have wanted to say "Let us toast the dear old queen," but what he actually said, "Let us toast the queer old dean," has a different meaning. People laughed at Spooner's remark since they recognized that what he meant to say was different from what he actually said. As with speech acts, so with ordinary acts: they have a public meaning. And normally people mean what they say and mean or intend what they do.

Intention in the psychological sense (what I want to do) has no political significance except insofar as it is embodied in appropriately expressive word and action. It is possible that in the 1890–1910 period the German kaiser Wilhelm II and his ministers had no intention of going to war with any of their neighbors, and that, like John Spooner, they were singularly incompetent in expressing this in their foreign policy. They may not have understood the full political significance of their aggressive behavior. But even as other major powers also wondered if the kaiser was fully rational or if the German government was really aware of the diplomatic signals it was sending, they still found its behavior threatening and aggressive and felt they had little choice but to react accordingly. The motives and political desires of the kaiser may have been obscure, even to him; but the policies of his government could not but express a certain logic, a set of developing intentions with political implications.

I am claiming that right intention in *jus ad bellum* is to a significant extent morally right insofar as it is an appropriate response to the intentions of other governments or groups. The intentions of governments or groups are in principle publicly observable in their statements and actions. Thus, what we are concerned with is not inner psychological intention or motive but the political meaning of actions and policies. Determining whether right intention is present has nothing to do with psychoanalyzing politicians and everything to do with analyzing their policies and their reasonably expectable impact. That moral analysis is related to how well they have responded to the intentions of other states, international bodies, or groups: criteria of reasonableness, justice, fair-mindedness, prudence, and avoidance of aggressiveness and naïveté are all relevant to assessing how good the response has been. More than any other *jus ad bellum* criterion, intention with respect to war is grounded in the government's prewar policies.

The right intention criterion is the point where Clausewitz's principle that war is an instrument of policy connects to the just war tradition. His principle is not an ethical judgment legitimizing war. It is an acknowledgment of the fact that international politics, whether in peace or war, involves the intentions and policies of different states and some nonstate agents, with many of those intentions arising as a response to the perceived or apparent intentions of other states.

On Clausewitz's view, resort to war is an option that, while not desirable as such, may be required in response to the intentions of other states. While resort to war is always regrettable, it is tragic when its occurrence is attributable to policy flaws arising either from failure to communicate the intentions embodied in that policy or from serious misreading of the other side's intentions.

In general, a right-intentioned state will conduct policy so as to minimize the probability of having to resort to armed force. Subject to contextually sensitive political analysis, keeping the peace is an important goal that governments should intend. It is always more than, and in many cases different from, merely avoiding war. Peace does not keep itself, and the assumption that peace is the natural state of things is not borne out by the record of history. Donald Kagan argues:

> What seems to work best, even though imperfectly, is the possession by those states who wish to preserve the peace of the preponderant power and of the will to accept the burdens and responsibilities required to achieve that purpose. They must understand that no international situation is permanent, that part of their responsibility is to accept and sometimes even to assist changes, some of which they will not like, guiding their achievement through peaceful channels, but always prepared to resist, with force if necessary, changes made by threats or violence that threaten the general peace. (Kagan 1995, 570)

It is notable that Kagan makes little reference in this context to the role of the United Nations. He is more impressed with the achievement of the 1815 Congress of Vienna in creating the subsequent "concert of the powers" that managed to avert general European war for the next hundred years.

Thus, analysis of the legitimate or competent authority's intention is not a matter of considering the psychological states of the head of government on the eve of war. It is a matter of looking at the public intentions embodied in the actions and policies of the state that have led up to the war. That a state's actions and policies have been involved in an overall causal process leading to war does not necessarily imply that the state has acted wrongly, attacking or undermining the good of peace. The state's role is to promote the general public and international good, of which peace is only part. Whether right intention has been present depends on how its policies can be evaluated in light of that overall good.

Preemptive Strike and Preventive War

Intention is relevant to evaluating the moral status of launching a preemptive war or a preventive war. Military strategists and ethicists differ as how to distinguish between preemptive war and preventive war. In the ethicist's view, a preemptive war seeks to forestall an intended and imminent attack, whereas a preventive war seeks to forestall an eventual and probable but not now intended or imminent attack. Military strategists tend to take a different view: "Preemption was an idea that grew from the operational level of war; it was a military concept, whereas preventive war was a political one. Preemption was not necessarily linked to war's causation, but was part and parcel of war's conduct. Linked to stratagem, ruse, and deception, it embodied the core strategic principle of surprise in war" (Shue and Rodin 2007, 27). Thus, military strategists viewed preemption as applicable to attack or strike rather than to war as such, since they took it that in such cases war was already decided on (by one side or the other). Where this was the case, preemption solely concerned which side would launch the first assault.

Launching a preemptive strike is relatively easy to justify. The difficulty lies in determining how imminent the threatened attack is. A restrictive approach would take "imminent" to mean virtually certain to happen within days. In 1842, US secretary of state Daniel Webster stated that justifying a preemptive strike would require showing "a necessity of self-defense . . . instant, overwhelming, leaving no choice of means, and no moment for deliberation" (quoted in Walzer 1977, 74).[18] I shall refer to this as the strict interpretation. As Walzer notes, that would "permit us to do little more than respond to an attack *once we had seen it coming* but before we had felt its impact" (Walzer 1977, 74; emphasis in original). It could be understood in an even stricter sense of requiring that the other side fire the first shot.[19] It would not permit a preemptive attack by a country against another that had massed its army on their mutual border, with every sign of preparing to invade. Not until the massed German army had traveled the last kilometer to the border in the early hours of the invasion day could Poland in 1939 or the USSR in 1941 have been justified in fighting.

The strict interpretation is unreasonable for several reasons. First, contrary to Webster's view, decisions to go to war are too important *not* to be matters of deliberation. In general, Webster's view is fundamentally antipolitical, as if wars could never be understood as political in nature. Second, it may impose burdens on the just side (or the more just side) that lead to its losing the war. The changing modalities of how to conduct war may require the possibility of flexible response. In 1996, the International Court of Justice declined to find that initiating the use of nuclear weapons would, in cases where the state's existence was threatened, be illegal (Franck 2002, 98).

Consider the case of the Gulf War (1990–91), when Iraq concentrated its army on the Kuwaiti border in the summer of 1990. Other states assumed that the threat to invade was merely a bluff. In view of Iraq's subsequent invasion of Kuwait, it seems clear that those states had misread Iraq's intention, and that Iraq mistook the nonresponse of other countries to its troop deployment as indicating an intention not to oppose militarily a subsequent takeover of Kuwait. If attack is threatened, failure to respond may make attack more likely. In 1994, when Iraq again threatened Kuwait, the United States responded rapidly and forcefully.

In view of the success of Britain's sending troops to Iraq in the early 1960s and the United States' action in 1994 where in neither case was actual fighting required to stop Iraq from invading, and in contrast to the war that had to be fought to evict Iraq from Kuwait in 1991 in consequence of ignoring Iraq's massing of troops on the Kuwaiti border, the strict interpretation of justifiable preemptive attack will not do since it requires a response that violates practical reason. The strict interpretation may also hamper the military ability of the threatened country to defeat the attack by confining its military options to the purely defensive even when it is clear that attack is virtually certain.[20] In addition, the US secretary of state's insistence on a moral condition that deprives the threatened country of "choice of means" and of time for "deliberation" undermines the wider goals of *jus ad bellum*. The *jus ad bellum* theory is a theory of good governance that values prudence and practical realism, is critical of aggressiveness or foolish passivity alike, and requires both choice of means and deliberation.

The foregoing indicates that we should adopt a relatively permissive, or at least not strict, view of imminence. Once a government or the United Nations has sufficient evidence that a certain country intends to launch an aggressive attack on one or more of its neighbors or to carry out genocide against some of its own people, it is morally permissible to act militarily. It is understood, of course, as discussed earlier, that an intention is an intention to act, not a mere motive or desire to act. Imminent attack could apply to something that may not happen for some weeks or even some months. Regarding what is to count as sufficient evidence, it should follow the standard of proof in civil rather than criminal cases, where it is a matter of the balance of probabilities rather than proof beyond any reasonable doubt. Another way of putting it is to use the common law's standard of what the reasonable person would find convincing.

Launching a preventive war is far more difficult to justify because the key element of manifest aggressive intent on the part of the other side found in preemptive war and defensive war is usually missing here.[21] As discussed earlier, a key element in developing a right intention (with respect to policies of war and peace) is discernment of the intentions of other states. Discernment of the intentions and policy goals of other states as well as the probability that they will use force to attain them are the primary occupation of diplomats and foreign ministry departments. Accordingly, the key element (it may not, of course, be the only element required) for being justified in launching a preventive war is the presence of an aggressive intent on the part of the other side.

The mere fact that a great power A feels itself threatened by the rise of another power B, where it can be predicted that B will eventually be more powerful than A, could not suffice to justify a preventive attack by A.[22] Other factors would have to be present, such as a general aggressiveness or expansive policy that was more immediately affecting others. Without that, A could not possibly be justified in launching war against B.

In such circumstances, B will be politically and morally obliged in the interests of peace not to do anything to threaten A, and even to take steps to reassure A. To put that in less moralistic and more political terms: it is politically prudent if not necessary for B to avoid threatening its neighbors. An indifference or obliviousness on the part of B to its neighbors' concerns about future aggression is politically foolish and hence, in the context of right intention, the most political of the *jus ad bellum* criteria, morally blameworthy. If in future years B's indifference or insensitivity to its neighbors leads to the formation of a military coalition against it, as with the case of Napoleonic France or Wilhelmine Germany, its ability to have a right intention in resisting that coalition militarily will be impaired by its previous failure to have a right intention. Having a right intention in the context of decision to go to war requires having had a right intention prior to that with respect to such international goods as peace and stable international order.

In consequence, while the fearful and consequently aggressive anti-B coalition will probably not be justified in fighting a preventive war with B, B's moral status in *jus ad bellum* perspective will be weaker as a result of its failure to defuse a political threat created by its rise.

What could make a difference to the morality of launching a preventive war would be if B does intend to attack A at some point in the future when it has become stronger than A, although B has no intention of going to war under present circumstances and has no plans for attack later. (In the 1939–41 period, Germany wished to avoid war with the United States, so it had no immediate aggressive intentions directed against the United States. However, its aggressive intentions directed at conquering the other European powers posed a long-term threat to the United States, so it was predictable that, given Germany's current aggressive policies, it would eventually develop plans for war with the United States.) Here B has a remote intention of making war on A.[23] Under such circumstances, A could have some justification for fighting a preventive war against B.[24] The justifiability of preventive war against such a state is to be connected rather to the policy intent expressed in taking foresighted action to deal with threats before they become worse.[25]

In such circumstances, it would be difficult to have the requisite degree of evidence to warrant A's arriving at the conviction that B intended to go to war eventually; without it preventive war could not be justified. Yet in principle such knowledge is attainable (see Trachtenberg 2007).[26] Unlike motives that are often secret, even from the agent whose motives they are, intentions are public to a significant degree since they are expressed in action. If B had an intention to attack A, no matter how remote in the future the attack was intended, it would be manifest to some extent in B's behavior.[27] This is not solely an epistemic point to the effect that one could not know that the other intended something unless he or she acted in a way that indicated the intention. It is also an ontological point about the nature of intention—namely, that intention is embodied in action of some kind. Even the agent herself cannot know that she actually has a particular intention unless she is acting in some way designed, no matter how remotely, to achieve the goal of the intention. A motive or desire need not show up in action, but an intention necessarily does so.

The virtue of prudence is precisely what might lead A to contemplate going to war with B now rather than later. This may seem a dubious notion of what prudence involves. However, if one distinguishes here between going to war and merely contemplating war, it may be more acceptable. Ideally, one would wish A to intend to avoid war as far as possible; to make the most of any available time to deter, forestall, or prevent B from launching aggressive war; and, if deterrence fails and war is necessary, to take the initiative so as to maximize the chance of success and minimize loss of life.

Far from putting off all thought of war until, as in the American secretary of state's words, there is no other choice and no scope for deliberation, a government (or the United Nations) should be quick to discern the possibility of future war and deal with it. Admittedly, the secretary was speaking of actually going to war rather than of merely contemplating going to war. Nevertheless, the difference at the practical level of intention is not great. If A contemplates fighting a preventive war with B, it does so for practical purposes—that is, with a view to deciding whether it should actually fight such a war.

Deterrence is not just an important part of strategy. It is also of central concern in the task of exploring the topic of right intention since deterrence is essentially a matter of clearly communicating the state's intentions to the other side, and doing so in a way that makes them credible. Accordingly, the intention or threat expressed in the deterrent policy must be specific and not vague or overly general, it must be reasonable in the sense of being credible (A is able to deliver on it), and it must be reasonable in the sense of being proportionate (it is the kind of thing others would probably do in similar circumstances).

In none of these steps, however, must it communicate that it has categorically ruled out preventive attack. It cannot bluff and expect to deter, and it would be politically (and morally) wrong to enlist allies without being willing to protect them by force if the need should arise. It can do none of these things effectively without having decided that it is prepared to launch preventive war if they fail. Since keeping the peace is always more than avoiding war, right intention with respect to keeping the peace cannot be identified with avoiding war or threats of war. It must be understood as a commitment to pursue the policies that will preserve the peace.

Just as B appeared to have a remote, not proximate, intention of attacking A, so A's intentions can be categorized as remote and proximate. A has an appropriate remote intention of preventing B from launching aggressive war that might defeat A. Practical realization of that remote intention will require, as the previous paragraph intimates, the formation of proximate intentions oriented to actions to be performed or policies to be implemented in the near future. A's principal goal is to communicate effectively that it has no intention of awaiting its own defeat while at the same time it has no hostile independent intentions of its own toward B. Its goal is to change B's calculation of the relative benefits and costs of waging war.

As argued earlier on other grounds, the discussion of preemptive and preventive war also shows that the ethics of intention cannot intelligibly be confined to intention narrowly focused on going to war. Nor is the intention in going to war formulated only when war is imminent or unavoidable; it is inherently grounded in the political strategy of the state in question. Fighting a war is not an isolated act disconnected from policy.

Thus, right intention in *jus ad bellum* is not just about the specific intention of a particular war that shades into its strategic intention but also about more general intentions with respect to managing its affairs with countries with whom it may foreseeably find itself in conflict. Right intention concerns both winning the war and winning the peace, either by deterrence of aggression or by means of the political strategy of which fighting the war is a part.

Intention in War-Fighting

I turn now to what had been earlier listed as levels 3 and 4 in discussion of different levels of intention with respect to war. These include the intentions informing the decision to go to war along with strategic military decisions identifying the goals to be achieved by specific campaigns that are part of war-fighting at the strategic level of choice of where and how to fight.

The issue of intention here can also be expressed in terms of what it is that the government is fighting for: what will count as winning? Whether it be war-fighting or humanitarian military intervention, the goals must be made concrete so that appropriate strategic intentions can be clearly identified in a way that gives guidance to the military leadership.[28] Strategy is the answer to the question of what must be done militarily in order to achieve the political objective. The political objective must therefore be made specific enough so that strategic military options can be derived from it.

Specifying the political goal in the right way so that it can be linked to strategic military action is a task that requires close cooperation and communication between the political and military leadership (see Smith 2006, 12; Gray 1999, 17).[29] The relevance of this to the ethics of intention in *jus ad bellum* concerns the importance of having a clear intention. It is unethical to have wrong or immoral intentions since these involve direct wrongdoing. It is also unethical, in the sense of failure or serious incompetence where lives are at stake, to go to war with an intention that is so vague that no strategic sense can be made of it, so that the human costs will be either unnecessary or ineffectual. At the level of motive (insofar as it may be relevant), it is enough that the government is motivated by a concern for peace, stability, and the protection of human rights. At the level of what right intention must involve in *jus ad bellum*, that is not enough. The political leadership must have worked out with its military advisers whether its political goal can be made concrete enough to make it possible to outline plausible strategies for its realization. If the government's goal is so vague (e.g., "Something must be done to stop those massacres in country X") that no strategy for implementing it successfully can be outlined, then the right intention condition has not been fulfilled.

In reply, it might be objected that such an understanding of what right intention involves is not present in the literature on the just war tradition, and that it is unnecessary and irrelevant to the ethics of right intention.

To the first point, I reply that analysis of intention at strategic level is at least not forbidden or theoretically excluded from the tradition. Second, the just war tradition was well-developed before anything of lasting value (apart from Sun Tzu's *Art of War*) had been written on the nature of war. Clausewitz's and Antoine-Henri Jomini's work still lay far ahead in the nineteenth century. I fancy that Thomas Aquinas, at least, having the Aristotelian's interest in the natures and essences of things, would have endorsed the value of Clausewitz's goal of specifying the nature of war as relevant to application of ethical principles to it.

To the second point, a variety of replies may be relevant depending on the critic's interest. First, ethics is about more than motive or generalized psychological intention: intention is not just about what one wants to achieve but also about how one proposes to achieve it. Second, ethics is also concerned with character, and inability or reluctance to be practical and prudent is a character failing. It is easy enough to wish for world peace, harmony, and universal respect for human rights. It is much more challenging to learn how to use war and the threat of war as a tool or means to achieve those goals and in a way that is successful and minimally damaging to human life and the environment. That challenge is obviously ethical. Third, there is an art to applying ethical principles, and the tradition from which just war thought came valued casuistry. Fourth, it is irrational and hence unethical for political leaders to refuse to be advised by the military leadership that certain goals are beyond their strategic capacities. It is unethical to have an intention that is too sloppy to be coherent, and to be so indifferent to that fact that one will not listen to expert critique.

Different Kinds of War

Addressing strategic intention obliges us to advert to the diverse uses of military force. The first type of use is in traditional and formal interstate clashes along the lines of the major wars of the last three centuries, culminating in the near-total war of two world wars. This is one kind of war, which a few theorists have suggested may be on the wane, even if not altogether disappearing (see Smith 2006, ch. 7).

Closer attention to the roots and core ideas of the just war tradition brings a second kind of use of military power in policing actions into view, ranging from the Korean War, which closely resembles traditional interstate war, to various kinds of humanitarian military intervention, typically by the United Nations or else by UN-authorized states. It could include trying to restore order in places where the state has virtually collapsed.

Humanitarian intervention involving the military can be broken down into four kinds of goals, one or more of which may be the intention of the intervention and the mission assigned to the military: assisting aid delivery, protecting aid operations, saving victims, and defeating the perpetrators.[30]

The third type of use of military power is the use of nuclear weapons. Use of nuclear weapons on Hiroshima and Nagasaki did not change the character of that war drastically since only one country had them, and it used them at a time when its victory was virtually certain and the war all but over. Even though it never went "hot," the Cold War was a different kind of war in which nuclear weapons were central to deterrence, the time frame for measured response in traditional war had shrunk to hours if not minutes, and it was arguable that neither side could win such a war.

The fourth kind of war is the use of military force in decolonization wars or wars of liberation, counterinsurgency wars, terrorist wars, or certain kinds of UN military interventions. What the members of this diverse group have in common is that they are, to use Rupert Smith's apt phrase, "wars amongst the people" where winning hearts and minds is of vital importance to winning the war and achieving its goals.[31] The difference between this kind and the second kind is that winning hearts and minds is not an issue in the second kind.

As noted in the previous section, war-making must have a specific goal that can be translated into strategic language. It might be forcing the other side to evacuate occupied or conquered territory, defeating its army in such a way as to disarm that country for several years to come, or regime change. Regime change is insufficiently specific as a strategic goal. The government or the United Nations must also specify its further objective after the regime has been overthrown. It might choose to leave the task of setting up a new government entirely to the local population (i.e., abandon the country to its own devices), or to facilitate the emergence of whatever kind of regime is most likely to provide some kind of basic order, or to seek to establish a democracy under the rule of law. While there probably would be moral reasons to prefer one choice over another, the most basic requirement for a government seeking to have a right intention is to have a clear intention, which requires due consideration to the outcome it seeks and the likelihood of its being achievable.[32]

In the case of smaller states, their intention in war-fighting can hardly be credibly expressed without identification of the strategy for achieving it. In 1914, Belgium had not the means to expel or defeat the invading Germans. But insofar as it may have had reason for believing that delaying its capitulation by fighting would rouse other countries to its aid, its strategy was not unrealistic. Similarly, in World War II, neutral Ireland was prepared to resist invasion by either Germany or Britain. Ireland could not have resisted either belligerent for more than a couple of days. What gave the strategy of resistance some intelligible rationale was that resisting the invader would give time to enable the other side to come to the aid of the invaded island.

Conclusion

The notion of intention is complex and rich, as is illustrated by its being distinct from notions of cause and motive. It offers interesting possibilities for updating and elaborating what is involved in having good grounds for going to war. "Intention" must not be thought of as "meaning well" or "hoping for the best" in a general unfocused way. It must rather be thought of as directing attention to concrete, practical political goals. Right intention is a moral criterion that not only must take account of very general matters of ethical principle but also must be applied in some detail to political and strategic matters.

That is the central point of this chapter: right intention cannot be understood apart from the political context. An abstract definition can be given, but working out what it means will always be context-sensitive. For instance, a key role for right intention at the political level is the divining of the intention of a possible enemy and countering it earlier, thereby possibly avoiding war.

Similarly, the question of whether a competent authority could rightly intend doing more, or doing less, than reversing the injustice that has occasioned military action will depend on contextual analysis. Right intention addresses the question: "What will 'winning the war' mean in this context?" It also requires some worked-out idea of what kind of postwar political settlement the government or competent authority aims at. In consequence of the last point, a great deal of what has lately been considered under the heading of *jus post bellum* more properly comes under the heading of intention in *jus ad bellum*.

Notes

1. See Finnis 1998, 285: "Here 'intention' covers the whole set of nested ends (ends and means) from the overarching intention to promote peace and the well-being of decent people, right down to the exclusion of cruelty, fraud, and, by implication, intent to kill or harm innocents."

2. While these virtues resemble such classical virtues as Aristotle's *phronesis*, prudence, temperance, and fortitude, there are significant differences. See also Caney 2005, 191: "Values such as compassion, forgiveness, and mercy, for example, should inform how regimes respond to external wrongs."

3. See Walzer 1977, 117, for remarks along similar lines.

4. Johnson 2005a also draws attention to the bishops' conflation of just cause and right intention.

5. Here I slightly conflate reason, desire, and intention. I distinguish them later.

6. Holmes is one of the few writers to make the distinction. See Holmes 1989, 136.

7. See Caney 2005, 202–3, for conflation of intention with motive, in consequence of which he mistakenly rejects right or just intention as irrelevant to *jus ad bellum*.

8. See Wheeler 2000, 198–99, on the response of the American public to the killing of US Rangers in Somalia by local warlords in 1993.

9. Orend 2006, 160: "Conceptually, war has three phases: beginning, middle, and end. So if we want a complete just war theory—or comprehensive international law—we simply must discuss justice during the termination phase of war."

10. See Rawls 1999, 8, 16: he takes the claim as established.

11. Rodin 2002, 112, draws attention to the fact that a state fighting a legitimate war is not required in law to terminate the war when it has "vindicated its rights" but may continue to "final victory."

12. Although Ireland's neutrality in World War II was probably not immoral, it was not admirable: a European state can hardly claim to be glad that Nazi Germany

was defeated and simultaneously proud that it had nothing to do with that defeat. Ireland's subsequent refusal to join NATO in 1948 on the grounds that it could not be in alliance with a country (Britain) that still "occupied" part of "its national territory" (Northern Ireland) was morally wrong. It ignored the moral and political force of the argument that, in the light of the experience of World War II, all European countries, particularly smaller ones, needed to join together in solidarity in order to act decisively against possible future aggression.

13. Neutrality as a general policy is often claimed to be justified by the fact that being disarmed promotes peace and general well-being. Apposite here is Nietzsche's acerbic comment on the animals who think they are good because they have no claws. See Kaufmann 1982, 230.

14. Prudential strategic logic can be used to evil ends. It is precisely because of its practical value that one is glad Hitler so often refused to accept the conclusions of the "prudential strategic logic" of his generals.

15. Howard 1983, 22: "Whatever may be the underlying causes of international conflict, even if we accept the role of atavistic militarism or of military-industrial complexes or of socio-biological drives or of domestic tensions in fuelling it, wars begin with conscious and reasoned decisions based on the calculation, made by *both* parties, that they can achieve more by going to war than by remaining at peace."

16. Walzer 1977, ch. 5, also deals with this theme. As that chapter's title, "Anticipations," suggests, he focuses more narrowly on war than I do. Schelling 1980 is useful here, in highlighting both the primacy of the political context and the centrality of intention and its interpretation.

17. A report in the *New York Times*, June 3, 2007, discussed Sen. Hillary Clinton's vote in favor of going to war with Iraq in 2003. She referred to her husband, President Clinton, who, in the light of his experience in seeking to restrain the Iraqi government of Saddam Hussein in the 1990s, had been quoted as saying that Saddam was determined to obtain nuclear weapons and to use them. In an interview with Dan Rather of CBS on the eve of the Anglo-American offensive in 2003, Saddam Hussein stated that he had not "lost" the Gulf war of 1990–91. I take that to mean that he saw the war not as ending with the cease-fire in 1991 but as continuing during the 1991–2003 era of UN sanctions that he had successfully resisted. Clausewitz's definition of war identified its goal as the imposition of one's will on the other; Saddam's view was that the UN had not successfully imposed its will on him.

18. This is known as the Caroline doctrine or precedent; it is discussed in a number of the essays in Shue and Rodin 2007.

19. As late as the 1945 San Francisco conference establishing the United Nations the US delegation held that the inherent right of self-defense applies only

when an armed attack has actually occurred. Imminent threat of attack—for example, an invasion fleet approaching a country's shores—would not suffice to warrant armed response: the country under threat could dispatch its own fleet but could not order it to attack. To count as acting in self-defense, the first shot would have to be fired by the other side. See Franck 2002, 50.

20. See Walzer 1977, 80–85, for discussion of Israel's successful preemptive strike in the 1967 "Six-Day War."

21. For historical perspective on preventive war, see Trachtenberg 2007. He argues that the US policy enunciated in its 2002 National Security Strategy document of being prepared to fight preventive war (in the document's own words, "against emerging threats before they are fully formed") if deemed necessary is more in line with the policies of US presidents Roosevelt, Truman, Kennedy, and Clinton than is widely thought. Shue and Rodin 2007 (the set of essays that includes Trachtenberg 2007 and Luban 2007) is in many ways a set of responses to the 2002 document.

22. See Luban 2007, 172, for a particularly succinct articulation of the reasons why a general rule permitting preventive war against countries posing remote threats cannot be justified, including the fact that it would be far too permissive with respect to justifying war. China is currently a rising power both on the Asian mainland and in the Pacific, and its rise threatens the US naval hegemony in the Pacific. Nevertheless, neither China's rhetoric nor its behavior indicates intent to attack the United States or any of its neighbors at some point in the future.

23. On preventive war, Rodin refers to "an attack against a state which has not yet formed the intention of an aggressive attack, but which is about to achieve a decisive advantage which would seem to make a future aggressive intent likely and dangerous" (2002, 113). Decisive military advantage does not of itself constitute aggressive intent.

24. The intention of the other side to attack is the key element that (all else being equal) gives moral warrant for going to war. The imminence or remoteness in time of the attack is secondary. India's and Pakistan's respective intents in acquiring nuclear weapons seem primarily for strategic defense, not attack. Concern about Iran acquiring nuclear weapons arises not just because it might change the balance of power in the Middle East or because it might frighten some Arab states, but because it might use them on Israel: in short, the concern is to know the answer to the question, what would Iran intend to do with nuclear weapons?

25. It is surprising that in Shue and Rodin 2007, only Luban's essay takes note of the importance of the other side's intention; see Luban 2007, 172, 190–91. Uniacke 2007, 77–78, distinguishes usefully between a "future threat" and an "actual threat of future harm" and allows that in the latter case one could reasonably argue that self-defense allowed preventive attack, even where the future harm was

distant in time or not inevitable because it was conditional or contingent upon other events. While she does not refer to the other side's intention, her view has some similarity to mine.

26. McMahan 2006, 188, notes that people tend to support preventive war where (a) there is compelling evidence that the other state will unjustly attack, (b) the threat can be eliminated now but not later, or it would be impossible to defend ourselves later, and (c) peaceful means have been ineffective.

27. If it is in no way evident, it probably doesn't exist. For an alternative approach to mine, see Luban 2004, 230.

28. US administrations lacked clarity on the strategic goal of their military involvement in Vietnam 1963–73. In the last twenty years, the Israeli government has failed to grasp that fighting urban guerrillas in Lebanon and the Gaza Strip is different from fighting conventional Arab armies. This is reflected in the inappropriate specification of strategic goals, i.e., goals that cannot be achieved by the Israeli army.

29. See Smith 2006, 12. "By strategy I mean the use that is made of force and the threat of force for the ends of policy" (Gray 1999, 17).

30. This is taken from Seybolt 2007, 39–40, which elaborates at some length what is involved in each, including the differing implications for use of military force.

31. See Smith 2006, particularly the final chapters.

32. As the United States found in Iraq, it was much easier to overthrow Saddam Hussein's dictatorship than to establish a multiparty democracy to succeed it.

Chapter 6

Succeeding

No other national endeavor requires as much unshakable resolve
as war. If the nation and the government lack that resolve, it is
criminal to expect men in the field to carry it alone.

Sen. John McCain, 2002

Prudence and Pragmatism

Classic just war thought listed competent authority, just cause, and right intention as the three required criteria for being justified in going to war. Other
criteria were added in modern times; these include reasonable prospect or
probability of success, last resort, and proportionality.[1] In this chapter I address reasonable prospect of success.

Here we come to what in many ways is the most practically oriented of
the *jus ad bellum* criteria. With just cause and the right kind of intentions, a
state has what might be called minimally necessary or basic justification for
going to war. At that point other prudential conditions become relevant. In
this chapter, I focus on the moral implications of the rather obvious fact that
success matters. Naturally, the more specific and precise the competent authority's intentions are, the more able it will be to know whether it is likely to
be successful since success is to be defined with respect to the goal intended.
Neither the competent authority nor its generals will be able to determine
whether the reasonable prospect of success criterion can be met until the intention has been specified.[2] Thus, fulfilling the success criterion will necessarily enforce clarity regarding intention, if that clarity has been lacking. In
addition, as I note later, if there is no reasonable prospect of success, war will
not be a practical option and hence not a morally acceptable option.

The identification of this criterion in the literature is vague. The US bishops and Orend refer to it as "probability of success." Johnson labels it rather more subjectively as "reasonable hope of success" (Holmes 1989, 164; Orend 2008; Johnson 2005a). The bishops' document elaborates as follows: "Its purpose is to prevent irrational resort to force or hopeless resistance when the outcome of either will clearly be disproportionate or futile" (Holmes 1989, 164). That rules out going to war in circumstances where the probability of success is vanishingly small so that war-making is pointless and hence irrational. That much is uncontroversial and can be accepted.

However, avoiding "hopeless" options is only a minimal requirement. It may not be enough to qualify a decision to go to war as fulfilling the criterion. It is overly permissive to hold it fulfilled where going to war isn't absolutely hopeless or heading for certain defeat. A 10 percent probability of success is considerably better odds since it is not "hopeless," yet a 1 in 10 chance of success can hardly be described as a "reasonable probability" of success. It would be difficult to specify a precise mathematical figure as the required probability, but it seems plausible that the criterion should be read as involving a substantial likelihood of success rather than some minimal or slight chance of success. Governments and their military chiefs would usually want much better odds.

Sometimes the context may affect the judgment of the relevant authority with regard to what would count as a reasonable prospect. If the country is invaded or about to be invaded and the alternative to fighting is surrender, governments and generals might think a 10 percent chance of success is good enough to warrant fighting. Where there is no threat of invasion or attack, a government contemplating going to war for some other purpose would probably want far higher probability of success, perhaps in the order of 60 percent or higher. I incline to the view that politicians and generals are more realistic or objective in that latter judgment than they are in the case of the former. Since I think this particularly important as a practical criterion, I can see no good grounds for softening the requirement that there be a reasonable, which means at least substantial, probability of success in going to war.

Winning What?

First, the success in question is not precisely the achievement of the political intention or intentions that were part of the relevant context grounding the competent authority's decision to go to war. The success at issue is rather the achievement of the political intention embodied in the war's strategic goals. The latter may be slightly narrower than the former. The distinction is admittedly a fine one, and often the two will be indistinguishable for all practical purposes. But this is not always or necessarily the case. For instance, in World War II the United States and Britain might have had the political goal of wanting to replace the Nazi regime with a democracy governed by the rule of law.

If the Federal Republic of Germany founded in the late 1940s had, instead of flourishing as it did, collapsed into a quasi-dictatorial or strife-torn country, it would probably be a kind of political defeat for the United States, Britain, and France, but it would not mean that they had failed to achieve the war's strategic goal of defeating Nazi Germany's armies.

It is morally highly desirable to win the peace after winning the war. For political and, hence, moral reasons, the choice of military goals and methods of war-fighting ought to be such that they undermine that remote goal as little as possible. Nevertheless, winning the war is not to be conflated with winning the peace. Success in war must be what the military strategist, informed of the political goal of the war, would identify as success. The general or military strategist must never lose sight of the political context within which, and the political goals in relation to which, strategic plans for action are developed and implemented. At the same time, military strategy and politics are different, and the general staff cannot reasonably be expected to identify the political means required for stabilizing the country in the years after the war is over.[3]

Accordingly, the reasonable probability of success that *jus ad bellum* seeks is a matter for military strategy. The political is not excluded from it since it is that which gives the conduct of the war its overall strategic direction. The political leader seeks the advice of the general or strategist as to the probability of success—that is, as to the ability of the country's armed forces to achieve the strategic military goals connected to the overall political goal. Political success beyond that is a matter for the political leaders, not the generals.

Second, success in war does not necessarily mean winning the war. A number of examples may illustrate the point. In the Seven Years' War (1756–63) Austria mobilized a vast coalition including Russia, France, Sweden, and Saxony against Prussia in order to regain Silesia, which Prussia had seized in 1740. Britain gave financial support to Prussia until 1761, but Prussia had a dreadful time of it, enduring repeated defeats yet holding on grimly until the death of the Tsarina Elizabeth led Russia to withdraw from the war in 1762. The Peace of Hubertusburg left Prussia in possession of Silesia, and there were no other boundary changes.

Prussia could not be said to have "won" the war, nor its opponents said to have been "defeated," in the conventional sense in which we tend to use those terms. Nevertheless, Prussia was successful in holding on to Silesia. Indeed, given the fact that it faced a coalition of countries with twenty times its own population, Prussia's survival counts as a success.

While Belgium was on the winning side in World War I, it did not win its little war to keep the German army out of its territory in 1914. It had received earlier warnings that Germany would require transit rights for its army in the event of war with France, and had been urged to facilitate this peacefully on the grounds that it could not successfully resist. Nevertheless, although Belgium could not be said to have had even a 10 percent probability of succeeding in stopping the German army, it was successful in another way by drawing Britain into the war. By holding up the German armies, Belgium presented the picture of a small country fighting gallantly against the odds (and hence worthy of support), unquestionably the victim of unjust aggression by a much larger power (and hence owed the debt of justice), a victim that had been promised protection by Britain and that could yet be saved by military intervention (and hence worth acting for). That had a significant influence on British opinion, both at political and public levels, and contributed to Britain's decision to enter the war. Had Belgium not resisted, Germany would have overrun it swiftly and relatively painlessly, thereby not incurring bad publicity and being able to present the United Kingdom and the rest of the world with a fait accompli. (Whether the Belgian government's decision to resist was determined by this is secondary. Belgium's neutrality had been guaranteed by the great powers by treaty in 1831, and—more important—the Belgian government knew that France and Britain had direct and immediate interest in coming to Belgium's aid.) British hostility to the German invasion of Belgium is undoubted. But had Belgium acquiesced in German use of its territory to defeat France, the British ultimatum would have been less likely.

The first Battle of the Marne in September 1914 is a good candidate for the title of most significant battle of the two world wars. The French, with the aid of the small British expeditionary force, managed to halt the German offensive. Although it was a kind of German defeat, it was not seen at the time as a decisive victory for the Entente powers. But Germany never regained the strategic initiative on the western front that it briefly held at the outbreak of the war.

Sometime after US withdrawal from Vietnam in the 1970s, a US colonel is supposed to have remarked to a North Vietnamese colonel: "You never defeated us in the field." To which his Vietnamese counterpart replied: "That may be true. It is also irrelevant." In its Vietnam venture, the United States was never defeated in the field as were the French at Dien Bien Phu in 1954. The Tet Offensive of 1968, North Vietnam's largest offensive against American and South Vietnamese forces, was a tactical disaster for North Vietnam. Nevertheless, North Vietnam was strategically successful in the war and the United States was not.

  The foregoing examples suggest that success is relative to strategic goals and the political intention they express. In World War II, the Allies specified their political goals as the overthrow of Nazi Germany and imperial Japan in such a way that neither could be resurrected. The related strategic goal was unconditional surrender. In other cases, success might be understood to amount to no more than not being defeated, to keeping one's territory and army intact.

All else being equal, the more limited the strategic goal, the higher the probability of success.

Clausewitz defines war as "an act of force to compel our enemy to do our will" and goes on to identify that with rendering the enemy powerless (1976, 75). While that definition holds up well for the most part, it may not provide apt description for all cases. It does not appear to consider cases where war is fought for limited purposes, and where one side might eventually concede the relatively modest demand of the other without being reduced to powerlessness in the strict sense. Nor does it cover the case of Belgium in 1914, where Belgium's success lay in frustrating the German desire for a speedy move through Belgian territory to outflank the French armies before Britain could react. Clausewitz's terms may need to be interpreted broadly.

Success is partly defined by the goals set at the first, political level of Clausewitz's trinity. Winning might be defined as (a) conquering the other country in order to annex some of its territory or to impose a specific political system (e.g., multiparty democracy, socialism) or merely to change the regime; (b) defeating the enemy, thereby attaining a position where peace terms can be dictated; (c) fighting the enemy to a standstill—that is, to a situation where the other side decides that continuing the war is prohibitively costly and decides to treat so that peace terms can be decided through a negotiation between "equals"; or (d) holding the enemy at bay long enough to generate political or military support from other quarters that may change the balance of forces.

Connection to other Conditions

As can be seen from the previous paragraph, probability of success is closely related to having an intention that is right not just morally but also practically. Intention must aim at realistic political goals and, in the case of war, political goals that can be realized at the strategic military level. Thus, dealing with right intention at the strategic level points toward pragmatic consideration of how likely success is.

The other two criteria are last resort and proportionality. Both the US bishops and Orend put last resort ahead of probability of success, and Johnson places both last resort and proportionality ahead of probability of success. However, it is not clear that these authors see the ordering as having any significance. I have argued that there is a logical order to the criteria. That order is specified by the following rule: if fulfilling criterion A is logically necessary for fulfilling criterion B, A has logical priority over B.

Consideration of the probability of success criterion does not require that the last resort condition be met, so it is not logically dependent upon it. A particular state could have a better than 80 percent chance of success in a proposed war yet not have tried other ways to obtain its goals. In such a case, the last resort criterion has not been met although the probability of success criterion has been met. Thus, the probability of success condition does not depend logically upon the last resort condition. By contrast, if there is no realistic probability of success, then going to war is simply not an available option, so it can't be a resort of any kind, last or otherwise. One cannot rationally judge that war is now the only resort remaining if it is clear that one has no hope of winning any such war. The last resort criterion is logically dependent upon the probability of success criterion.

Proportionality requires that both the probability of success and the last resort criteria have been met. It seems intuitively obvious that it is disproportionate, to say the least, to fight a war that one has no realistic prospect of winning, or to fight a war that one didn't need to fight at all, since other methods would have achieved the relevant political goal. A choice to go to war is disproportionate under *jus ad bellum* if going to war is insufficient to achieve the goal (no chance of success) or unnecessary to achieve the goal (not the last resort). Lacking one of those, going to war is automatically disqualified as disproportionate.

The US bishops' treatment of probability of success, cited earlier, introduced the element of disproportion in order to explain probability of success. However, this confuses rather than clarifies since it would imply that probability of success depends upon the proportionality criterion. The dependency runs in the other direction. In other words, if going to war is without any prospect of success (on any definition of success) then doing so is necessarily disproportionate. On the other hand, there could be a high probability of success and yet going to war might be disproportionate for other reasons.

Ethical Aspects

Both Johnson and Orend take the view that competent authority, just cause, and right intention as ethical conditions are deontological in nature and have to do with justice. Orend takes probability of success, last resort, and proportionality to be consequentialist in nature. By that I take him simply to mean consequence-oriented. Johnson views them as essentially prudential and auxiliary to the primary conditions of authority, just cause and right intention.[4]

This line of thought is plausible. That they are secondary to competent authority, just cause, and right intention is clear. Whether the respective moral character of the two sets of criteria is as sharply different as Johnson and Orend imply is less obvious. First, deontological considerations are not utterly disconnected from concern about consequences. This applies particularly to the right intention criterion.

Second, deontological elements can be found in the prudential criteria of probability of success and last resort. It is imprudent to fight a war where one has no chance of success. It seems immoral, a kind of injustice, knowingly and deliberately to sacrifice the lives of one's soldiers and possibly of many civilians to no purpose. The primary injustice in such a case is no doubt attributable to the aggressor whose attack kills them. But one's own exercise of competent authority involves the duty of care, so far as is practicable. Good governance might well begin at the same place that medical practice begins: first, do no harm.

Governmental failure to evaluate the probability of success properly is a failure in prudence. Certain kinds of failure or carelessness shade into negligence, and negligence can be morally culpable.

Probability-Raising

What is to count as a reasonable probability of success must be, after all steps that can raise it have been taken, one that gives a good chance of success. "Good" here must not be purely comparative; the best chance of a bad lot is not good enough. "Reasonable" probability is often taken in a way that is too lax, as in a 10 percent chance, which is still better than a no-hope chance. If the probability of success isn't good enough, the proportionality criterion, which is logically dependent upon it as discussed at the beginning of this chapter, can't be met. Nor can just cause or right intention make up for a lack of adequate or good enough probability of success.

Consider a particular government that has ample cause for war and whose intentions are morally right and reasonably well focused. When it comes to considering the prospects of success, it may well find that the chances are not great, as would be the case where the professional military advice estimated a 40 percent to 50 percent probability of success. In such a situation, a prudent government would try to change the odds to make success more likely. That suggests that considering the probability of success condition is not simply a matter of passive review of the existing situation but also a matter of seeking (where possible) to improve it.

There are various success-making factors. First, increasing or improving its military resources in personnel or materiel could raise the odds of success. Of course, the military resources in question must be of the right kind for the proposed war. Doing this may require delay in going to war. Second, perhaps the political objective involved in right intention could be revised in a more modest direction yet without abandoning the politically necessary goal. In similar vein, a government could also improve its chance of success by facilitating the other side's coming to terms, perhaps by allowing it to save face, if this can be done with safety. The United Nations has often been used as a face-saving device, where one country can get out of a fight that is going badly by making a high-sounding statement to the effect that, in deference to the United Nations, it is announcing a cease-fire.

Sometimes such mitigating options are not possible or would violate right intention. The government may then have to face the fact that winning will be costly in lives, resources, and time. This brings us to the point that a state highly averse to taking casualties may not be willing to pay the price for victory and, hence, does not have the requisite probability of success. In the words attributed to an Irish freedom fighter in the 1920s, "it is not those who can inflict the most but those who can endure the most who will prevail." That is not a universal truth, but it is often true, and it has sometimes seemed to be the Achilles heel of US military engagement. In 1983, the United States sent the marines to Beirut as part of a peace-keeping mission in the teeth of opposition from Syria and other local groups. It took one suicide bomber driving a truck loaded with explosives into their compound and killing 241 marines to make the United States decide to pull out. It is possible that the United States had erred in sending troops there in the first place, but when it showed itself so ready to cut and run, it dismayed its friends and made its enemies think it morally soft.[5] This may have given Saddam Hussein, then ruling Iraq, the impression that the United States, while matchless in armament and technology, lacked the determination to prevail in war, as the Vietnam War had apparently shown.

A government's resolutely facing the fact that victories are rarely cheap may raise the probability of winning. In addition to political clarity about the objective and the objective's being realistically achievable, there must also be the will to achieve it and the nerve to withstand political opposition and military reverses.[6]

Motivating the People

As well as moderating one's war aims and expanding one's armed forces, a third way of increasing the probability of success is to create public support for the war. Clausewitz was acutely aware of the military impact of France's successful mobilization of its population in the revolutionary and Napoleonic wars and was more uncomfortably aware of the military impact of the rise of German nationalism in and through the final struggles with Napoleon from 1812. His remarks about war being a kind of trinity involving the political leadership, the army, and the people are apposite here.[7] War-making is in part a mobilization of popular will to go to war. British success in galvanizing popular support for continuing to oppose Germany in 1940 was strategically important, as was the US failure to recognize the effect on American public opinion of television portrayals of the Vietnam War. By contrast, Édouard Daladier, returning from Munich to Paris in 1938, expected to be execrated by the public for betraying Czechoslovakia and was dismayed to find people cheering him (see Larkin 1988, 71; Kagan 1995, 405).

The degree of public support for the war has an important bearing on the probability of success.[8] Strong public opposition, even in nondemocratic countries, acts as a drag upon the war effort, and an unpopular war may undermine the government or even the state itself.[9] In democracies, overwhelming opposition to going to war may convince the government that it would be politically unable to sustain the cost in lives, materiel, and money. This applies particularly to long and protracted wars.[10] It can also be extremely difficult in democracies for the government to convince its people and their elected representatives that vital national interests are in danger and that their support for war may be needed.[11] Before December 1941, President Roosevelt was politically unable to go to war with Japan or Germany despite his awareness of the threat they presented to US interests.

Political leaders are thus obliged to consider such moral factors as the potential willingness of their own population to endure sacrifices. People seem prepared to make larger sacrifices when it is a question of driving invaders out of their own country than in other cases: the huge losses suffered by the Red Army and the enormous sacrifices sustained by the USSR's population in World War II did not undermine public support for fighting the war.

The inference to draw is that the government needs to persuade the people that war is necessary. It cannot do so without giving reasons and providing justification for its position. In the eyes of some, this will look like propaganda. Something needs to be said on this point.[12]

In most cases it is necessary for the government, if it is to have a realistic hope of success, to shape public opinion: in other words, it must use propaganda. This will doubtless outrage some readers, but unless we agree that the term "propaganda" is to be confined to meaning false, seriously misleading, or mendacious communication, the outrage is misplaced. If the reader strongly objects to the term because it carries such connotations, another term could no doubt be found. However, a government convinced of the need for war but facing the fact that the public through ignorance are most unwilling to accept will have to do more than simply explain to the people; it will have to promote its cause vigorously, to persuade and cajole, and that will look like propaganda. In consequence of having just cause and right intention, a competent authority will have some moral responsibility to persuade its people of what needs to be done.

Nor should it be thought that governmental persuasive efforts in such matters necessarily run only in a war-making direction. Sometimes the government's job may be to damp down public desire for military confrontation. Regarding the 1871–1914 period of European history, Kagan notes the relative ease with which public opinion in any of the five great powers (Russia, Germany, Austria-Hungary, France, Britain) could become inflamed against a neighboring country (Kagan 1995, 114–18, 131–32, 142). In the 1871–90 period, Otto von Bismarck was often a lone voice in the German government promoting the importance of avoiding war and behavior that could be interpreted as threatening by other countries. The popularity of going to war in August 1914 is amazing (even appalling) to read of today. At the time of the heaviest US bombing of North Vietnam in winter 1972, the USSR was attempting to reach an agreement with the United States in the SALT I (Strategic Arms Limitations Talks). Had the extent of the bombing of its Vietnamese ally been known to the Soviet people, public opinion would have been hostile to any such agreement with the United States.

The alternative to propaganda is for a government to let itself be led by public opinion. Such an abdication of leadership is morally unacceptable given the serious moral implications of war-related decisions. The moral responsibility is the government's and it may neither yield it nor lose the battle for public opinion by default. The most obvious application of that consideration is related to ethnic/nationalist/tribal conflict in different parts of the globe, where often there is no real dividing line between combatants and civilians, and where nationalist or tribal emotions can run high in ways that lead to serious outbreaks of violence.

The morally objectionable element in what is conventionally called propaganda is knowingly disseminating falsehoods. That the government should seek to inform and persuade is not just morally permissible but morally desirable as well. Right intention is inherently reasonable and inherently morally plausible or it's not right. It may not be the sole reasonable or morally plausible course, but to require that it should be would require too much. The reasonableness and moral plausibility should be communicable to the public in a way that would change the minds of a sufficient number of voters.

This is not a matter of presenting the issue to the electorate and asking them to decide. The decision must be made by the government. It can, of course, listen and consult as widely as it pleases. But the responsibility to decide lies with the government. It is up to the government to do what it can to bring the people along, and to weigh the implications for going to war against its degree of success in doing so.

Sometimes, a government may not be able to persuade the electorate that it would be just and prudent, even necessary, to go to war. In such cases, if the government judges that it cannot educate the public in the matter, there may be no reasonable prospect of success.

The Time Factor

Since, as noted earlier, the probability of success may increase or diminish with time, the condition of probability of success is time-sensitive. Britain and France's prospects of success in war against Nazi Germany diminished after their failure to go to war over Czechoslovakia in 1938. While delay gave them more time to rearm, it gave the same advantage to Germany, and at that time Germany's economy was more geared to rearmament. More significant was the fact that Germany acquired a considerable amount of war materiel from Czechoslovakia after its fall in early 1939. Czechoslovakia had a more modern army than did Poland. Finally, the USSR and Poland had been prepared to help Britain and France in 1938. However, when it came to Germany's aggression against Poland in 1939, the USSR abandoned Britain and France by signing the German-Soviet nonaggression pact in August 1939, technically becoming Germany's ally and subsequently joining Germany in invading Poland.

The point is important. Once the just cause and right intention criteria are fulfilled (or as much fulfilled as these things ever are), the primary moral considerations are satisfied. That is enough to warrant an "in-principle" decision to go to war. Consideration then moves to when and how to go to war, with the most immediate concern being that of winning or being successful. It may be that circumstances are then so unfavorable that going to war may have to be postponed indefinitely. In such circumstances, anything that changes the balance of forces and factors in favor of winning must be pursued, as discussed earlier. The most important of these conditions is the time factor as it bears on the probability of victory. Writing on strategy, Colin Gray remarks: "Performance in all but one of strategy's dimensions— politics, ethics, military preparation, technology, and so forth—can be improved. The sole exception is the dimension of time. Time lost is literally irretrievable" (1999, 16; see also 42–43). As with the dimensions of strategy, so with the conditions affecting the probability of success: time is a dimension that we cannot control.

Accordingly, it is the probability of success criterion that determines the right time for going to war. Against this, it may be argued that last resort has not yet been discussed, and surely it is the condition determining the time for going to war. But contrary to what might be expected, the last resort condition is not time-sensitive in the same way. If "last" is taken to be a temporal notion, there will always be some sense that if we wind up in the situation where war appears to be the last resort, then we have not tried hard enough at making the other options work. That line of thought leads to a situation wherein practical judgment falls victim to a kind of unrealistic idealism.

The only way the doubt can be settled and a time limit set to consideration of the last resort is by connecting doubt to the practical issue of probability of success. The time factor should not be understood as governed by whether all nonbelligerent options have been tried. It is rather to be understood along the following lines. Given the probability of having to fight, the time for going to war is determined by the balance of forces as that time when one has not just a good prospect but comparatively the best prospect of success. That is the moment at which one reviews all options other than war, and if none will work at that time, the last resort has arrived. The time to go to war is when one has the best chance of success. It is then, and only then, during that time frame or window of opportunity, that consideration of whether the last resort has been reached should be carried out. In this area, the government depends heavily on military advice. It has an obligation to listen to the general staff's recommendations and adopt them unless it has strong reasons for not doing so.

Finally, it might be noted in passing that the probability of success condition has interesting implications for the use of nuclear weapons. While concern to prevail in war led both sides in the later stages of the Cold War to seek breakthroughs in the area of conventional weaponry, there always remained the awareness that while a war might start off without resort to nuclear weapons, it was probable that the side losing the conventional fight would turn to nuclear weapons. Thus, nuclear weapons, when available to both sides, seemed to put the probability of success beyond fulfillment, at least when success involved prevailing over another nuclear power. On the other hand, if success were a matter of deterrence of attack, possession of such weapons could be very successful indeed.[13]

Humanitarian Intervention

The issue of humanitarian military intervention was discussed earlier in chapter 4. As has been noted, when the question arises of whether the United Nations or other countries should be entitled to intervene by force if necessary to protect people from genocide or other gross violations of human rights visited upon them by their own government, lawyers, politicians, and the general public nowadays are less inclined to assume that sovereignty should trump or outweigh human rights. The focus of attention has shifted significantly away from issues of sovereignty and just cause to concerns about practicality and probability of success. We are less worried about violating sovereignty and more focused on whether intervention will work.[14] Accordingly, it is the probability of success criterion that is most relevant to humanitarian military intervention.

Assuming that there is a moral and legal responsibility to protect people from government-sponsored genocide and comparable oppression, practical realism will tell us that in many cases it will be a duty impossible to discharge. This is because intervention may fail to improve matters and may even make them worse. However, there are different kinds of intervention, and operational clarity on what is to be done and on the limits of the mission may show certain kinds of intervention to be more likely to be successful. Seybolt's grading of kinds of intervention into (a) delivering aid, (b) protecting aid delivery, (c) protecting victims, and (d) defeating the perpetrators ranges from involvement that might involve hardly any combat and be relatively easy of achievement (a), to outright defeat and possibly removal of oppressive regimes (d). In general, operations aimed at (a) or (b) are more likely to succeed than those involved in (c) or (d).

Hearts and Minds

Rupert Smith has developed a sustained argument for the claim that the era of industrial war (e.g., the two world wars) is largely over, and that most contemporary instances where troops are put in harm's way concern what he calls "war among the people" (2006). It sees winning hearts and minds as a major strategic concern.

It is relevant to humanitarian military intervention where the intervening force may have to win the trust of the very people for whose welfare the intervention has been undertaken. Winning hearts and minds may also involve showing respect for local custom since the interveners' intent is to leave as soon as possible and hope that normality returns. It may also involve getting along with local officialdom for the same reason.

It is also relevant to operations related to the so-called war on terror of 2000–2011. In Afghanistan and on the margins of Pakistan, NATO countries fought a war in which they needed not merely to win hearts and minds but also create enough stability and local security so that a security vacuum would not arise when NATO troops left. In addition to guerrilla forces such as the Taliban, there are also ideas and visions that have to be fought in the struggle for minds and hearts if the war on terror is to be won. It is no longer acceptable to "pacify" peoples the Roman way, so the minds-and-hearts battle is not optional.

Smith's line of thought leads to a wariness in regard to hubris about great military power. Today, the United States is the world's only military superpower, spending more on its military than most other countries put together.

It would presumably win a traditional conventional war with any other country. It does not follow that it is capable of winning any kind of war, for example, a guerrilla war such as in Vietnam. Nor does great military power necessarily facilitate the winning of minds and hearts. As was found in Vietnam, and as Clausewitz emphasized, moral factors also matter, and it is these that are most closely connected to the task of winning hearts and minds.

At present, Israel has reason to be on its guard against Hezbollah in Lebanon and Hamas in Gaza. While many Palestinians are less than convinced that Hamas or Hezbollah have their welfare at heart, Israeli military tactics in its 2008–9 offensive against Hamas would appear to have driven Palestinians further into the embrace of Israel's enemies. Listening to speeches from Israel's leaders, it sounds sometimes as though they thought that the kind of tactics that drove back Syrian and Egyptian armies could uproot an urban guerrilla group from its natural habitat. There was no reasonable prospect of success of doing so, and so the Israeli offensive was unjustifiable.

Against Fairness

The probability of success condition may not require that one always have a better than even chance of winning. But I think it does require one to take advantage of everything that would make victory more likely. It would not be morally acceptable to content oneself with a 75 percent chance of winning if one knew that certain strategies would raise that to a 95 percent chance and those strategies were to hand. After all, the goal is to achieve or protect certain goods or prevent certain evils. If it should become possible to improve one's strategic position to the point where the other side recognizes that it has no realistic chance of winning and accordingly surrenders or withdraws, victory has been won, and won without bloodshed or loss of life. War is too serious not to intend winning, and doing so as soon as possible and as bloodlessly as possible.

Accordingly, I have difficulty with David Rodin's claim that fairness is a value in the just war tradition, and that the interests of fairness in the fight require placing a heavier moral burden on the stronger side. He states:

> Yet there are forms of war that do not embody the symmetry and equality implicit in the chessboard image of war. It will be the argument of this chapter that when conflict diverges too drastically from the assumptions implicit in the chessboard image of war we experience serious difficulties in interpreting and applying standard judgments of just war theory. In short, when war ceases to be roughly equal and symmetrical the considerations of justice and fairness, rather than supporting and reinforcing each other in a symbiotic relationship, begin to dangerously diverge. (2006, 153)

Recalling the image of chess, we may observe that, as well as justice, fairness is a form of moral assessment relevant to war. In a conflict that is highly unequal, how can it be fair to require the overwhelmingly weaker party to abide by the same rules as the stronger? . . . The tactics of asymmetry may be the only way the weak can restore any measure of equality to a conflict. Although asymmetric tactics conflict with principles of justice in that they attack or expose non-combatants to excessive risks, they are justified by a principle of fairness to restore balance in radically unequal conflicts. (2006, 158–59)

The chessboard image of war, which appears to be a controlling metaphor in the passages quoted, is analogous to the idea of war as a duel to be played by the rules and monitored by a referee and seconds. While that line of thought about war was not uncommon in the early modern period, it is at odds with classical or contemporary just war thought and with any view of war as analogous to law enforcement against criminals.[15]

For a start, fairness does not turn up in any list of criteria that I know of, either for *jus ad bellum* or for *jus in bello*. Rodin's advocacy of fairness introduces a novelty into just war thought, and he offers no supportive argument for introducing it. As he himself admits, it collides with other values in the just war tradition. He thinks this a theoretical problem to be solved; I think the problem artificial, and the mistake is to introduce fairness into just war thought at all.

The analogy of a game or a duel misleads when applied to war. It is reasonable to assume that war is a rule-bound activity with respect to *jus in bello* for the treatment of prisoners and noncombatants. But that does not suffice to warrant taking war to be analogous to a game. The practice of the courts is also rule-bound yet not assimilable or analogous to a game. Even when we allow that the courts are concerned with fairness to all sides, their goal is not the drama of a trial but the doing of justice. Fairness is merely a procedural value in court proceedings. By contrast, in duels or games, fairness is more than merely instrumental since the goal of the game is the playing of the game regardless of who wins or loses.

Rodin's approach has elements of the idea that war ought to be a gentlemanly duel. A fair fight would mean trying to level the playing field to give all sides an even chance of winning. But good governance should seek the opposite for the sake of the public good. It should aim to have the greatest possible chance of winning, ideally so great that the other side caves in without fighting. That's the moral ideal, and it points against fairness. Deontological constraints are allowed, but fairness is not one of them.

Rodin's pitch is for the weaker side in a war to be given a certain moral leeway or permission with respect to using "asymmetric tactics" under which he includes chemical, biological, and nuclear weapons; terrorism; guerrilla warfare; hostage taking; various innovative methods in cyberwarfare; and more. Use of some of those weapons and tactics would violate just war norms on discrimination between combatants and noncombatants as well as norms on proportionality (of the *jus in bello* kind). What is ironic, in view of his concern for fairness, is his suggestion that **one side be given moral permission to break some of the rules—and for no other reason than that it is the weaker side.** His argument is not along the lines of holding that the side of justice should, *in extremis* and facing defeat, be allowed to ignore those deontological moral constraints. It is purely because one side is weak that it should be allowed to do so. But it is an odd notion of fairness that would seek to make the rules of the game optional.

Rodin's position may arise from a confused notion of what *jus in bello* prescribes.

> The problem [whether justice or fairness is to be preferred when the two values conflict] is a component of the well-known tension between *jus ad bellum* and *jus in bello*. . . . The one set of rules tells us when fighting is morally appropriate and why, indeed, it may be morally valuable and important to fight and to win. The other places constraints on the means of fighting, even though this may impinge on the ability to fight effectively and to win. . . . In this sense, at least, the just war theory represents the subordination of *jus ad bellum* to *jus in bello*. This is made absolutely explicit in just war theory, for fighting in accordance with the *jus in bello* is one of the necessary conditions classically identified for war to be *ad bellum just*. (2006, 160)

There are a number of points on which I differ. First, the *jus ad bellum* rules are described in an oddly weak way. They cannot tell us that fighting is morally appropriate without also telling us that it is morally appropriate for only one side. There's no "may be" about the moral value of winning a war fought for just cause to achieve a right intention. If it is morally necessary to go to war, it is morally obligatory to win. One has no business going to war except to win, and one shouldn't go to war unless one has a substantial probability of success.

Second, *jus in bello* rules place deontological constraints upon what may be done in the conduct of war: avoid intentional attacks on noncombatants or civilians, treat prisoners humanely, and observe proportionality in the use of weapons and infliction of death and destruction. All can be justified on grounds independent of other moral considerations bearing upon war. It is mistaken to analogize them to the rules of fair play in a game. Their purpose is not to limit or obstruct a decisive result in the interests of giving both sides a "sporting chance."

Third, following from the second point, there is no good reason for thinking that fairness is a kind of *jus in bello* rule. It is possible that the idea of fairness as morally relevant to just war thought arises from thinking that there is some neutral standpoint from which to assess the moral nature of a war, but it is not clear that there can be any such standpoint from which to judge equally the armed criminal and the police, the rogue state and the United Nations. Further, the leeway Rodin suggests might allow actions that would violate other *jus in bello* rules.

Fourth, it seems exaggerated to take the deontological limits imposed by *jus in bello* as amounting to a subordination of *jus ad bellum* to *jus in bello*, or that violation of them also nullifies the *jus ad bellum* moral case for going to war. The two parts of just war thinking can stand more or less independently of each other. Fulfilling the reasonable probability of success criterion requires doing what is possible to raise that probability. But that does not involve violation of *jus in bello* prescriptions since *jus ad bellum* is not concerned with the conduct of war but with the prior decision to go to war and with whether it can be justified.

Whether such *jus ad bellum* criteria as competent authority, just cause, and right intention are met has nothing to do with how the war is conducted later. A state might be justified in going to war, and its conduct and those of its troops in war-fighting might be morally appalling. The state's bad behavior does not mean it was unjustified in going to war. Merely because one can give definite answers to questions like "Was country *A* justified in going to war?" and "Did country *A* show morally appropriate restraint in fighting it?" does not mean that one can add up the answers to give an answer to some question like "Was the war just?" Moral evaluation of war is primarily moral evaluation of action, and *jus ad bellum* and *jus in bello* concern different actions. No coherent sense, I submit, can be made of interpretations of just war thinking that see *jus ad bellum* as subordinate to *jus in bello*.

Jus in bello conditions impose deontological constraints on what may be done to win the war. However, the right intention condition also imposes deontological constraints of a more immediate and significant kind on what may be done. Intentions to annihilate or subjugate peoples are ruled out as morally wrong. Intentions that would destroy the very good that the war aims at are similarly excluded. A well-conceived right intention is broadly consistent with *jus in bello* criteria such as not directly attacking noncombatants, using minimum necessary force, and respecting the rights of prisoners. Consistency between *jus ad bellum* and *jus in bello* is not the same as subordination of one to the other.

Conclusion

The success criterion is the most practical in nature of the *jus ad bellum* criteria. Even if its development as a criterion was relatively late in the history of just war thought, one can see how it follows naturally from the right intention condition. If right intention is concerned with goals to be achieved and broad strategic policies implemented to achieve those goals, the success criterion asks whether those goals are actually achievable and how likely those strategic policies are to work.

The success criterion also directs us to other practical matters. One is the issue of when to go to war, which turns out to be at the time when success is most likely. Another concerns other success-making factors, including the attitude of one's own citizens as well as the winning of hearts and minds of the population where military operations are to be conducted. Finally, taking the success criterion seriously means rejecting the claim that fairness is a criterion that can be integrated into just war thought.

Notes

1. See Fotion and Coppieters 2002, 79, 89n1, and Statman 2008, 659, for the suggestion that Grotius may have been the first to identify success as a requirement in *jus ad bellum*.

2. After the mid-1970s, many senior US Army officers believed that the US military had labored under a lack of clarity about the strategic goals of their involvement in Vietnam in the 1960s, thereby rendering battlefield victories ineffectual and ultimately demoralizing the troops. Unless the government identifies the goal of going to war clearly, the generals won't know what will count as victory and hence cannot win.

3. On the relationship, see Smith 2006, 12. In 2008–10, US generals concerned identified various political goals (e.g., eliminating or reducing political corruption, reform of the Afghani government, stabilizing local law enforcement) as necessary to ensure a NATO victory in Afghanistan. The generals were aware of the wider political benefit and significance of achieving such goals, but their interest in achieving them arose primarily from their likely contribution to achieving military victory.

4. Johnson 2005a comments: "Exactly when and under what circumstances these began to be used is unclear. John Eppstein, writing *The Catholic Tradition of the Law of Nations* between the World Wars, argues that proportionality and last resort are to be found in the arguments of the Neoscholastics, but the texts he cites do not clearly make the case. It is likely that these prudential criteria reflect the same uneasiness with modern war that gave rise to modern-war pacifism. Argu-

ably they are elements in the prudent exercise of statecraft, but including them as specific requirements of the *jus ad bellum* is a comparatively recent development."

5. The US secretary of defense and the Joint Chiefs of Staff had strongly opposed the mission on the grounds that it had no clear goal and that the marines were likely to become a target.

6. Lincoln's leadership in the US Civil War (1861–65) and Churchill's leadership of Britain after the fall of France in 1940 made just such a difference. In both cases, powerful and influential figures (many of Lincoln's cabinet and generals such as Winfield Scott and George McClellan at the beginning of the war, and British foreign secretary Lord Halifax and former prime minister Lloyd George in May 1940) wanted to stop fighting and come to terms with the other side. In Britain's case, with the Britain-and-France versus Germany phase of the war over and Germany decisively victorious, it is not obvious that Britain had a reasonable probability of success. With the USSR technically Germany's ally and the United States sympathetic but determinedly neutral, Britain had at best a 20 percent chance of defeating Germany. Even after the United States and the USSR became its allies, the failure of the Anglo-Canadian sea-borne assault on Dieppe in 1942 was a forceful reminder that victory was by no means highly probable.

7. See Clausewitz 1976, 89: "As a total phenomenon its dominant tendencies always make war a paradoxical trinity—composed of primordial violence, hatred, and enmity, which are to be regarded as a blind natural force; of the play of chance and probability within which the creative spirit is free to roam; and of the element of subordination, as an instrument of policy, which makes it subject to reason alone. The first . . . concerns the people; the second the commander and his army; the third the government. . . . Our task is to develop a theory that maintains a balance between these three tendencies."

8. In an updating of US policy on use of troops in 1984, Secretary of Defense Caspar Weinberger listed a number of conditions for committing US troops, which became known as the Weinberger Doctrine. The fifth condition was that "troops should not be committed to battle without a 'reasonable assurance' of the support of US public opinion and Congress." See Weinberger 1984.

9. Although hard to quantify, it appears that the casualties suffered by the USSR in Afghanistan in the 1980s played a role in discrediting the Soviet political system. The state of Somalia did not survive its protracted war with Ethiopia in the 1980s.

10. US general George C. Marshall, chief of staff during World War II, is supposed to have remarked once: "Democracies cannot fight a 7-year war."

11. Kennan 1951, 65–66, emphasizes the point. See also Kagan 1995, 202–4, on Britain's vacillation in 1914: as late as August 1, 1914, three days before Britain declared war on Germany, Foreign Secretary Sir Edward Grey had not succeeded in persuading his cabinet colleagues that they would have to stand by France.

12. Perhaps it should be noted that the general public the government must persuade is not to be likened to a group of ethicists or professors; different standards apply (not necessarily lower ones). At the same time, logical arguments are often persuasive; they can make good propaganda.

13. Quinlan 1997, 19: "A nuclear state is a state that no-one can afford to make desperate."

14. See Seybolt 2007, 15, on the absence and the need of serious work on probability of success.

15. Nor would it find any sympathy in Clausewitz, who holds that the nature of war is incompatible with the duelist's ideal of a fair fight.

Chapter 7

Last Resort

Now war broke out in heaven.

—Revelation 12:7

The last resort condition appears to have an intuitively obvious meaning: it would be wrong for a state to go to war until all other options have been tried and failed. Thus, any rapid move to war would appear suspect, as probably violating that condition. Yet appearances can be deceptive. It is possible that the moment of last resort, when war ought to be chosen, might arrive earlier than desired or expected. It is also possible that its arrival might not be recognized by the relevant government.

Britain and France had good reason to think the moment of last resort when war had to be declared had arrived in September 1939 when Germany attacked Poland. But if they were correct to think so, it is hard to see why they should not have judged that it had arrived in 1938 when Hitler threatened war against Czechoslovakia, or that it had arrived in early 1939 when he tore up the Munich agreement and invaded the remnant of Czechoslovakia. There is much to be said for the claim that Britain and France should have gone to war with Germany over Czechoslovakia, thereby implying that the last resort had arrived in 1938.

Natural reluctance to resort to war may hinder democratic states from accepting that the last resort has arrived, much less that it might arrive quickly. The only clear exception governments make to that general attitude is when their own country is being invaded, when one can no longer deny that the last resort has come. But apart from that, there seems to be a common notion that a government can never really be certain that the last resort has arrived since the moral horror of war is surely such that there is always some other option that could be tried instead. There may be options that have not yet been tried, or options already tried that could be tried again: to hold that nothing but war will serve is sometimes viewed as a counsel of despair.

It seems, then, that of all the *jus ad bellum* conditions, the last resort condition is that which we are most likely to see as impossible of fulfillment in practice. It is part of the purpose of this chapter to argue that clarification of the last resort condition shows that this is not so. As a tradition in practical morality, the just war tradition's criteria are capable of fulfillment even though certainty on the matter is usually hard to come by. But it cannot really be questioned that the last resort is sometimes reached if only because a government resisting an invasion can be in no doubt that the last resort has come.

Success and the Last Resort

Throughout this book I have argued that there is a logical ordering of the *jus ad bellum* criteria. Thus, without having a just cause in war, a government cannot have a right intention; without a right intention, having a reasonable prospect of success becomes irrelevant. In this chapter the relevant logical link is the relationship between the probability of success criterion and the last resort criterion.

Without an adequate probability of success, going to war would be irrational; hence, it could not be a practical option for rational choice. If in a given instance there is no reasonable hope of success, it cannot be rational to go to war. If it is irrational to go to war, war is simply not available as an option, even as a final option or last resort. Thus, failure to meet the probability of success condition means that the last resort condition cannot be met, and consideration of it becomes irrelevant.

As a corollary of that claim, the reasonable probability of success condition must also play a key role in identifying the period of time within which going to war would qualify as a practically possible option. If after a certain point in time a previously high probability of success dwindles sharply so that success is now unlikely, the moment of last resort must come—if it comes at all—prior to that point.

Consider the following question: Assuming that competent authority, just cause, and right intention are present, when may a state go to war? It is commonly thought that the correct answer is when the moment of last resort has arrived. It is assumed that the last resort condition has a temporal element to it.

A more accurate answer to when a state may go to war is when the state in question has the best prospect of success. Only during the period in which there is a satisfactory probability of success can the last resort condition be fulfilled. This factor serves as a corrective to the idea that the moment of last resort always recedes into the future, with there always being some other non-belligerent option that can and should be tried first (see Decosse 1992).[1] It can also counter the criticism that claiming the last resort has arrived necessarily manifests a war-hungry aggressiveness.

Because of the importance of meeting the success criterion, the last resort is affected not just by whether other courses of action have been tried or considered but also by factors outside the control of the relevant competent authority. If the state's strategic position relative to its opponent is likely to decline in the coming years, then the last resort—if it comes—must come earlier. That decline may result from factors in international politics, or from growing national economic weakness and consequent military weakness, or from the aggressor's progressively increasing armaments program, or from some similar factor.

A second type of consideration raised in the discussion of intention suggests that part of what having a right intention requires is a shrewd and realistic estimate of the intentions of the aggressor or potential aggressor. The way in which the aggression is threatened or the other political signals that enable the state to discern the intentions and thinking of the other side could indicate either that a slow ratcheting up of pressure, with military action coming much later, is appropriate or that a very rapid military demonstration of will is required.

A third type of consideration affecting the last resort criterion has to do with the strategic nature of any likely conflict. Some states might have large reserves of troops and armaments, or might be able, in the event of an outbreak of hostilities, to afford temporary ceding of a substantial amount of territory to an invading force. Other states might not have such options: for them, the last resort will come earlier.[2]

In all three types of cases, determining whether the last resort has arrived depends on factors that are independent of whether all other means of achieving the appropriate goals of reasonable peace have been tried.

Interpreting Last Resort

Treating the importance of avoiding war as a paramount consideration may be excessive. This is evident in cases where analysis of just cause and right intention has determined that there are important goods at stake. Failure to use force or long delay in doing so may reflect a weakening in commitment to securing or obtaining those goods.

The questions of the nature and importance of those goods and of the degree of urgency with respect to securing them are addressed under the headings of just cause and right intention. The question of how likely in a given instance those goods are to be achieved by force concerns the success condition. The question of when force could be used to achieve those goods is a matter for the last resort condition. The more important those goods are, or the greater the harms that result from not securing those goods, the sooner they should be secured. The last resort criterion should not be taken as mandating as much delay as possible: the cases of actual invasion or genocide are clear examples militating against that interpretation, as also are cases where there is overwhelming evidence that these calamities are imminent.

In view of that, the claim that the *jus ad bellum* theory carries a strong presumption against war is erroneous. It undermines the practical nature of the theory by making the moment of last resort appear to recede constantly and never be reached.[3]

James Turner Johnson criticizes the US bishops' interpretation of last resort:

> The US Catholic bishops in *The Challenge of Peace* [held]: "For resort to war to be justified, all peaceful alternatives must have been exhausted." Stated in this way, the criterion of last resort is effectively impossible to satisfy, for it is always possible to introduce yet another "peaceful alternative," however difficult or unlikely its achievement may be. The language may be that of just war, but the result is pacifist, always ruling out resort to force. For the last resort requirement to be meaningful as a guide to prudence in political decisions, it has to have a different meaning: that a broad range of nonmilitary alternatives must be carefully thought through, and any genuinely promising ones must have been tried and failed to produce the desired result. (Johnson 2005b, 58)[4]

Johnson contrasts requiring that "all peaceful alternatives have been exhausted" and requiring that only "genuinely promising" alternatives have been tried and found wanting. Thus, the contrast is between the range of conceivable alternatives and the narrower range of the alternatives that are not merely practical but "promising" as well. The former suggests that there is a moral requirement to delay going to war as long as possible in order to give time to think up and try out all kinds of nonviolent strategy regardless of their practicality. Johnson supports trying out only those that seem likely to succeed.

I suspect that those who do not consider themselves pacifist yet who hold to the strict interpretation of what last resort requires are assuming that when the last resort arrives, its arrival will be so unmistakable that it will virtually compel the state to go to war. As has been argued, this is a mistake. It is possible that the moment of last resort may arrive and may either not be recognized or not be accepted. In hindsight, the British government that went to war with Nazi Germany in 1939 over Poland would have had good reason to think that the last resort had actually arrived a year earlier. The strict interpreters are afraid of the moral risk of going to war prematurely; they tend not to see that there is also a moral risk of leaving it too late to go to war. Of course, a pacifist would naturally reject such reasoning. But if one is not a pacifist and claims to hold to the just war tradition, then one must be aware of both risks. The US bishops' position on the last resort lies in a kind of incoherent middle ground between pacifism and just war thought arising from a commitment to the idea that the *jus ad bellum* theory contains such a strong presumption against going to war that it converges asymptotically on pacifism.

I am in sympathy with Johnson's idea that it is mistaken to hold an overly strict interpretation of what is required in order to be justified in claiming that the last resort has arrived. This fails to allow that the last resort might, under certain circumstances, arrive very quickly. This is also mistaken in that it forgets or fails to grasp that the last resort condition is an integral part of a theory involving interrelated criteria grounded in a public policy aimed at the good. The individual *jus ad bellum* criteria are not like independent hurdles disconnected from each other, which a judgment in favor of going to war must surmount one by one. An individual criterion cannot be interpreted in a way that ignores its connection to the other criteria: a significant part of the standard for interpreting the individual criterion and for avoiding either excessive laxity or excessive strictness in the interpretation is to make it fit well with the earlier criteria, and thereby with the overall orientation to the good that drives *jus ad bellum*.

Another consideration to bear in mind with respect to the just war tradition's view of the last resort condition has to do with the overall context of the tradition. As is argued in the earlier chapters of this book, the tradition sees the use of armed force under appropriate conditions as an exercise in governance. It does not see it primarily as an act of self-defense. Self-defense, or defense of the national territory, may be involved as part of that good that the state seeks to protect or promote by going to war, but it is not the element that explains or justifies going to war. When a country has suddenly come under unjust attack in the form of invasion, few would argue that the last resort has not come: it must be taken that the goods to be protected by armed resistance require protection so urgently that the last resort is to be presumed to have arrived. However, in the case of the Gulf War of 1990–91, it is odd that people who presumably would have accepted that the last resort had arrived for Kuwait as the Iraqi army crossed its borders in 1990 did not think that the last resort had arrived for the United Nations in going to war against Iraq to liberate Kuwait. It was as though they could not see that the goods were the same, regardless of whether they were viewed from the perspective of the Kuwaiti government or from that of the United Nations or any other interested party. Once Iraq invaded Kuwait, the last resort had arrived. That doesn't mean there was no longer room for negotiations of any kind, and successful negotiations (leading to Iraq's withdrawal from Kuwait) would obviously have removed the need for further war. But what would not be morally acceptable in the *jus ad bellum* view would have been treating those negotiations as taking place between nonbelligerents, where some compromise may be morally acceptable. To assume that attack on one's own state automatically means the last resort has arrived but that this is not necessarily true when an attack is launched against some other state is to misunderstand the fundamental principles underlying *jus ad bellum* thought. It is to give self-defense a moral weight exceeding that of international order, justice, and the rule of law, or even to fail to take the latter seriously as warranting decisive action to maintain them.

In connection with preemptive attack, Johnson writes:

Classic statements of the just war idea did not stigmatize first resort to force because their concern was with responding to injustice, however it might be manifest. They did not prioritize defense against armed attack, and certainly did not define just cause in terms of such self-defense, reflecting Augustine's conception of just war: a Christian might not use force in self-defense because Jesus had forbidden that in his admonition to respond to violence against oneself by turning the other cheek; yet, a Christian might justifiably use force to protect an innocent neighbor against harm. Augustine's aim was not, as Ramsey later saw clearly, to justify use of force to respond to prior use of force—one did not have to wait until the neighbor had been harmed to act—but to show how force might be morally justified to prevent the harm from being delivered. (Johnson 2005b, 116)

Johnson's remarks recapitulate some of the themes of the earlier chapters of this book. In this instance, I am interested in its implications for understanding how to interpret the last resort condition. Taking self-defense as moral paradigm for war is misleading since this suggests that the last resort cannot actually arrive for that state until a violent attack has been made on it. The individual citizen has no moral right to launch a preemptive attack on a likely assailant unless the attack is imminent: the last resort for a person defending himself or herself comes no earlier than minutes before an assault. By contrast, the last resort for a police force seeking to prevent armed attack by a gang on ordinary citizens comes much earlier. The police are both empowered and expected to protect the public and take whatever preventive action—including use of force—is necessary to prevent it.

Accordingly, it is not to be assumed that preemptive military action probably violates the last resort condition. In cases where genocide is credibly threatened and credibly believed to be imminent, not only would preemptive military action not violate the last resort condition; it would also be morally praiseworthy. It would be praiseworthy precisely because it demonstrated shrewdness, foresight, and prudence, thereby saving lives. In such cases, the sensible view of the last resort criterion is that it can be met simply on the basis of the existence of credible threats of imminent genocide.

The Relevance of Intention

In chapter 5 on intention, I argued that governments needed to be clear on what they hoped to achieve by going to war and on how going to war would achieve it. One couldn't really know whether the right intention criterion had been met unless there was a certain degree of specificity about strategic intentions and military goals. Intending peace and justice in a vague and general way does not provide specificity adequate to determine whether the right intention criterion has been met. The last resort criterion increases the pressure for specifics with respect to what the competent authority seeks to achieve. As long as the goal is vague, it will be hard to have clarity as to whether the last resort with respect to achieving it has arrived.

The last resort criterion requires reviewing the range of means for achieving the goal. If a morally appropriate and strategically concrete intention has been identified, it will lead naturally to consideration of possible means for realizing that intention. In that context, the last resort criterion can be taken to be another expression of the point that, since there are certain goods for which it would be appropriate to deploy force, it is necessary to deploy such force in time to secure those goods. In other words, it may be understood not just in the permissive sense of "You may use force only if all other means fail, and you must not be too hasty in resorting to force" but also in the imperative sense of "If on the balance of probabilities you have good reason to believe that all other means are likely to fail to achieve or protect a certain morally valuable good, then you must use force and not be too tardy in doing so."

The greater the specificity of the right intention, the clearer the range of options for achieving it. In some cases, greater intention specificity may show that the only effective way of achieving right intention's objective is by force. This points to a reinterpretation of what the last resort condition involves. The very term "last resort" suggests that typically there is a variety of choices open to the relevant authority, only one of which involves force. With that interpretation in mind, criticism of rapid resort to force in a crisis may well arise from a belief that, regardless of practical considerations, there is always a range of choices. But in some instances, there may be no choice about using force if the good at which right intention aims is to be protected or secured.

Accordingly, the last resort criterion could more aptly be thought of as the necessity criterion. The emphasis should be put not on whether there are other options but on what is the option most likely to be effective in achieving the objective. It is only where, all else being equal, a nonviolent option would be just as effective as using force that the last resort criterion requires choosing the nonviolent option.

The just war tradition does not consider resorting to force as a course of action grudgingly given moral permission. It views the resort to force as something that may be morally required to secure certain important goods. These goods are specified in the right intention criterion with the consequence that the last resort must be relativized to the right intention criterion in a certain sense.

Thus, depending on the moral importance of achieving the goal specified by a right intention, failure to do all that is possible to achieve it may be morally wrong as well as irrational. That claim cannot be deflected by pointing out that *jus in bello* has certain deontological restrictions on going to war, or attempting to argue that these are overriding with respect to *jus ad bellum* criteria. Those restrictions—not attacking noncombatants, not maltreating prisoners, not using disproportionate force—all have to do with preserving the good that is necessarily part of what is intended by a right intention. Thus, they dovetail or harmonize with the idea underlying the right intention criterion that whatever is necessary to achieve the good must be intended and enacted. Delay may be morally culpable not merely because it is delay in bringing about an important good (e.g., stopping genocide) but also because it may compromise its achievement.

The context of application of the last resort criterion is not to be thought of as necessarily involving a number of choices, each of which is equally available to the relevant authority and equally suitable for attaining the objective, with the resort to force being the one that may not be deployed until all the others have been tried. No doubt last resort sometimes is like that. But to see it as generally like that would be mistaken, for it would interpret the last resort as a criterion that required a state to view decision to go to war as something extraordinary, a kind of choice permitted only in extreme and rare conditions.

Given that a government may have to go to war (e.g., because it is morally obliged to use force to preserve good international order or prevent massive human rights violations), the last resort criterion both warns of the necessity of doing so and requires that there be no other viable choice. The combination of the two yields certain implications. One is that a state ought to be ready and able to use force in such circumstances and in proportion to its abilities. It ought not think that war need never be chosen since there are always other options. A second implication is that a state must not stumble into war, being taken unawares and left with no room to maneuver or even being quite unprepared for war. A third is that a state must understand the use of armaments for communication, as in deterrence postures or communicating that it has the political will to undertake certain kinds of conflict.[5]

Negotiation

If going to war is to be the last resort, what are the alternatives to be considered? In some cases, negotiation might be an alternative to going to war. But that applies only to cases where there is such a previous absence of diplomatic contact that the two sides seriously misunderstand each other, and one or both sides is disposed to take precipitous action. Such cases of unnecessary war are rare. With respect to the last resort criterion, however, such cases cast little light precisely because they are cases where just cause is probably lacking. These apart, it is important to see that negotiation is not an alternative to going to war in the way that sanctions, blockade, or other forms of pressure might be. Negotiation as political communication is an intrinsic part of the political context within which alone war can make any sense. Political communication or negotiation does not necessarily stop when war begins and is often resumed even while fighting continues. In addition, the issuing of an ultimatum and the going to war are themselves communicative and hence not disconnected from negotiation.

In cases where country *B* genuinely misunderstands the implications of its policies for country *A* and does not appreciate that its action may constitute a *casus belli*, either *A* has failed to communicate its position clearly or *B* has failed to hear the message. Sometimes one or other of these does happen. In such cases, could one conclude that the last resort has not arrived for *A* or that there is no moral entitlement to claim that it has arrived?

The short answer is that it is never too late to pull back from the brink. *A* is responsible for communicating clearly, particularly with respect to conditions under which it might resort to force. Where *A*'s position was unclear to the wider world as well as to *B*, *A* may have the option of acquiescing to *B*'s behavior without loss of face, assuming *A* is willing to live with the consequences of not resisting *B*'s action. The question of whether *A* would be wrong to do so concerns issues of just cause and right intention. The alternative for *A* is to deliver an ultimatum privately or publicly, thereby providing a final and unambiguous communication so objections that the last resort condition was not met in such cases are easily taken care of by delivery of the ultimatum. *A*'s moral position is not directly undermined by the fact that a climb-down in the face of an ultimatum may be humiliating or politically difficult for *B*.

Where *A* has hoped and intended that *B* will do something foolish or inadvertent to generate a *casus belli* and has not warned *B* clearly, *A*'s good faith is

open to question, and *A* appears to lack what would qualify as a right intention.[6] In that case, whether *A*'s going to war passes the last resort criterion is
irrelevant.

Normally, it is reasonable to assume that communication and negotiation
have been ongoing in attempts, successful or otherwise, to explain to the other
side what would be unacceptable and might lead to armed response. It would
be misleading to suggest that here negotiation is in any strong sense an alternative to war since in such cases it may effectively involve communicating
threats to resort to war.

The presence or absence of the threat of force obviously makes a significant difference to the nature of negotiations. If force has been excluded with
respect to some issue, then war can never be the last resort—not without
being open to the charge of culpable misrepresentation or of misleading communication. If it is not excluded but intimated in some way, then negotiation
is not an alternative, a different strategy opposed to war, but part of the larger
context within which war's role is to be understood.

There is a clear difference, even if it sometimes seems more a fine line,
between indicating that military action may be used in certain foreseeable circumstances and threatening military action outright. It is generally mistaken
and counterproductive to start by threatening.

Sometimes, leaving the other side in uncertainty may be helpful in deterring it or bringing it to negotiate seriously. There are no hard and fast rules
on these points. But if resort to force is an option that may well be contemplated, it is necessary to avoid giving any impression at odds with that to
the other side. In such cases, one negotiates with weapons in the room but
not in one's hands. Two points can be added here. First, ambiguity or uncertainty about what degree of military action may be taken might be helpful
but not ambiguity about the fact that there will be some significant military
reaction. Second, uncertainty is likely to deter only where the consequences
to an opponent of miscalculation are very severe, for example, if they might
involve the use of nuclear weapons. An uncertainty that generates prudence
is welcome; an uncertainty that leads to the opportunist's gamble is not.

Democratic governments may, through making explicit in negotiation
their normal, morally appropriate reluctance to go to war, give the impression
that they are reluctant to go to war on this occasion and hence are not determined to hold their ground and are willing, provided a face-saving formula
can be found, to yield ground for the sake of peace. If that gives the other side
the impression that the government won't fight over the issue, it violates the
last resort criterion for two reasons. First, the criterion requires that the state
be prepared to go to war under certain circumstances, and, second, it requires
that the state not mislead its potential opponent on this matter.

One can't negotiate from a position of strength unless one is prepared to use that strength; one has communicated to the other side, in addition to the broad conditions under which one would use force, one's political determination to use it in those circumstances; and one's threat to use force is credible.[7] In the summer of 1990, as Iraq massed troops on the Kuwaiti border, the US government might not have wanted to contemplate the possibility that Iraq would invade Kuwait and thereby cause war, so it refrained unwisely from even mentioning that possibility to the Iraqi government.

Alternatives

The last resort criterion directs attention to whether there is any alternative with a reasonable degree of probability of being effective within a definite period of time. As with the reasonable prospect of success condition, these are matters of prudential judgment where apodictic certainty is not to be had.

With respect to alternatives, the question arises as to whether meeting the last resort criterion requires that each alternative shall have been actually tried rather than merely considered and rejected as impractical. Brian Orend claims that it does not: "It seems much more plausible to contend *not* that war be the literal last resort—after all other imaginable means have been totally exhausted—but, rather, that states *ought not to be hasty in their resort to force*" (Orend 2006, 58). He goes on to argue that "attention must always be focused on the nature and severity of the aggressor and its actions," suggesting that desires to avoid going to war prematurely or to try alternatives are laudable, but they must not distract attention from the main focus. I agree.

In *The Responsibility to Protect*, the International Commission on Intervention and State Sovereignty (ICISS) has some interesting remarks to make on the topic of last resort:

Every diplomatic and non-military avenue for the prevention or peaceful resolution of the humanitarian crisis must have been explored. The responsibility to react—with military coercion—can only be justified when the responsibility to prevent has been fully discharged. This does not necessarily mean that every such option must literally have been tried and failed: often there will simply not be the time for that process to work itself out. But it does mean that there must be reasonable grounds for believing that, in all the circumstances, if the measure had been attempted it would not have succeeded. (ICISS 2001, 36; sec. 4.37)

The reference to the "responsibility to prevent," whether it be genocide or other massive and widespread human rights violations, is an appropriate reminder of another constraint on understanding the last resort criterion. However, the passage is ambiguous. The first two sentences suggest that the "responsibility to prevent" humanitarian crises can—and ought—be "fully discharged" by nonmilitary means only. This presumes that it is only if such crimes have actually commenced that military force will be used, in the sense of troops engaging in combat.[8] The minor objection to this is that, even if deployment is to prevent genocide by deterring or disarming those threatening to commit it, it still is an instance of military coercion. The major objection must be to the view that the responsibility to prevent could be fully discharged without embracing all possible means, including military means. The duty to prevent genocide has to be one that involves all possible means, and the *jus ad bellum* tradition indicates that it is precisely to fulfill such duties that resort to force is justified.

That said, the main point of interest here is that the authors of the ICISS document do not require that alternative options be actually tried. The context of the ICISS document is the issue of whether and under what circumstances there is a right or duty of humanitarian intervention in a state's internal affairs by outside bodies. The passage in question reflects awareness of the fact that alternatives to military force may seem unlikely to be effective at the period of time when it is crucial that they should be effective. In view of that, the authors of the document take the view that it is not necessary to have actually tried alternative means; it suffices to have good grounds for believing that alternative means would not work. In my view, this is in line with the practical orientation of the just war tradition. It also reflects the idea that, in cases where humanitarian intervention is needed urgently, delay in using the means most likely to be effective may be morally wrong regardless of whether those means involve force.[9]

Accordingly, meeting the last resort criterion is a function not just of giving appropriate attention to alternative strategies but also of assessing how urgent the situation calling for action is. In some cases, for instance, where genocide or massacre or international aggression is imminent, it is appropriate to rely on a reasonable judgment that measures other than force are unlikely to be effective in the short run and hence useless for prevention. Thus, even though no attempt to use the alternatives has been made, the condition can be deemed met since the urgency of the situation allows of no further delay.[10]

When Britain, anticipating an Iraqi attack on Kuwait in the early 1960s, sent a regiment of soldiers to Kuwait, which led to a removal of the Iraqi threat, it did not thereby violate the last resort condition, nor should it have refrained from doing so simply because it was not absolutely certain that invasion was imminent. Had its doing so failed to have that deterrent effect, would we make a different judgment as to whether the last resort had arrived? I doubt it. There are no good grounds for holding that such a response by Iraq would make Britain's decision violate the last resort criterion.

In recent times, arguments for prompt intervention and the use armed force and arguments against excessive emphasis on force being the last resort regularly cite the genocide in Rwanda in 1994. In that case there were frequent warnings of what was likely in the lead-up to the massacres. While serious doubts could be raised as to whether the intervention of foreign troops would have been likely to succeed in preventing genocide, no such doubts apply with respect to the last resort criterion. If we can assume that armed intervention would at least have significantly reduced the death toll, it seems reasonable to suggest in hindsight that the last resort had arrived when those warnings were received (see Wheeler 2000, ch. 7; Seybolt 2007, 70–78).

Accordingly, the idea that the just war tradition contains a strong presumption against war is seriously misleading since it gives the impression that the tradition concerns how to give as limited and grudging a permission as possible to the use of force. It never sees going to war as something morally required but only as something that may be reluctantly permitted on rare occasions. Such a view blocks seeing that the same theory is not just about when going to war is permissible but when it may be, in the interest of prudent policy aimed at the common good, morally required in cases where it is necessary to protect civilian populations against genocide or massacre. The presumption against war should be taken as meaning no more than that war is to be avoided as much as possible. But the just war tradition is not to be taken as endorsing a strong presumption against war since doing so would undermine or sabotage the primary goal of that tradition.[11]

The strong presumption against war tends to suggest that last resort never comes or comes only after a long period of time during which every alternative is exhausted, no matter how ineffective. In view of the arguments advanced in this section, a more appropriate way of understanding last resort is to think of it as simply the least desirable option, but choosing it does not necessarily mean a moral failure on the part of the relevant competent authority. The moral consideration involved in the last resort criterion is of lesser weight than the moral considerations involved in the earlier *jus ad bellum* criteria.

Deterrence

Deterrence is not often viewed as an alternative to war, and for some writers it may seem too warlike to qualify as an alternative. In the Cold War era, talk of deterrence was often confined to talk of the deterrent effect of nuclear weapons, but it is obviously applicable to deployment of other types of military power. While deterrence involves use of armies and weapons systems in the sense that standing armies must be maintained, weapons systems regularly upgraded, and appropriate support systems put in place to make the armed forces effective, this is done partly to ensure that it won't be necessary to use them in an actual shooting war. In that sense, deterrence can count as an alternative strategy in that, adopted well enough in advance, it may work effectively to achieve goals or protect goods that might otherwise have to be fought for.

Like negotiation, deterrence is a kind of communication.[12] It is not a negotiating kind of communication since deterrence is more of a drawing-a-line-in-the-sand kind, informing potential opponents what kind of actions will not be tolerated and will evoke a military response. It is one of the elements shaping a framework for negotiating since it is a way of indicating the limits of tolerance. It communicates the circumstances when the last resort will be reached for the state enunciating the policy. The state must be resolute in its deterrence posture, communicating that resolution to its opponent as well as to its own people. Otherwise, it cannot negotiate from a position of strength.

The 1962 Cuba crisis is generally viewed as the closest that the planet came to World War III, and the hair-trigger readiness on both sides during the Cold War helped to keep in the public mind the fact that the possibility of nuclear war was all too real. But generally, counterfactual wars, unactualized possibilities of armed conflict, are not taken very seriously. Vivid awareness of the horrors of actual wars swamps awareness of wars that nearly were and thankfully were not. That factor may partly explain why people are sometimes skeptical about the claim that deterrence can succeed. But the plausibility of the challenge "Tell me of one war that was avoided" is superficial.

Modern history—starting, say, from 1815—would find many instances where one state has been deterred from courses of action that would have caused war. During the Cold War, US troops were stationed in Western Europe, communicating to both the United States' Western allies and to its opponent, the USSR, that the presence of the American troops would function as a kind of trip wire. Invasion of Western Europe by the USSR and its allies would automatically involve the United States so that it would trigger US military response and would no longer be a matter of choice for the United States. By adopting this policy the United States communicated as clearly as possible that invasion of Western Europe would mean the arrival of the last resort for the United States to use force against the USSR, and arrival in a way that would remove the matter from further deliberation by the US government. To say it worked seems something of a generalization, but the fact that no general war broke out between NATO and the Warsaw Pact for a period of forty years supports the claim. NATO did not intervene to save Hungary in 1956 or Czechoslovakia in 1968, and the USSR drew back from attempting to force the Western powers out of Berlin in 1948 and 1961.

Similarly, in contrast to the frequency of general European wars in the eighteenth and early twentieth centuries, the absence of any such large-scale European war between 1815 and 1914 is striking. In the late nineteenth century, there were instances where pressure from well-armed neighbors induced more aggressive states to refrain from going to war or to make peace, and there were some instances where failure to do so contributed to war.[13] Thomas Schelling argued in his classic work *The Strategy of Conflict*:

> Thus strategy . . . is not concerned with the efficient *application of force* but with the *exploitation of potential force*. . . . To study the strategy of conflict is to take the view that most conflict situations are essentially *bargaining* situations. . . . Viewing conflict behavior as a bargaining process is useful in keeping us from becoming exclusively preoccupied either with the conflict or with the common interest. . . . A "successful" employees' strike is not one that destroys the employer financially, it may even be one that never takes place. Something similar can be true of war. (1980, 5–6; emphasis in original)

While Schelling is referring primarily to limited war, the final sentences of the passage show that he sees it as applicable to forms of deterrence. Once in progress, a war may develop a logic of its own, overriding rational or moral considerations, moving in the direction of absolute or total war. But such occurrences are probably rare. Prior to going to war, and generally during war, a state may have a great deal to lose and is likely to respond to developments in a way that serves its own self-interest. As already discussed, it is not just immoral but also irrational to fight a war one has no hope of winning. Appropriate military deterrence is both a preparation for war and often an effective way of preventing war through its appeal to the rational self-interest of the potential opponent.

Sanctions

Sanctions are often cited as an alternative to war. But the track record of their effectiveness is discouraging. The most significant effect of sanctions imposed by the United States on Japan in the 1930s in response to its military expansion in China was probably that Japan realized that it would have to fight the United States if it wished to achieve its political ambitions in Asia. In that instance, the idea that, for the US government, imposing sanctions was an alternative to going to war makes little sense. At best, it was a prelude to war. If US leaders in the administration or Congress had seriously believed that the imposition of sanctions would prevent war, they were naïve.

One success story may be that of the effect of sanctions in the 1980s in inducing South Africa to dismantle the apartheid system. By contrast, UN sanctions against Iraq that sought to compel Iraq to terminate its weapons development program failed in the 1991–2003 period. The sanctions may have done more harm than good in that the Iraqi dictatorship seems to have manipulated them to hurt the poorer sections of the Iraqi population, thereby arousing international sympathy for their plight and opposition to UN policies.

Overall, sanctions do not seem to work against dictatorial regimes, regimes that have decided to embark on external military aggression, or regimes indifferent to international public disapproval.[14] In the rare case where sanctions were so severe and universally enforced that they threatened to strangle the economy, they might work. The moral objection to such sanctions is that they would heavily penalize and even threaten the lives of a civilian population that had no control over the offending regime. If sanctions were successful within a short period of time, the suffering imposed on the civilian population might be proportionate compared to the alternative suffering of war. Unfortunately, sanctions usually take a long time to work.

The case of the 1991–2003 sanctions on Iraq shows that sanctions can be resisted, and successful resistance may give a state a victory it could not have won on the battlefield.[15] The Iraqi dictator, Saddam Hussein, effectively said as much when, in an interview with Dan Rather of CBS on the eve of the Anglo-American invasion of Iraq in spring 2003, Saddam stated that he hadn't "lost the Gulf War"—that is, the war of 1990–91. In his view, he might have been defeated on the battlefield in 1991, but he was still resisting the will of the United Nations and the United States, so sanctions that had been meant to last only a few months in 1991 but had lasted for more than a decade were to no avail. All he had to do was wait them out and eventually the United Nations would lose the will to enforce them. At that point he would be able to declare victory. Insofar as the imposition and maintenance of sanctions on Iraq had been a continuation of the actual fighting in 1990–91, Saddam could reasonably claim to have defeated the United Nations and the United States in the sanctions phase of the struggle.

In general, it seems clear that in most cases sanctions fail as an alternative to war that will achieve the goal. Only when they are conceived as integral to a larger strategy, of which war is a part, have they much chance of success. In such cases, they function as a deterrent, communicating a convincing threat to resort to force.

Sanctions also tend to be ineffective as a communicative tool designed to prevent war or deter the aggressor because they usually impose no costs on the agent (whether the United Nations or other countries) who imposes them. A threat to go to war involves an undertaking to accept costs, possibly heavy ones, in order to stop the aggressor. The aggressor will typically have some idea of those costs along with his own estimate of whether the country threatening response is willing to accept them. While certain kinds of deterrent strategies may involve costs and hence be more convincing, sanctions rarely involve costs. It is, at present, difficult to understand what message the United States and its NATO allies are trying to communicate to Iran over its alleged program of building nuclear weapons. That the sanctions express displeasure with Iran's policy is obvious enough. Although the United States has said no option is "off the table," thus leaving open recourse to war, it is not clear how the sanctions themselves forward US political goals. The sanctions do not put the United States at risk or impose costs on its allies. At the time of writing, the current or likely future sanctions regime to be imposed on Iran cannot be taken as a convincing deterrent move in the direction of war.

Conclusion

Let me summarize the principal moral aspects of the last resort condition, as discussed in this chapter.

1. Effectiveness in achieving the political good is the central or primary moral value informing the last resort condition. War is often ineffective (as well as costly) with respect to achieving the relevant political goal. The last resort criterion requires prudential evaluation of the practical effectiveness and, hence, moral rightness of sanctions, deterrence, war, or alternative strategies.
2. It is morally obligatory not to resort to war if the same political goal can be achieved effectively and within a reasonable period of time by other means.
3. It may often be morally obligatory and not just morally permitted to use force to achieve the particular good indicated by the just cause and right intention criteria.
4. Because going to war is a serious choice, it may be morally blameworthy for a government or competent authority to find itself with no choice but to go to war if this predicament arises, even in part, from its own earlier political naïveté or lack of realism. In such cases the government, even though blameworthy for its earlier naïveté, does not thereby become unjustified in resorting to force.

5. The last resort criterion is subordinate to the reasonable prospect of success criterion: war cannot be an option of last resort unless there is a reasonable prospect of military success. If there is a window of opportunity, a limited period of time in which there is a reasonable prospect of success but not thereafter, consideration of war as a last resort should be undertaken at that time even if nonviolent alternatives have not been exhausted.

6. Moral considerations relevant to the evaluation of a policy of deterrence include that it be put in place sufficiently in advance to give the potential opponents time to factor it into their calculations and that it be credible.

7. It is morally necessary to be realistic about the effectiveness of sanctions. If the sanctions merely inflict pain but are unlikely to achieve the desired effect, it is irrational to use them and morally wrong to impose pointless suffering on the civilian population. It is also self-deceptive to use them as a way of putting off needed action.

The idea that the just war tradition expresses an overriding presumption against war is particularly misleading with respect to the last resort criterion. It generates two erroneous impressions. The first is that any and every attempt on the part of the relevant authority to avoid war thereby acquires some moral credit or weight that cannot be easily outweighed, and the second is that the sole role of ethics is to object to war and raise the moral barriers against it as high as possible. Points 1, 3, and 4 are incompatible with the presumption against war since it makes it hard to accept or even understand that it might ever be morally wrong not to go to war.

In conclusion, I give some brief schematic comments on when the last resort arrives. First, in cases where armed interstate aggression is imminent or the aggressor's attack is about to commence, the last resort has come for the threatened state. It may well be argued that it arrived earlier, but there can be no question that it has arrived when attack is imminent. This applies even where alternative means of settling the imminent conflict have not yet been tried.

Second, generalizing from the first type of case, in cases where intrastate ethnic conflict, genocide, and the like put civilian populations at imminent risk of armed attack, the last resort has come for the United Nations or other states in a position to intervene. The fact that they may be unwilling to respond is irrelevant to the condition's obtaining. The United Nations or other interested outsiders are not precluded from trying other means at the same time, but whatever good might be done by use of force will often in such cases require immediate military action. In addition, the principle "justice delayed is justice denied" militates in favor of holding that the last resort has come. Justice delayed amounts to letting the aggression and wrongdoing increase. Sanctions are problematic here since—if they work—they work slowly. Thus, last resort is partly determined by the nature of the injustice or aggression and its increasing with the passing of time.

Third, the advent of the last resort may also be determined in part by circumstances peculiar to the side threatened with attack, a point reflected in meeting the reasonable prospect of success criterion. The last resort can be determined to have come in cases where a state has substantial grounds for thinking that there is a high probability that it will be attacked unjustly by another state, and in cases where, even though the attack is not imminent and may be some months away, alternative means to resolve the issue appear ineffective and the state's chances of winning are likely to fall if there is further delay.

Notes

1. The Vatican journal *Civiltà Cattolica* held (in the context of discussing the 1990–91 Gulf War) that the last resort is never reached: "there are always peaceful mechanisms for settling conflicts" and "in practice there is no *extrema ratio*" (Decosse 1992, 117, 123). One could hardly have said that to the Polish government in the early hours of September 1, 1939, as the German army charged into Poland. It is true that there are always peaceful means for settling conflicts (one side can surrender), and it is true in a kind of transcendent sense that all wars are unnecessary. It does not follow that peaceful means are always morally available to the side with just cause, nor does it follow that it is never necessary for the side with just cause to go to war.

2. See Walzer 1977, 83–85, on the Arab-Israeli 1967 Six-Day War. The larger Egyptian and other Arab armies could have fought a long defensive war, whereas the smaller Israeli army depended heavily on reservists who could not be kept mobilized for long. For Israel the last resort would come much sooner than it would have if it had had a much larger army.

3. Michael Walzer takes a tough line on exaggerated ideas of what it means for some course of action to be the last resort. "Taken literally, 'last resort' would make war morally impossible. For we can never reach lastness, or we can never know that we have reached it. There is always something else to do: another diplomatic note, another United Nations resolution, another meeting. . . . Assuming that war was justified in the first instance, at the moment of the invasion [of Kuwait by Iraq in 1990], then it is justifiable at *any* subsequent point when its costs and benefits seem on balance better than those of the available alternatives" (2004, 88).

4. Oddly, some authors fail to make this commonsense interpretation of the criterion. Stanley Hoffmann remarks: "One of the criteria of the theory of just war is deeply flawed: the idea that the resort to force must be postponed until the failure of all attempts at peaceful settlement . . . when a genocide is foretold or predictable, this idea could have disastrous consequences" (2008, x). His misinterpretation of the last resort criterion arises from thinking of it as fulfilled only after one has systematically tried all other nonviolent options, regardless of their effectiveness.

5. It would be too crude to understand this as implying that avoiding war requires arming oneself to the teeth. In some cases that may be what is called for, in other cases it may be a matter of building up certain branches of its military capacity, and in yet others it may mean reducing armaments. Understood in a nuanced fashion, the maxim "If you want peace, prepare for war" holds good since it is another way of saying that peace does not keep itself.

6. Bismarck's engineering Prussia's wars with Austria in 1866 and France in 1870–71 are cases in point.

7. See Schelling 1980, 6–7, for these and other aspects of deterrence.

8. For the ICISS proposals to the UN Security Council in 2001, see Bellamy 2009, 56–58. It is interesting to note that it cites virtually all of the *jus ad bellum* criteria.

9. See Seybolt 2007, 69–70, on the futility of an intervention (in the case of Bosnia 1992–95) involving substantial forces but without a clear mandate to take action and accept casualties.

10. For a judgment to be prudent or reasonable, it is not required that the judgment turn out in hindsight to have been correct. It requires no more than that an unbiased observer would have thought that the agent making the judgment had good grounds for doing so at the time. That applies even if the observer did not necessarily think those grounds were adequate.

11. The presumption against war, deployed as a metaprinciple for the just war theory, leads to pacifist distortion of the theory. See Johnson 2005a: "First, in a phrase invented and popularized by the United States Catholic bishops, Catholic just war thought is represented as beginning with a 'presumption against war,' so that the function of the just war criteria is redefined as only to overturn this 'presumption' in special cases." I concur that this line of thought departs radically from the just war tradition and renders it unusable.

12. As Schelling indicates, it is communication for a certain kind of context: "The deterrence concept requires that there be both conflict and common interest between the parties involved; it is as inapplicable to a situation of pure and complete antagonism of interest as it is to the case of pure and complete common interest" (Schelling 1980, 11).

13. Kagan argues that, had Britain grasped before 1914 the strategic necessity of having the kind of large conscript army the other great powers had, it might

have convinced Germany that it could not win in the west and thereby deterred it from going to war in 1914 (1995, 210–14).

14. In 1998, the United States had various sanctions in place against twenty-six foreign states. For comments on the United States' extensive use of sanctions, their ineffectuality, and the vulnerability to pressure of US politicians from US businesses negatively affected by the sanctions, see "US Backs off Sanctions, Seeing Poor Effect Abroad." *New York Times*, July 31, 1998.

15. Bear in mind Clausewitz's idea that the imposition of one's political will on the opponent is central to what war is about.

Chapter 8

Proportionality

"But what good came of it at last?"
Quoth little Peterkin.
"Why, that I cannot tell," said he:
"But 'twas a famous victory."

Robert Southey, "The Battle of Blenheim"

Proportion and Judgment

Proportionality is the final and most obscure criterion in *jus ad bellum*. Some of its obscurity can be removed if it is accepted that it is logically dependent on the other criteria. If any of the earlier criteria are not fulfilled, the proportionality condition cannot be met.[1] I also hold that proportionality's obscurity is partly unavoidable since it is a kind of "catchall" for any moral concerns not addressed by the other more specific criteria.

The absence of just cause or right intention would mean that in a given instance going to war or resorting to military force would be morally wrong and unjustifiable. Whether there was a reasonable prospect of success or the last resort had come would then be irrelevant since neither would change the fundamental immorality of going to war in those circumstances. Similarly, regardless of how proportionality was defined or understood, it could not compensate or make up for the lack of just cause or right intention.

Oliver O'Donovan highlights a significant aspect of that point in an interesting way:

Proportion . . . has to do with the rational form which [an act of judgment] assumes, i.e., with the shape of a successful act of judgment. The question of proportion has to be raised at two distinct points. On the one hand, since an act of judgment is reflexive, backward-looking, pro-

180

nouncing on a preceding act or on an existing state of affairs brought about by previous acts or failures to act, it has to be proportioned by a truthful description of the wrong done. On the other hand, since an act of judgment is also forward-looking, constituting a law-governed context within which future acts, private or public, are to be performed, it must be proportioned to the state of affairs which it attempts to realize. (2003, 48)

O'Donovan does three things here. He relates proportionality to the wrong or the threat that generates just cause. That's the backward-looking pronouncement on a preceding act. Second, he relates it to the morally appropriate goal or right intention aimed at by the competent authority deciding on war. That's the forward-looking aspect of judging, oriented to achieving a law-governed intention. It is clear that he takes these two as distinct from each other, taking it that right intention is not automatically to be identified with rectifying injustice.

Third, he emphasizes the act of judgment.[2] In discussing just cause and right intention in earlier chapters, I focused on the data, considerations, historical experience, and other contextual factors relevant to making an informed judgment but without adverting to the judgment. In the context of the current discussion of proportionality, I argue that if just cause is lacking or substantially deficient, resort to war will not be a proportionate response. O'Donovan is arguing that the act of judging must be conditioned, limited, or proportioned by the purported just cause or grounds for going to war.

As he notes later, much of the discussion in the literature on the proportionality condition has viewed proportion solely as a relation or balance between the cost of going to war and the hoped-for gains from doing so. In consequence, the judgment of proportionality is treated as purely prospective. That ignores the retrospective aspect of the judgment of proportionality whereby it judges the moral and political significance of the events that constitute just cause.

As should be clear from the earlier chapters, the competent authority empowered and required to make the kind of judgments that bear on war and peace cannot qualify as having a right intention unless its intention is in some way balanced by a reasonable judgment about the cause. However, the proportionality condition contains more than that balance, as will be discussed presently. It suffices here to note that just cause, and not only right intention, is a necessary precondition for passing the proportionality condition. Where the fundamental moral elements of being justified in going to war are missing, going to war would necessarily violate the proportionality criterion.[3]

Finally, meeting the reasonable probability of success and last resort criteria are also necessary for proportionality. If there is no reasonable prospect of
success, there can be no gain to warrant incurring the cost of war. There will
be only cost without gain, loss without benefit, and suffering without justice, so no proportion of any kind can obtain. If the gain or benefit could be
obtained by peaceful means, the loss involved in war is unnecessary. Where
the gain or the good can be had without loss, no proportion can obtain in
resorting to war.[4] It is only when the loss incurred by war is both sufficient
(because it has a high probability of success) and necessary (because it is the
last resort) to achieve the benefit that the possibility of its being proportionate obtains.

Judgment: Then and Now

As in many other areas of practical concern, we can distinguish two kinds of
judgment. There is the judgment made with a view to a decision about practical action, and there is the judgment of hindsight, reviewing the earlier event.
While the latter has the advantage of hindsight, it is not necessarily blessed with
20/20 vision, and its objectivity may be as prone to being compromised as is
that of the earlier judgment. However, for the sake of argument, I will allow
20/20 status to hindsight and assume a high level of objectivity in the retrospective judgment.

The retrospective judgment of hindsight might hold that country A was (or
was not) morally right, justified, or prudent in going (or not going) to war in
a given instance. Insofar as it has an ethical aspect, the historian's judgment is
of that variety.

Ethicists would disagree among themselves regarding the relationship between the two kinds of judgment. The utilitarian or consequentialist holds
that moral evaluation of action depends on actual—not expected—consequences, and on consequences alone. Thus, she would hold that there is no
principled difference between judgment for the purpose of decision and action and judgment in hindsight. The fact that the earlier judgment of consequences, but not the latter, is made with a view to decision is irrelevant to the
evaluation of the earlier judgment. She would also hold that the fact that the
earlier judgment was made under uncertainty and with some lack of knowledge of the consequences is irrelevant.

By contrast, nonconsequentialists would argue that the judgment prior to
action must be evaluated from the context, if not the point of view, of the
agent. The focus cannot be exclusively or even primarily on the actual outcome or consequences but rather on the reasonably foreseeable consequences
at the time of decision and the agent's knowledge and its limits at that time.

In addition, the judgment leading to decision to act has a practical moral significance that consequentialism fails to accommodate.

While the differences between consequentialists and nonconsequentialists are well known, there is a tendency in the literature on proportionality in *jus ad bellum* to conflate the two moments of judgment, adopting the consequentialist stance of hindsight judgment based on the actual outcome. The following passage from Thomas Hurka illustrates the resulting confusion:

> Each proportionality condition [i.e., that in *jus ad bellum* and *jus in bello*] allows two formulations. An objective version assesses a war or act in light of its actual effects, that is, the relevant good it actually produces and its actual destructiveness; a subjective version does so considering only an item's likely effects given the evidence available to agents at the time. Both versions must make some probability estimates: of the likely effect of alternatives that are not chosen . . . and of the magnitude of evils the war does good by preventing. But given their different assumptions about a war's positive effects the two can yield different results, so a war can be objectively proportionate but subjectively disproportionate, or vice versa. (2005, 38)

The utilitarian approach appears in the focus upon actual consequences as the only factor determining the rightness or wrongness of going to war and, hence, as the only thing that can make moral judgment objective. By contrast, the judgment made at the time when the decision to go to war is on the table can be only subjective, which Hurka implies lacks objectivity, having no epistemic access to the actual future consequences.

Several objections can be raised to this. First, this implies that moral theory is not action-guiding in any objective way, and that judgment with a view to action is always the prisoner of an ignorant and distorting subjectivity. That means giving up on the idea of practical moral theory, for a moral theory that requires knowledge of actual consequences of one's action is not action-guiding but merely action-evaluating in hindsight. Such a stance cannot be reconciled with *jus ad bellum* thought since that is meant to guide a government trying to judge whether it would be morally justified in going to war. *Jus ad bellum* thought is not intended for the historian or the pundit trying to determine with the benefit of hindsight whether the decision to go to war was wise. A utilitarian perspective might be of some use to the historian's hindsight judgment but is useless or even misleading to the competent authority seeking to make a prudent judgment with a view to action.

Second, a further objection to Hurka's position is that the judgment of hindsight might not be objective either. Can we say that all the consequences of World War I are now known so that historians can definitively allocate blame between the Triple Entente and the Central Powers? Or all the consequences of the Anglo-American overthrow of Saddam Hussein in their war on Iraq in 2003? Hurka avoids this question, speaking of objective versions of proportionality as if they are accessible with a utilitarian God's eye viewpoint. But a God's eye viewpoint is irrelevant since it is inaccessible, and introducing it may even derail development of a practical conception of proportionality. Besides, without a principled means of drawing a limit or cut-off point for consequences of some event (and utilitarianism explicitly rejects the possibility that there is such a means), it would seem that objective judgments about proportionality are unavailable even a century after the event or war in question.

Third, Hurka's objective/subjective contrast is misleading because it ignores the nature of judgment. All judgments are subjective in the trivial sense that they are made by cognizers or judges: there is no knowledge without a knower, no judgment without a judge, and both knowing and judging are conditioned by the epistemic characteristics (e.g., epistemic virtues) and epistemic context of cognizer or judge. Whether the judgment is to be made prior to decision and action or whether it is a hindsight judgment of evaluation of an earlier decision does make the judgment more or less subjective. In addition, objectivity in judgment is promoted by the subject's epistemic virtues.[5] In light of that, one could argue that objectivity is the fruit or outcome of virtuous cognitive subjectivity, not something divorced from or necessarily at odds with the inherent subjectivity of any judgment. The historian's judgment made in the light of actual consequences could be quite lacking in objectivity owing to intellectual laziness or incorrigible prejudice on the part of the judge. The distinction between the practical judgment oriented to action that the political leader must make and the theoretical judgment the historian may make is useful. But it has nothing to do with the distinction between being objective and being (pejoratively) subjective in cognition.

Fourth, the utilitarian line admits the strange phenomenon of moral luck so that whether the decision to go to war passes the test of proportionality depends, to a significant extent, on luck or chance. We cannot hold people responsible for what they could not be expected to foresee, much less the vagaries of chance. If moral luck is allowed into the theory, it will undermine the moral value of right intention. But since the just war tradition holds that use of armed force can be an important tool for rational action to promote the public good, right intention is central to moral evaluation of that decision. Allowing in moral luck would thus destroy the coherence of *jus ad bellum* since it makes results outweigh the nature of the intention.

As emphasized, *jus ad bellum* is a theory of practical judgment that offers guidance to the competent authority required to decide whether to resort to force. Accordingly, the ethicist's focus is not on the results but on the decision, not on how posterity judges but on how the government judged when it made its decision to go to war or avoid it.

Hindsight claims that the government in question "should have known that such-and-such would have resulted" are sometimes made too easily by journalists, the public, and even on occasion by historians. That the government could have foreseen the actual outcome as one of a range of possible—and foreseeable—outcomes is often correct. But that will not suffice to show that they could have foreseen the actual outcome as the most likely or even highly likely. That Neville Chamberlain and his cabinet did not foresee (and probably could not have foreseen) how terrible World War II would be does not provide evidence that their decision to declare war on Germany in September 1939 violated the proportionality condition. A line of argument that says, "War X led to appalling slaughter and suffering extending well beyond the country suffering the aggression that caused the war, so the decision to go to war cannot pass the proportionality condition" is simplistic since it fails to give adequate attention to the agent and context of moral judgment and decision. Stated in those terms, it dismisses, not explicitly but indirectly, such factors as just cause and right intention. Casualties and suffering are relevant to assessing the proportionality of a decision to go to war, but the idea that they are the only relevant factor arises from an unsustainable utilitarianism. A decision that brings about a war leading to appalling suffering is not thereby shown to be disproportionate. Similarly, a decision to go to war that led to minimal suffering or to immediate capitulation by the other side with no actual fighting is not thereby shown to be proportionate. The focus must remain on how the agent, the competent authority, ought to have chosen given the available knowledge and its limitations.

In the case of Britain and France going to war with Germany in 1939, the example to which I have so frequently referred, it can be misleading to suggest that because and only because of the later war Britain and France acted wrongly in appeasing Hitler over Czechoslovakia. It is not what happened subsequently that should lead to a negative moral evaluation of the British and French governments in 1938–39 but what was known to them at the time of their decision at Munich to give way to Germany and pressurize Czechoslovakia to cede territory.

Applying the foregoing to the issue of proportionality, I claim that *jus ad bellum* is concerned with proportionality in the judgment of the government or other competent authority in going (or not going) to war. It is not concerned with hindsight's verdict or judgment. The historian or other observer may, with hindsight, claim that if that government had known certain things, or if it had paid more attention to what it did know, then it should have decided differently. It also seems to be the case that popular judgment of government action is heavily influenced by perception of actual consequences. However, that should not distract the ethicist from the focus on the evaluation of the moral agent and his or her actions.

The Price of Not Going to War

In weighing whether to deploy and use armed force, the government must try to estimate the costs that result from going to war, including loss of life, destruction of human habitat and degradation of the environment, expenditure of financial resources, political harm, and so forth. It then must consider the goods promoted or harms averted by resorting to arms and must weigh or compare them in some way.

When a government has to weigh going to war and make a decision, often there is also a price to be paid for *not* going to war. One can reasonably expect that in some cases this cost will be less than the cost of fighting. But it should not distract from the salient point that there usually is a cost.

It may be the case, for example, that the cost of war has merely been deferred, not avoided permanently. The deferred cost being foreseeably greater adds weight to the scales in favor of earlier action. That these matters are hard to quantify and weigh is unquestionable, but such an objection would be irrelevant here. A government faced with a situation where international aggression or massive violation of human rights has created the prima facie conditions for armed response, and faced with deciding whether to act with military force, will normally have to weigh the consequences of using force against those of not using force.

Different Views

Attempting to define proportionality would probably yield something uninformative, if not tautologous. Explaining it has to be indirect or circuitous. The first element of its explanation has been generated by considering the logical or conceptual relations between the different *jus ad bellum* criteria, showing that proportionality requires the fulfillment of the earlier criteria or even that the concept of proportionality entails key elements in the other criteria. A decision to go to war that is defective regarding just cause, right intention, reasonable probability of success, or last resort cannot be proportionate. Accordingly, we can take it that understanding what the other conditions involve unpacks some of what proportionality involves.

The earlier conditions, while not absolutely precise themselves, are still more precise than is proportionality. Proportionality is the vaguest of the conditions and the most expansive. We may be able, as I suggest, to explain part of what proportionality involves by explaining what right intention or last resort involve; we cannot explain them by appealing to proportionality.

The second element in explaining or exploring proportionality is to focus on the question, what is to be proportional to what? What kinds of things or states of affairs are to count as costs and what as gains? What are to count as evils and what as goods, whether incurred or averted, gained or lost? There is a wide range of possible candidates.

Alex Moseley sees proportionality in *jus ad bellum* as a relation or balance between the means and the end.[6] However, seeing proportionality as between means and end seems to be a minority view. Brian Orend takes it to involve weighing expected good outcomes against expected evil outcomes (particularly casualties).[7] The US bishops juxtapose the expected good to the damage and costs imposed by war.[8] David Rodin takes it as relating harms inflicted, presumably through war, and goods preserved.[9] Thus, Orend, the bishops, and Rodin see proportionality as about comparing the costs or evils of the war with the gains or goods secured by the war. Casting the net more widely, Hurka suggests that the proportionality condition is about comparing the benefits and harms arising from going to war with those relating to not going to war.[10]

Moseley's formulation is too restrictive since some of the costs may not be part of or integral to the means used to fight the war but may instead be side effects or indirect consequences, not integral or necessary to the means used, rather reasonably foreseeable effects. His way of putting it tends toward conflating *jus ad bellum* proportionality with *jus in bello* proportionality. The latter is more clearly limited to the strategies, tactics, and weaponry deployed in war. By contrast, proportionality in *jus ad bellum* must also take into account longer-term political and economic outcomes, both good and evil, of waging war, and these are not relevant to *jus in bello* proportionality.

Rodin's and the US bishops' views focus on harms and costs incurred by war as what is to be compared with the goods to be protected by war. Orend's formulation is preferable since it more clearly indicates that there may be other relevant harms involved in addition to the casualties and destruction caused by the fighting.

Hurka's line is different in that it directs attention to comparing the outcome (good and evil) of going to war with the outcome (good and evil) resulting from not going to war. That wider perspective suggests a different balancing.

With respect to a particular instance of going to war, Orend's approach places the goods preserved or attained in one scale and the harms incurred in the other scale. If we follow Hurka's line, it could mean using two pairs of scales: the going-to-war scales (that Orend suggests) weighing resulting goods against harms and the not-going-to-war scales weighing resulting goods against harms. Alternatively, one could set the goods preserved or gained by going to war along with the harms incurred by not going to war against the goods preserved by not going to war combined with the harms incurred by going to war.

This wider comparison has some interesting possibilities. It is difficult to compare the harm done by war, including deaths and environmental destruction, with the good preserved by it. Suppose preserving the independence of a small state of two million people from aggressive conquest will involve the sacrifice of eight hundred thousand troops and a national debt that burdens the country for the next twenty years and inflicts significant poverty on its inhabitants. At that price, is the country's independence worth a war? It is hard to say since the goods and harms are so different from each other as to seem incommensurable. If we were to say that the proportion could be quantified, as in "x number of troops may be sacrificed provided the size of the population is not less than y in number," we would be opting for a consequentialist calculus for all values. Since nobody has ever satisfactorily worked out such a calculus, that is not a viable option. Besides, deontologists would tend to hold that such values are incommensurable.[11]

Hurka's approach suggests not a solution to the difficulty but an option for some progress. It allows us to compare like with like. There might be some hope of comparing the goods protected by going to war to those protected by not going to war, and likewise comparing the evils or harms incurred by war and those incurred by not going to war. There may be some commensurability found this way.

Time Sensitivity

An important point to bear in mind in making a comparison is that it must be indexed to a particular time or times. Thus, it is sloppy to speak of going to war or not going to war in the *jus ad bellum* context, as though these were tenseless events. A decision to go (or not to go) to war is made at a particular time in a specific context. Assuming a decision not to go to war against a particular state, a decision made a year later to go to war against the same state would be a different decision. The fact that it is made at a different time points to a different context. Britain and France's decision to go to war against Germany over Poland in September 1939 was not a revisiting and reversing of their previous decision not to go to war against Germany over Czechoslovakia in 1938.

The last point finds concrete application in the exploration of proportionality. A practical decision by a government not to go to war against a certain country is contextual, and part of that is its being a decision not to go to war at that point in time. From 1935 on, the British and French governments were well aware that they might have to go to war with Germany eventually; even Neville Chamberlain hardly thought, after he returned from Munich in 1938, that Britain could never find itself having to face war with Germany. Thus, in considerations of proportionality, the comparison will, among other things, be a comparison of the costs of going to war now set against the costs of going to war later. Consider the following example.

Assume that in 1938 Britain and France had been more politically determined and better armed and had, in alliance with the USSR and Poland (both of whom claimed to be willing to support Czechoslovakia if Britain and France would), gone to war with Germany over Czechoslovakia. Assume that the war lasted one year, and ended in Germany's defeat, with two million dead, mainly Germans and Czechs. Two million dead is a heavy price to pay, regardless of the value of the independence of a democratic Czechoslovakia or the overthrow of the Nazi regime. But if we compare two million dead with the actual number of dead in World War II, we would be glad to accept a cost of two million dead, a far smaller number than the number of those who actually died. Two million dead compared to nobody dead seems seriously disproportionate; two million dead compared to more than forty million or fifty million dead does not seem so disproportionate at all.

The last example may seem like a typical philosopher's hypothetical example and of little practical relevance. Yet it has been the received view among politicians, historians, and the public that Britain and France were right to go war with Nazi Germany in 1939, and that while they may have been well intentioned earlier, they were definitely mistaken in not resisting Nazi Germany over Czechoslovakia. If such moral intuitions are correct, it seems to follow that the proportionality condition must have been more or less met in their decision to go to war with Germany in 1939. While Édouard Daladier and Chamberlain could not have foreseen how destructive the war would turn out, they knew that the USSR would be not be their ally (as it would have been a year earlier in a war to defend Czechoslovakia) but would be Germany's ally, so they necessarily knew that victory would come at a higher price. Insofar as proportionality involves comparison of costs regarding going to war with an aggressor at one time as opposed to going to war with that aggressor at another time, some kind of measuring may be feasible. There is reason to think that the cost of war over Czechoslovakia in 1938 would have been much less than the cost resulting from going to war over Poland in 1939. Insofar as proportionality is comparative, Britain and France's going to war over Czechoslovakia would more clearly have passed the proportionality criterion whereas their going to war over Poland in 1939 does not so obviously pass it.

In 2003, the US government advanced a similar line of thought with respect to Iraq. Given the failure of sanctions, the political resistance of Iraq to the United Nations, Iraq's apparent desire to rearm, its attempt to attack Kuwait again in 1993–94, and the ineffectiveness of military punishments of

Iraq meted out by the US government under President Clinton, was it not the case that sooner or later Iraq would go to war again when it was ready? A war fought later at a time of Iraq's choosing would probably be more bloody than a war fought while Iraq was still weak. Ceteris paribus, the proportionality criterion would be more likely to be met by going to war earlier.

Where that competent authority has reason to think that sooner or later it must confront the aggressor by force, proportionality probably requires it to do so at the time when casualties and other evil effects will be at their lowest.[12] In its dependence on context, meeting the proportionality criterion is rather like paying a reasonable, low, or bargain price. What may count as a bargain price for a house when the market is booming may be seen as exorbitant when the market is in a slump. It is pointless to try to discover what is a low price as such.

Main Elements of Proportionality

First, proportionality is logically dependent upon the other *jus ad bellum* criteria. The dependence is immediate and obvious in the case of the reasonable probability of success criterion and the last resort criterion, both of which (like proportionality) can be seen as prudential or oriented to consequences. They are necessary, though not sufficient, conditions for proportionality to obtain. The relevance of all three depends on the basic justice of the case for going to war, which is a matter of just cause and right intention. As is discussed later, the goods and the justice or rightness involved in just cause and right intention both provide candidates against which the cost of going to war can be measured with a view to assessing its proportionality.

Second, proportionality is a residual criterion. After the other criteria are met, proportionality is meant to capture whatever other relevant moral intuitions may remain with respect to the decision for or against war. Hence, it is in connection with proportionality more than any other of the *jus ad bellum* criteria that the importance and centrality of judgment is apparent. When the competent authority says, "Given that we have adequate grounds for resorting to force, what we intend to do is reasonable and just, we have good probability of success, and no other means is likely to work, is it worth going to war?" in popular parlance, this is the judgment-call moment.

Third, the judgment is (as Oliver O'Donovan claims) both retrospective, concerned with the just cause or grounds for military response, and prospective, oriented to what outcome is desired and sought. At first glance, it would seem that the decision to go to war must be proportionate in both directions—that is, proportionate to both the cause and to the intended outcome.

Fourth, proportionality does not concern solely the costs and gains of going to war on a given occasion. It also concerns the costs and gains of not going to war since not going to war on a given occasion may be merely postponing the inevitable. Democratic states are rarely faced with decisions about going to war where there is no cost arising from not going to war (see Rawls 1999, 92–93).

Fifth, proportionality is a relation between two entities or sets of entities, which could be acts, outcomes, or states of affairs. The question is, what is to be proportionate to what, or in relation to what *x* is *y* a proportionate policy, action, or outcome.

There are two approaches that could be adopted to answer the question. The first seeks to identify, for a given instance where a decision is to be made about going to war, all the goods and evils, benefits and harms, gains and costs connected to choosing war as well as those connected to choosing not to go to war. Included under that heading are goods and benefits foregone or lost as well as evils and harms averted. That will be treated later in the chapter.

The second approach is narrower in focus. It is based on the idea that the proportionality criterion is part of the *jus ad bellum* theory, one of a set of integrated criteria. In this theory, the reasons for going to war are primarily expressed in two of the earlier criteria—namely, just cause and right intention. Assuming that the reasonable prospect of success and the last resort criteria have been met, meeting the proportionality criterion is a matter of showing that the practical response generated by a right intention is not disproportionate to the evil or harm constituting just cause. The underlying idea is that the relevant goods and harms have already been brought into consideration in dealing with the just cause and right intention criteria, and it distracts unnecessarily to cast the net more widely. In addition, the goods and harms figuring in those conditions are those for which the competent authority carries a direct responsibility. This approach will be treated later.

Goods

The just war tradition is one of practical ethical thinking oriented to clarify a particular role of the public authority in promoting the good. As discussed in chapter 2, certain goods are relevant to *jus ad bellum* thought. Some may be directly involved in the just cause and right intention conditions. Together they provide a moral background or context for understanding proportionality. As suggested earlier, the proportionality condition in *jus ad bellum* is a kind of residual criterion directed to asking whether, after the other criteria have been met, there remain any other moral considerations to take into account. For that reason, review of relevant goods is necessary to clarify proportionality.

Each good has some claim to be basic in that none is obviously reducible to any of the others. The goods relevant to judgments of proportionality include (in no particular order) the following.

Human Lives and Physical Integrity

The good of human lives and physical integrity is probably the most important of the relevant goods. The goods involved here can figure on both sides of the ledger, whether preserved or lost as a result of going to war. In intervention to prevent genocide, the deaths resulting or likely to result from genocide will figure on one side of the scale while on the other will be the likely deaths of the intervening country's soldiers or other personnel as well as those of the soldiers of the genocidal regime. In the case of the Anglo-American invasion of Iraq in 2003, the American and British governments cited the good of ending the gross violation of human rights perpetrated by the Iraqi dictatorship against its own citizens over the previous twenty years as a contributory justification for their action of invading with a view to overthrowing the regime.

Material and Economic Well-Being

Even though war may benefit certain industries or sectors of the economy, such benefit is not something that should be weighed in the scale of benefits achieved by going to war. On the other hand, the destruction of crops, food supplies, factories, and all other physical objects and resources negatively affects human material well-being always to some extent and not infrequently to such a serious extent as to verge on life-threatening. Since the advent of nuclear weapons, damage to the environment as a basic life-preserving resource has to be factored into consideration.

The Good of Order

This includes both national and international order. It is less obvious as a good than the previously listed goods. Perhaps it can best be illustrated by considering states that have collapsed following military defeat. It is one thing for the particular government or regime to be removed (for instance, that of the Hohenzollern emperor in Germany in 1918) and replaced by a new regime. It is another thing for the state itself to collapse or for the functioning of government to become impossible. Following a long war with Ethiopia in the 1980s, the Somali state more or less collapsed in the early 1990s. No successor state has clearly emerged as of the time of writing. After the overthrow of Iraq's Baathist regime headed by Saddam Hussein in 2003, moves were made by the occupying powers (with the subsequent support of the United Nations) to establish a democratic regime. However, the violent insurrection or civil war that broke out, much of it aimed indiscriminately at the civilian population, showed the new Iraqi government as lacking the means to impose minimal order for some years after the overthrow of the Baathist regime.[13]

At an international level, there exists no order comparable to that of a well-run state. Nor can the United Nations substitute, except in a fragmentary way, in the case of a failed state. At the same time, the development of international law, treaties, alliances that are not aimed at aggressive and sweeping alteration of the existing international order, as well as the United Nations, and other world bodies all constitute a major part of the fabric of international order.

Justice and respect for human rights can be seen, depending on one's ethical theory, either as goods in themselves or as important elements of what is known in philosophical circles as the Right—that is, that nexus of normative actions, procedures, customs, practices, rules, and laws that promote the Good. Their realization and vindication depend on the existence of basic social order. While promoting democracy and removing oppressive dictatorships is oriented usually to promoting the good of individual freedom and respect for human rights, armed intervention or policies aimed at political destabilization of the dictatorship may attack the good of order, where the overthrow of the dictatorship leads to the collapse of the state.

Moral and Spiritual Well-Being

The notion of moral and spiritual goods can sound vague. They are connected to such notions as that of human dignity, even of national dignity or ethnic dignity. Violations of human rights can easily be seen as attacks on moral and spiritual goods. In the case of the American war of independence (1776–83), the "No taxation without representation" slogan expresses the idea that while a benevolent dictatorship might not attack such goods as human life or economic well-being, it significantly obstructs the realization of the human goods involved in and expressed through participating in legislation and governance and taking civic responsibility.

Even if a particular country decides to submit rather than fight, as Denmark did in April 1940 when invaded by Germany, there is a certain good being denied or undermined by living under a dictatorship, no matter how benevolent, that the people have not chosen. Without a realistic chance of success, a decision not to resist is prudent and hence morally correct. Nevertheless, it may have a moral cost in terms of its inducing national feelings of helplessness, weakness, and submissiveness.[14]

On the other side, going to war often damages people's moral and spiritual well-being, where emotions that are jingoistic, racist, or hate-filled are generated against the peoples of those countries with which their own country is at war.

Honor and Dignity

Somewhat more ambivalent are such goods as honor, prestige, or national dignity. They may appear to have little to do with moral goodness, but appearances may be deceptive. Donald Kagan draws attention to Thucydides's remark that nations go to war from motives of "honor, fear, and interest." He goes on:

> I have found that trio of motives most illuminating in understanding the origins of wars throughout history. . . . That fear and interest move states to war will not surprise the modern reader, but that concern for honor should do so may seem strange. If we take honor to mean fame, glory, renown, or splendor, it may appear applicable only to an earlier time. If, however, we understand its significance as deference, esteem, just due, regard, respect, or prestige we will find it an important motive of nations in the modern world as well. (1995, 8; see also 569)

Selfish national interests and irrational fears can be dismissed here as lacking any moral value and not directed toward objective goods. Reasonable self-interest on the part of national governments is acceptable and is implied in much of what I have said, particularly in the chapters on governance and intention, so no more need be added here.

The idea that honor, respect, due deference, and the like could be moral goods relevant to our topic deserves attention.[15] Perhaps the idea can be illustrated by examples. In the decades prior to Britain's handing Hong Kong back to China in 1997, China could easily have seized it without fear that Britain would attempt to retake it by force of arms. China was much too powerful for Britain to have any hope of successfully resisting, as was generally agreed. By contrast, Argentina's seizure of the British-occupied Falkland or Malvinas islands in the south Atlantic in 1982 was reversible, and that duly happened. While forceful eviction would have been humiliating for Britain in either case, failure to use military force in response to the seizure of the Falklands would have been much more damaging to Britain's international image, causing loss of respect, regard, and prestige. Britain could not have defeated China militarily, so nobody would have expected it to attempt to do so. But failure to stand up to Argentina, a much weaker power that Britain was capable of defeating, would have dismayed its friends and made its allies wonder about its reliability, thereby damaging it politically.

Accordingly, honor (understood in the way Donald Kagan suggests) is a good that is often perceived as important enough to make countries go to war.[16] Regarding proportionality, it is not a good that should rank highly as giving grounds for going to war, although it is reasonable to assign it some weight depending on context. In addition, proportionality considerations should factor into account the honor of the other country. A reasonable degree of respect and deference is one of the goods that must be weighed in discerning a proportionate response.

On this, it is possible to err in either direction. In Britain's dealings with Germany in the 1930s, it probably gave too much weight to Germany's sense of hurt honor that arose from its feeling of being humiliated by the Treaty of Versailles.

The goods listed here are central to questions of proportionality. They can be damaged or undermined by war, they can be promoted by war, and they are worth defending by force against serious attack. For those reasons, they have to be factored in to considerations of whether proportionality would obtain in a decision to go to war or in a decision not to go to war, each decision being subject to the proportionality constraint.

As can be seen, I cast the net widely. First, one must consider the goods and evils involved in going to war as well as those involved in not going to war. Second, potential as well as actual goods and evils are to be considered. Thus, for example, a weighing of goods with a view to deciding whether the proportionality criterion can be met must attend to actual goods that could be lost by war, to actual goods that need to be defended by war, and to possible goods that could be attained by war. Given the well-known futility that besets utilitarianism's project of trying to assign a numeric value to each good or value, I can offer no weighting of the goods listed. All that can be asked of the competent authority deciding on war is that, after considering those goods under attack (figuring in the just cause condition), the goods to be protected or achieved (figuring in the right intention condition), and the cost of achieving that intention (figuring in the success condition), the authority in question must consider whether there are other goods or evils that will be directly or indirectly affected by the decision to be made.

In any case, the onus of proof must lie on the side arguing in favor of going to war.[17] Its proponents have to show how going to war will tend to realize certain goods. This is usually done by directing attention to the values vindicated by going to war in a given instance.

Pursuit of Values

When the basic goods relevant to matters of war and peace are listed, it can often seem as though the cost of going to war can never be proportionate to the goods expected or evils averted. However, it is important to see that the goods in question are not static outcomes but are partly realized in the actions and policies that pursue the values arising from the goods listed earlier. Goods are typically concrete (e.g., food); values are more abstract, having to do with the intelligibility of goods (e.g., nourishment). A state goes to war to protect or regain certain concrete goods (e.g., its independence, its being respected internationally, the lives of its citizens or of the citizens of other states, or access to an important natural resource like water or oil). In so doing, it expresses its commitment to certain values, and thereby seeks to vindicate them (e.g., international order, international law, mutual respect between states, respect for human rights as a universal value, or a modicum of justice with respect to states' access to material goods). A man who resists attack on his wife or child by using force to defend them even if he knows he cannot succeed still vindicates a certain value by being willing to lose the concrete good that is his life in the effort, however futile, to protect them. Some of the values listed in the following as sought in action seem to be among those that could be weighed in any consideration of proportionality in action. (Where there are good reasons for thinking that there is just cause, it will be the case that several of those listed will apply.)

Vindicating the Worth of the Victims

Jean Hampton has drawn attention to the fact that light sentences for relatively serious crimes such as rape involve more than excessive leniency to the offender.[18] They also communicate a sense of how much, or rather how little, the victim's dignity and rights are worth. When Neville Chamberlain in 1938 expressed his abhorrence at the idea of launching a war for, in his words, "a people of whom we know little," he was expressing a sense that the people of Czechoslovakia, or at least Czechoslovakia as an independent state, did not represent a value for which Britain should go to war: they were not worth fighting for. Holding to the worth of persons also implicitly rejects the utilitarian calculus that considers that relatively few victims would not warrant sacrifice of a large number of troops.

Reversing or Undoing the Harm Done to the Victims

Sometimes certain aspects of the harm can be undone or overturned. In the case of a state that has been violently annexed without the consent of its citizens (as in Czechoslovakia in 1938–39 and Kuwait in 1990–91), its liberation is a reversal of that particular harm. In other cases, the possibility of compensating them or making reparations may be realizable.

Preventing Further Harm to the Victims

The harm inflicted on those suffering genocide, gross violation of human rights, or conquest is not necessarily accomplished rapidly. Many of these harms can be ongoing, so there is a value to be vindicated in stopping the genocide, human rights violations, and so on.

Preventing Potential Harm to Others

Whereas the value in the previous instances had to do with the victims, here the value concerns those other groups or peoples likely to be affected by unchecked aggression. Similarly, it can apply to those threatened but not yet affected. This value is obviously relevant to consideration of preventive or preemptive war.

Punishing Aggressors

During the Cold War (1948–89) the idea of just cause being constituted by the need to punish wrongdoing fell out of favor for understandable reasons. Even for ideological partisans on either side, the value of punishing the other side or its leaders was clearly outweighed massively by the costs of doing so. Since the early 1990s, the idea of using military force not merely to stop but also to punish the perpetrators of war or ethnic cleansing (e.g., in Cambodia, Rwanda, or the states of the former Yugoslavia) has gained greater acceptance. In the 2000–2010 period, the European Union made handing over alleged war criminals to the International Criminal Tribunal for the former Yugoslavia in The Hague a condition of granting accession to the European Union or more favorable trading relations with the European Union for Croatia and Serbia.

Thus, more recent developments suggest that the value of punishing aggression is not irrelevant to the moral issues concerning going to war, although there may be circumstances in which its value is slight indeed. The crucial idea is that aggression, like crime, must not pay.

Deterring Future Aggression by That State

In giving sweeping guarantees to Poland following Hitler's aggression against Czechoslovakia, Britain and France no doubt hoped to deter Hitler from any aggression against Poland, but their credibility on that point had been badly damaged by their capitulation over Czechoslovakia. In the late 1940s, the United States developed a policy of seeking at least to contain any further expansion of the Soviet Union's influence. To Western eyes, the coming to power of communist governments in many central and eastern European states appeared to threaten both democracy and the interests of the United States. Particularly in the case of the Korean War, where Soviet- and Chinese-backed North Korea had attacked South Korea in 1950, regardless of whether there had been any provocation, the United States and its allies felt under threat and needed to convince the other side that they were prepared to draw a line in the sand. Attempting to overthrow communist governments in Eastern Europe seemed likely only to provoke war, and that seemed unjustifiable even if the condition of the peoples of those states was one of oppression and absence of freedom. But the values of preventing any further expansion and of convincing the other side that the Western powers were prepared to fight seemed important enough to risk war.

Fighting a limited war is sometimes done in hope that the opponent may refrain from similar aggression in future. It was hoped in 1991 that the speedy defeat of the Iraqi army would deter Saddam Hussein from future attempts to attack Kuwait or any of his neighbors that had contributed troops to the UN campaign to evict Iraq from Kuwait.

Restoring International Order

As noted in the list of goods earlier, international order is an important value. The kind of international order that Germany, Italy, and Japan wished to establish in the 1930s and 1940s would obviously have involved the subjugation and conquest of many other countries on a long-term basis. In many ways that order would have been much like the order produced by any of the great empires of the past in their rise to power through conquest. What was objectionable about the Axis powers' goals was not just the nature of the new order they wished to establish, in all its exploitation and brutalization of others, but also the fact that they intended to bring it about by conquest. That the international order should change is not in itself objectionable; but deliberately bringing change about by force without good reasons is unacceptable.

At the same time, the collapse of various states around the world in recent times and the United Nations' relative impotence to resurrect them suggests that the international community should be slow to overthrow an oppressive regime if it is not ready and able to help put a new government in place. Accordingly, the idea that tolerating a less-than-just order is reactionary and unacceptable now seems impractically idealistic. Even relatively unjust states, provided they are not genocidal, are better than anarchy.

Putting the foregoing more positively, the value involved here is the value of international law. It is a value worth fighting for.

Dissuading other States from Aggression

The failure of the League of Nations in the early 1930s to deal with aggression, particularly in the case of Japan against Manchuria in 1931, encouraged other states to fall back on their own resources and to regard collective security as a mirage. It also encouraged those who wished to resort to force or threats to secure their interests. Determined action to deal with armed aggression or genocidal assaults on one's own population sets a clear standard for other states or groups that might be tempted to do something similar.

Reinforcing One's Own Moral Character by Accepting Some Cost in Defending the Right

There is a positive value in grasping that, just as no town can do without a police force and support from the citizens of that town, so no peaceful or half-just world is possible without willingness on the part of the nations of the world to defend that peace and defend the rights of others. A citizenry jingoistically longing for war against one of its neighbors is in need of reeducation, and the same applies to a citizenry that is strongly wedded to the idea of staying out of other nations' problems, regardless of the consequences or the moral values at stake. Both are bad for what one might call national character or national moral fiber. Following World War II, such small countries as the Netherlands, Norway, Denmark, and Belgium—neutral prior to the war—grasped the futility of neutrality as a way of preserving their independence and committed themselves to collective security.

All the values listed could figure in any calculation or weighing of the proportionality of resorting to force. Proportionate values may center on the victim, on potential victims, on the aggressors, on the world at large, or on one's own country. Such values are not as independent of war as are the goods outlined earlier. They are values significantly expressed through being willing to fight. They may figure in the cause or in the intention with which the state goes to war.

All of the values listed are candidates for filling the role of that for which the suffering and destruction of war might be proportionate. The demand that the world be made a better place in the sense that there be a net gain (usually material gain) in well-being as a result of going to war is a demand that—on the surface, at any rate—is not realizable. Where proportionality is conceived of as a matter of weighing gains and losses in material well-being, it is a condition that probably cannot be satisfied. An approach that focuses on evils avoided rather than gains achieved might be more viable.

Most of the values listed earlier are moral and political in nature. They are not reducible to monetary or material equivalents. A notion of proportionality that could not accommodate them would be impractical, incapable of being used in *jus ad bellum* thought.

Since they are values, ethical theory can accommodate the idea of their being partially realized. Unlike rights, which frequently have an absolutist character, it is possible to accept that a particular value can be vindicated or a particular good achieved only in part or only under certain sets of circumstances. Perhaps the most important moral imperative with respect to those goods and values is that a government's decision with respect to the choice of going to war should not act directly against—that is, attack—those goods or undermine those values.[19]

Putting the preceding two points together, it could be argued that proportionality is not then about achieving good in the sense of making matters better or achieving a net gain in general well-being but about avoiding evil. It involves making a choice between evils rather than between goods, coupled with (or constrained by) the deontologist prohibition of actions that directly and intentionally attack goods.

Proportionality: Between Just Cause and Right Intention

The alternative approach to proportionality identified earlier moves from a focus on goods and values in general to consideration of those goods, and only those goods, directly involved in the particular just cause and particular right intention relevant to the pending decision to go to war.

That the costs of war should be proportionate to what is involved in the just cause seems intuitively correct as a working notion. However, it has a weakness. It assumes that the goal of going to war is simply to reverse or prevent aggression, genocide, gross human rights violation, or injustice in general.[20] Sometimes that is the case, but not always. Where it is the case, we can say in respect of proportionality that the amount of suffering or harm likely to be caused by going to war, including harm to the aggressors, must be proportionate to the harm of the injustice or aggression. If the harm caused by going to war is less than that of the aggression, particularly if resorting to force is successful in preventing or forestalling the aggression, the proportionality criterion has been met. If it is far greater than that of the aggression, proportionality probably does not obtain.[21] If it is equal to or slightly in excess of that of the aggression, it is still possible that proportionality does obtain, since the values of stopping aggression and protecting the innocent and the weak could balance the extra harm caused by war.

In the foregoing case, a course of action's being proportionate to the cause turns out to be the same thing as its being proportionate to the intention.

In cases where good governance requires more than merely reversing the injustice, so that perhaps regime change is judged necessary, just cause is not a useful guide to proportionality. Here, as noted in the earlier chapter on intention, just cause and right intention part company since right intention cannot be "read off" from the just cause as simply the reversal or prevention of injustice. In such cases, since right intention specifies a goal or goals, proportionality has much to do with the intention, and probably right intention is more important than just cause to specifying what would be proportionate.

A key consideration will have to be whether the intention or goal is too ambitious. Assuming that the goal is realistic and that there is a substantial prospect of success, it could still be prohibitively costly in that the use of force may tend to undermine other goods. Thus, considerations of proportionality tend to exercise a restraining influence, seeking to restrict war by limiting what may rightly or prudently be done to realize the intended goal.[22] Even with a right intention and a high prospect of success, the cost could be such that it might be prudent, if not morally required, not to go to war.

The just war tradition understands being justified in going to war within the framework of the exercise of competent authority in suppressing lawless violence and armed aggression against the innocent. In cases where the United Nations or coalitions of willing states intervene to stop genocide or widespread life-threatening oppression, a kind of rough symmetry, proportion, or balance could be expected between the cause and the response: the punishment will fit the crime; the intervention will try to stop the oppression. However, given that the world is not yet at such a level of law-abidingness, such a proportion may not obtain in many other cases. Whether it does or not, for both types of case, it is to the intention of the state under unjust attack or the intention of intervening states that we should primarily look in order to judge whether the proportionality criterion is fulfilled. What is to be proportionate is the response to aggression or injustice so that is more closely related to right intention than to just cause.

In addition, the state or states or the United Nations considering intervening by force may have to weigh other factors to which focus on just cause is not sensitive. The intent that involves the use of force by the relevant legitimate authority must not be disproportionate; it would be unjust to resort to force without adequate reasons. But there is also the kind of force that the aggressor may unleash if confronted; the legitimate authority must take account of that even though it is not morally responsible for the aggressor's unleashing it. This is the prudential element in the proportionality criterion.

Conclusion

The conceptual boundaries of proportionality are wider and less clearly delineated than those of the other criteria of *jus ad bellum*. My principal concern in this chapter has been to cast the net wide enough to include any element that might play some role in judging whether it would be right or permissible to go to war. Here, I summarize those elements briefly.

First, the logical ordering of the *jus ad bellum* criteria and the dependence of the later criteria on the earlier ones tells us a lot about proportionality—namely, that without just cause, right intention, reasonable probability of success, and last resort all being met, the proportionality condition cannot be met. As I have put it, it cannot even arise as a relevant practical consideration if any of them are not met. Where those criteria are met, there will be a strong case for going to war. In such cases, the elements of proportionality will be residual not in the sense of being unimportant but of not needing to rehearse or reexamine the concerns already settled by the other criteria being fulfilled.

Second, precisely because it is the last criterion, one that looks to any residual factors, its application is more dependent on the judgment of the ruler or government than the other conditions. That judgment must pay attention to a number of goods as well as to the values inherent in alternative courses of action.

Third, proportionality need not necessarily be about goods gained or secured. It could be met by a course of action designed to prevent evils or harms. In the decision whether to go to war or not, very frequently the issue will not be a matter of choosing between war or peace but of choosing between war now or war later. In that choosing, consideration will have to be given to the price of peace as well as the price of war.

The vagueness that is perceived to surround proportionality arises from failure to distinguish between the different criteria. I suspect that once they have been met, the issues that might raise concerns about proportionality will stand out clearly. They may be difficult to decide, and it is true that the role of the judgment call is more pronounced here than in the other criteria, but at least they will be identifiable.

Notes

1. For a similar line of argument, see Hurka 2005, 36–37. He suggests that the proportionality condition "incorporates" the other conditions. I think that way of putting it is less clear than speaking of proportionality as presupposing the other criteria or stating that its fulfillment logically entails the fulfillment of the others. Hurka's line risks collapsing the earlier conditions into proportionality.

2. While I have not hitherto adverted to the act of judgment to the degree that O'Donovan does, its importance is implicit in the earlier chapters of this book. My approach is broadly in sympathy with his on this point. In emphasizing the importance of avoiding reification of war, and directing attention to the acts of choosing and fighting war, I direct attention also to the judgments from which such acts emerge. The assessment of whether there is a reasonable prospect of success or whether the last resort has been reached obviously involves judgment or "judgment calls." Less obviously, perhaps, but more importantly, the evaluation of the grounds for war given under just cause calls for a judgment as to the morally and politically appropriate response: judgment is central to right intention.

3. Moseley 2009 touches on this point, arguing that using another state's aggression as an excuse to annex territory or otherwise punish it after having defeated it would violate proportionality.

4. Hurka concurs with respect to the probability of success criterion, but not regarding the last resort condition. "A war can be proportionate, because the destruction it will cause is tolerable compared to its benefits, but not a last resort, because the same benefits could be achieved by less destructive means" (2008, 129). Given the suffering war inflicts, I fail to see how choosing an unnecessary war could ever qualify as proportionate.

5. On the role accuracy, adroitness, and aptness play in good knowing and judging, see Sosa 2007, 22–23.

6. "The final guide of *jus ad bellum* is that the desired end should be proportional to the means used. This principle overlaps into the moral guidelines of how a war should be fought, namely the principles of *jus in bello*" (Moseley 2009). Two points should be noted. First, the desired end must also be foreseeable and achievable: a high-minded but unrealistic end won't do since it tilts the proportionality balance toward war for bad (i.e., unrealistic) reasons. Second, *jus in bello* is irrelevant here. Unless a government, in making its decision to go to war, actually intends to ignore all *jus in bello* conditions or restraints on how it conducts its war, the *jus in bello* conditions do not bear upon the morality of the decision to go to war.

7. "Proportionality: A state must, prior to initiating a war, weigh the *universal* goods expected to result from it, such as securing the just cause, against the *universal* evils expected to result, notably casualties. Only if the benefits are proportional to, or 'worth,' the costs may the war action proceed. (The universal must be stressed, since often in war states only tally *their own* expected benefits and costs, radically discounting those accruing to the enemy and to any innocent third parties.)" (Orend 2008).

8. "The damage to be inflicted and the costs incurred by war must be proportionate to the good expected by taking up arms. . . . This principle of proportionality applies throughout the conduct of the war as well as to the decision to begin warfare" (US Bishops 1983).

9. "The proportionality that is required is between the harm inflicted and the good preserved, not between the types of force employed" (Rodin 2002, 42; see also 114–15).

10. "The proportionality conditions . . . require us to identify the benefits and harms a war will cause, a process that requires comparing the situation that will result from the war with the situation that would have obtained had it not been fought" (Hurka 2008, 129).

11. See Walzer 2004, 89–90, and 137, where he expresses skepticism that anyone knows how to weigh or compare goods and harms in the way that the proportionality criterion appears to require.

12. This is obviously an implication of the reasonable probability of success criterion.

13. Order is a political good, "since the only real political justice is an ordered justice. . . . The failure of the United States to come to the aid of the Hungarian freedom fighters [during the 1956 Hungarian uprising] may have been an instance of the requirements of order warranting the tragic permission of injustice. If so, this was not only because not all of the *ought to be* (the world political good) ought to be by us done, but only that part of it that is congruent with our national good. It was also because the preservation of political order against graver disorder is a part of the good of politics no less than the defense of justice against injustice" (Ramsey 1968, 11).

14. That this was avoided to some extent in the case of Denmark in World War II is reflected in the relatively successful Danish resistance to the attempts to round up Jews for extermination.

15. For some discussion and further references, see Statman 2008, 681–86.

16. Commenting on Kagan's introduction of the idea of honor, Rawls accepts it in part, understanding it as the kind of "proper self-respect" a people or nation is entitled to have. However, he thinks that Kagan fails to give sufficient weight to the different meanings such a notion can bear. Rawls distinguishes (correctly, in my view) between a kind of national self-respect that is "compatible with satisfied peoples and their stable peace" in contrast to the kind of national self-respect that is not thus satisfied, "setting the stage for conflict." See Rawls 1999, 34–35, esp. 34n38.

17. I say this with some anxiety as to how it will be understood. On the one hand, it is morally wrong for states to go to war lightly; there needs to be weighty reasons for doing so. That seems to place the onus of proof that the conditions are met on the advocate of going to war. On the other hand, excessive rigor, holding that the *jus ad bellum* theory contains a strong presumption against war, is to be avoided.

18. See Jean Hampton for an argument in support of the importance of punishment as an expression of the victim's value. "A retributivist's commitment to punishment is not merely a commitment to taking hubristic wrongdoers down a peg or two; it is also a commitment to asserting moral truth in the face of its denial" (1991, 398); and "How society reacts to one's victimization can be seen by one as an indication of *how valuable* society takes one to be" (1991, 412).

19. I follow an idea of John Finnis here, although not necessarily in his sense. See Finnis 1980, 118–25.

20. "Some restriction is needed on the goods that count towards proportionality, and it seems obvious what it should be: the relevant goods are only those contained in the just cause. If a war has certain just aims, the goods involved in achieving those aims count towards its proportionality but goods incidental to them, such as boosting the economy or science, do not" (Hurka 2005, 40). I agree with his desire to screen out irrelevant goods. However, I reject his assumption that the goods involved in just cause are identical to those involved in having "just aims" or right intention.

21. Unless going to war has the effect of preventing or forestalling a significant amount of harm; in that case, such counterfactual harms would also have to be counted. This suggests another reason why right intention may be more important than just cause for pinning down what proportionality involves.

22. See Johnson 1981, 208, and Clark 1988, 70. The line of thought known as limited war tradition places greater weight on proportionality than does the just war tradition.

Conclusion

The Primacy of the Political

The central point of this book on *jus ad bellum* is: politics first. With respect to the decision to go to war, the political must be neither excluded by the moral nor swamped by the legal.

The just war tradition, of which *jus ad bellum* is part, is fundamentally moral in nature. It is good that it has influenced international law, and that international law has gained wider acceptance, however cautious we have to be in making that optimistic judgment. But attempts to make *jus ad bellum* into a precise moral decision procedure are unlikely to succeed, and insofar as the illusion of success is generated, it will typically arise from a depoliticized reading of the *jus ad bellum* criteria. The application of *jus ad bellum* criteria is impossible without giving due weight to the contextual politics. The historical record clearly shows how remote, from one point of view, the *jus ad bellum* criteria are from the complexities of decisions to initiate war. That consideration sometimes leads to a kind of dismissive impatience toward the just war tradition for not quickly rendering a verdict on a particular conflict. But the impatience is unreasonable. To borrow a Kantian analogy, the set of criteria is like a formal schema largely empty of empirical content until filled by the data of historical cases and political tensions.

Regarding the law, it goes only so far: the judicial branch of government cannot usurp the role of the executive, and judicial overreach typically only brings the law into disrepute. Even allowing that the scope of the political is bounded by the law, effective government requires that the scope be broad: overregulation makes for inflexibility, and inflexible policy hinders responsive government.

Accordingly, I have sought to persuade the reader that treatment of the ethics of war must, above all, be historically informed and sensitive to the political context within which decisions to go to war are made, regardless of whether the decision is made by a government, the UN Security Council, or an insurgent group. The judgment made in hindsight by ethicists about the rightness or wrongness of the decision, or made by professors of law about the decision's legality, is a different kind of judgment, typically a nonpolitical judgment. In any case, the legal judgment is necessarily confined to what the law provides and must generally be silent about what the law does not address, so legal theorists have warrant for restraint regarding judgment with political implications.

The ethics professor has no such alibi. A detached stance on his or her part often reflects lack of awareness of the need to give content to the individual criteria, typically yields a judgment lacking political nuance, and too quickly finds the government in question failing to pass the criteria. On the other hand, an official historian may be so close to the events that he or she is either unable to see the big picture or is at risk of rendering an overly sympathetic verdict on the government decision to go to war or not go to war. Still, I deem the danger of the ethicist being too close to the events less than the danger of being too detached from them. Clausewitz's point that war abstracted from the political is meaningless could well be adapted by the ethicist: *jus ad bellum* is a fragment of a moral theory that is useless unless its application is understood as framed by the political.

Uncertain Judgment: The Need for Theory

Description of the political context in a particular instance quickly reveals complexity and obscurity. Not surprisingly, the decision to go to war is rarely made lightly. Even when the government choosing war is bellicose in its outlook or previous track record, there is at least some awareness in that government that the outcome of war is uncertain, and that resorting to arms is inherently dangerous. Judgment that going to war is necessary is a classic instance of judgment under uncertainty.

The uncertainty is firstly epistemic. It is often hard to know if the relevant interests of the state or the people are endangered in such a way that the situation warrants resort to force. It is particularly hard to know what the outcome and consequences of war will be, whether some sort of victory will be achieved, or whether the intentions for which it is undertaken will be realized.

The uncertainty is also moral. Even when it seems clear that war is necessary, the uncertainty of success, the certainty of loss of life, and the unpredictability of the extent of the damage it may wreak will usually weigh heavily upon those who carry the moral responsibility of deciding to go to war. As I have presented the concept of proportionality in *jus ad bellum*, it reflects the uneasy moral sense that probably should be present around decisions to go—or not to go—to war: after just cause, right intention, and probability of success have been determined to be present, there remains the need to judge whether going to war or avoiding war will ultimately "pay off" in a way that is morally acceptable.

Given the epistemic and moral uncertainty, the question may arise for some people: is just war theory any use at all? Given the importance of filling in political context, is an abstract and formal moral theory of much value? The answer to both questions must be yes. It is precisely because of the uncertainty involved that theory is needed. Limited though it is, and unable to provide a decision procedure though it be, some theory to apply in the face of the moral challenge of war and peace is better than to have nothing to follow but the individual's intuitions at the moment of decision. Common sense and ordinary intuition are too subject to bias, too vulnerable to prejudice to substitute for theory. The all-too-human tendency to give excessive weight to one's personal experience needs the corrective of impersonal theory; the emotions that war or the threat of war arouses, whether exultation or terror, require balancing by something more dispassionate in nature.

Claims that the just war tradition is "now out of date," if made as the threat of war looms, ought be suspect as lacking objectivity. It is true that no ethic of war is beyond improvement or criticism, but attempts, in the very moment of decision, to correct the theory or abandon it altogether should be resisted. The theory may (and probably should be) corrected or refined subsequently, when not under the great political pressure generated by war-threatening developments; but it should not be modified when immediate interests and emotional states are all too likely to distort judgment.

Theory is needed not just for good moral decision making about war but also to understand war itself. There are more than a few examples in history of people who are at one point too high-minded or pacifist even to contemplate war as anything other than evil and not long afterward are prepared to support unrestricted warfare regardless of its impact. Some French citizens who were virtual pacifists in early 1939 were prepared by 1942 to commit acts that might nowadays be classified as terrorist. There are many more examples of those who, like the crowds who cheered for war in the summer of 1914, became shortly thereafter utterly disillusioned with all war. One suspects that in such cases what has taken place is not a change in their moral thinking but a change in their understanding of the nature of war. War is not simply a physical phenomenon but one with social, political, and moral dimensions. Those are the dimensions that define war.

Future Conflicts: Goods and Rights

States often seek to deter potential opponents or prepare for the possibility of war with another state in the hope that by so doing they will communicate their resolve to the other country in such a way that war will be averted or that if it comes they will enter it well prepared.

I have suggested it is reasonable to hold that the ethical considerations that are the concern of *jus ad bellum* are also relevant in these earlier stages of political development that might lead to war. It seems odd to hold that the *jus ad bellum* criteria suddenly become relevant only when war is imminent. I have also suggested, particularly in my treatment of the right intention criterion, that failure to be cognizant of and responsive to threats to peace and aggressive policies by certain states may well violate the right intention criterion. While the *jus in bello* part of the just war tradition deals with how a state and its troops should conduct themselves in actual war, the *jus ad bellum* part deals with how a state should conduct itself relative to the possibility of war: it is as much an ethic of how to avoid war as it is an ethic of deciding to go to war.

In 2011–12, the US government initiated its "pivot" to East Asia, seeking to reduce its military commitments in Europe and the Arab world and build up its military and naval presence in the western Pacific. This development was understood as aimed at containing the rising military and naval power of a newly rich China. The ground had been partly prepared for this move some years earlier by development of more cordial relations between the United States and India. The US move was also encouraged by the unease of some of China's neighbors at its perceived aggressiveness in pressing its claim to extended territorial waters in the western Pacific and the South China Sea.

How is US policy in this matter to be related to the concerns that ground just war thought? China does not threaten war at the time of writing, nor can it be claimed that territorial aggressiveness is exclusively found on the Chinese side. The United States might argue, reasonably enough, that it seeks, by a judicious display of political will and military power, to enjoin caution upon China. It has no desire for war with China, nor does it seek to destabilize the Chinese state. At the same time, it is also the case that the United States is signaling its preparedness to resort to force if China should, for instance, engage in war with any of its neighbors in a way that would be perceived as one in which China were culpable.

How could the United States morally justify a policy that may eventually bring it into armed conflict with China? It is here that the emphasis I gave early in the book to the goods that government seeks becomes relevant. At present, China has not clearly violated the rights of other countries or their citizens, so the moral justification of the US policy cannot rest on the value of protecting human rights or states' rights. What are at stake in this matter are the goods of international order. I hold that human rights and their protection are central to any modern conception of the public good. But the public good is not exhausted by human rights or states' rights. There are goods of international policy that, while they cannot override or outweigh (generally) the goods of human rights, are not reducible to the goods of human rights.

The fact that China might grow more powerful militarily and the United States might decline relative to China is not in itself a cause for war. There can be no question of canonizing a particular international order as the best of all possible worlds since the international order is always unjust in some way. But there is a good in some kind of international order, even in a kind of balance of power. A country may rise to become a great power as others decline, and the international order may change accordingly. The primary thing desired is that the rising power will rise gently in a way that does not disturb or alarm its neighbors or make them move into defensive alliance out of fear. It is hoped that China learns the lesson that ancient Athens failed to learn in relation to Sparta, and that modern Germany failed to learn in 1890–1914: do not make your neighbors so fearful of your intentions that they band together against you. There are important goods involved here—goods of a moral nature because they are goods of a political nature—that cannot be interpreted as human rights goods.

It is the goods of the political order, including but not confined to human rights, that constitute what is to be protected and promoted by prudent public policy. Just war theory can only be understood as instrumental to protecting and promoting certain goods, and those goods go beyond human rights.

Updating the *jus ad bellum* Criteria

In this book I have sought to illuminate, clarify, and suggest amended interpretations of the classical just war criteria to be met when a government or the United Nations decides to resort to armed force, or when the leaders of an insurrection decide to take up arms against oppression. While I have argued that the criteria are logically interconnected in ways that have often not been noticed, it is also clear that they do not jointly constitute a decision procedure for going to war. In that regard, the *jus ad bellum* tradition is much like moral theories designed to assist practical judgment, where certainty as to the correct course of action is not to be had. The judgment that war is or is not necessary and the decision to act accordingly are an exercise of practical reasonableness, with all the uncertainties that attend on such exercises.

Because of its integral political dimension, *jus ad bellum* belongs to a theory of governance. While talk about going to war in self-defense might seem analogous to an individual exercising her right to self-defense, the analogy is limited at best and obstructs any kind of informative application to the sociopolitical world which is the context of war. It is also largely inapplicable to historical cases, and an ethical theory concerning war that has only tangential intersection with historical wars is of little use.

Since *jus ad bellum* concerns a certain dimension of political governance, the competent authority criterion can only be met by a political authority. On the other hand, political authority is not to be thought of, as it was in classical and early modern thought on war, as available only to the state. It is true that private individuals cannot constitute a competent authority. Even a ruler cannot constitute a competent authority in the case where his decision to go to war arises from a sense of personal injury or insult, as happened with certain medieval lords and princes. The goods for which a war is launched, whether in attack or defense, are political and public by nature: they cannot be private goods. When a section of the population revolts against oppression, many of those involved may be motivated by outrage at particular incidents of oppressive behavior. But it is only insofar as they form a group cohering around the sense of the public weal in danger and with the goal of political liberation or social justice of some kind being their target that their leadership can qualify as a candidate to be a competent authority in the sense required by just war thought.

Turning to just cause, the concept of what is to count as such has also changed in recent decades. Where once it tended to concern only the security of the state against external attack by other states, it has recently come to be oriented to the rights and well-being of persons and communities, with state security or sovereignty viewed as secondary. It is increasingly felt in much of the world that massive and forceful human rights violations are the moral concern of all humanity. This development, while by no means universal in scope, has significant implications for *jus ad bellum* thought that have yet to be fully worked out.

Much of what is involved in just cause has its counterpart in international law. In some quarters it even appears to be thought that without legal warrant there cannot possibly be any moral justification for going to war or for pursuing any policy that might be perceivable as preparation for possible future war. Of course, one can only applaud the drive to update international law so that it is sensitive to the diverse range of circumstances in which there might be a case for resorting to war so that the goal of appropriate legal regulation of war might be promoted. However, it is unlikely in the foreseeable future that the rule of international law will be so effective that the law alone can determine whether a state has sufficient reason or cause to resort to force.

I have argued at length that *jus ad bellum* is not a moral theory that becomes applicable only when war is looming but one that is relevant to the general conduct of foreign policy. Future possible conflicts ought to be anticipated with appropriate strategies for avoidance, deterrence, or advance preparation. Such policies cannot be covered by international law. Any adequate approach to understanding just cause has to go well beyond what is covered by international law. If, for instance, we assume that Britain and France had just cause to go to war with Germany in 1939, the question arises as to when they first had just cause: at what point did Nazi Germany's policies become a serious threat to the peace and stability of Europe? The point in question was not an occasion of it breaking some law: just cause cannot, without loss of the explanatory power of a flexible political interpretation, be reduced to a matter of breaking international law. A serious violation of international law helps provide legitimacy to the aggressor's opponents, but just cause in *jus ad bellum* is not to be understood as mere law breaking. There could be violations of international law that do not require resort to war, and there could be political and military initiatives taken which do not violate international law yet which give political warrant to others to prepare for defensive war.

At the time of writing, Iran's apparent determination to acquire nuclear weapons has alarmed the United States and European states, not to mention various Arab states with Sunni governments. The Western powers have sought to pressure Iran to modify its policy. Israel has a particular interest in the matter since prominent figures in the Iranian government have publicly made threats to wipe Israel off the map, presumably by using nuclear weapons. The combination of the attempt to acquire nuclear weapons coupled with the explicit and repeated threat to destroy one's country (even if such threats may be mere saber-rattling) constitutes just cause for Israel to go to war. This seems to be the case regardless of whether Iran has formally broken any international laws. Whether Israel would be justified in launching a preemptive strike on Iran is another matter since other criteria must also be fulfilled. The objection to Israel's launching such an attack (which would amount to initiating war) is the substantial possibility that it might not succeed in destroying Iran's nuclear arsenal or that, even if it did, it would be hard to prevent Iran from simply rebuilding its arsenal from scratch.

Right intention is one of the most underdeveloped themes in *jus ad bellum* thought. This is partly due to a tendency to conflate the concept of right intention with, or collapse it into, the concept of just cause. A legalistic approach reinforces this tendency by being inclined, in an ahistorical interpretation, to view right intention as simply a matter of intending a legally sanctioned response to actual or imminent armed attack. The long chapter on intention lays out several reasons why this approach won't do. It also argues that even in the world of law enforcement, more than one morally acceptable strategy might be available. In the world of international politics, a wide range of realizable intentions is possible, although the range may shrink the closer a crisis approaches. During a war, the intentions of the protagonists may change as the war develops. With respect to this criterion, there is much work to be done by ethicists.

Competent authority, just cause, and right intention are the explicitly moral criteria that concern goods, duties, and rights: who has the right to go to war, under what circumstances may they go to war, and what may they permissibly intend in going to war. Reasonable prospect of success, last resort, and proportionality are criteria oriented to pragmatic considerations, arising only when the more directly moral criteria have been met. They are focused on whether the war's goals are achievable and whether, all things considered, it is worth fighting.

The reasonable prospect of success and the last resort criteria are relatively easy to clarify. The most distinctive point in my treatment of them is to propose that it is the reasonable prospect of success criterion, and not the last resort criterion, that is most relevant to the time factor—that is, when to go to war. As writers on strategy have emphasized, the time factor is the one factor that is not within the control of any of the relevant agents. It is when there is both a substantial and the best prospect of success that the moment of decision about last resort arrives.

Proportionality is the most mysterious, vague, and open-ended of the criteria. I argue that clarity about it first requires delimiting it as a residual criterion, covering whatever the other criteria do not touch. There is no point in raising considerations of proportionality until the other criteria have been addressed. A decision to go to war that clearly violates any of earlier criteria cannot be proportionate. But if the decision passes those criteria, it has moved a long way toward passing the proportionality criterion: what needs to be asked then is whether there is any moral consideration left out that reasonably ought to be considered. This is the point at which outcomes and consequences can be weighed, insofar as they have not already been addressed.

The second phase in explaining proportionality is to identify what is being compared or weighed in seeking to identify due proportion. There is a range of options available for answering the question "What is to be proportionate to what?" I favor a comprehensive perspective that considers four factors: the costs and benefits of going to war at a particular time as well as the costs and benefits of not doing so at that time. The relevance of considering those costs relating to not going to war has to do with the fact that, in a case where the other criteria seem to be passed, the authority in question will often have good reason to fear that not going to war on this occasion may merely postpone the evil day to a later time.

There is also a question of whether to consider all harms and benefits with any relation to a particular possible war, or to confine consideration to those harms and benefits directly implicated by the specification of just cause and right intention. Another way of expressing that contrast is to distinguish between, on the one hand, all possible or foreseeable practical effects, whether benefits or harms, as one candidate for proportionality consideration and, on the other hand, only those effects directly intended or foreseen as highly probable, whether desired or merely tolerated, of the decision to go to war. Here lies another area for significant work in the future.

Sadly, war in one shape or another will be with us for the foreseeable future. The task of developing moral theory and reflection must still be pursued.

References

Andréani, Gilles, and Pierre Hassner. 2008. *Justifying War?* New York: Palgrave Macmillan.

Annan, Kofi. 1999. "Two Concepts of Sovereignty." *Economist*, September 18.

Aquinas, Thomas. 1988. *On Law, Morality, and Politics*. Edited by W. P. Baumgarth and R. J. Regan. Indianapolis: Hackett.

Arbour, Louise. 2007. "Time for States to Act on Agreed Responsibilities." *Irish Times*, November 22.

Augustine. 1998. *The City of God against the Pagans*. Edited by R. W. Dyson. Cambridge: Cambridge University Press.

Beiner, Ronald, and W. J. Booth, eds. 1993. *Kant and Political Philosophy: The Contemporary Legacy*. New Haven, CT: Yale University Press.

Bellamy, Alex J. 2009. *Responsibility to Protect*. Cambridge: Polity Press.

Benhabib, Seyla. 2006. *Another Cosmopolitanism*. Oxford: Oxford University Press.

Besson, Samantha, and John Tasioulas, eds. 2010. *The Philosophy of International Law*. Oxford: Oxford University Press.

Bricmont, Jean. 2007. *Humanitarian Imperialism: Using Human Rights to Sell War*. New York: New York University Press.

Buchanan, Allen. 2006. "Institutionalizing the Just War." *Philosophy and Public Affairs* 34, no. 1: 2–38.

Buchanan, Allen, and David Golove. 2002. "Philosophy of International Law." In *The Oxford Handbook of Jurisprudence and Philosophy of Law*, edited by Jules Coleman and Scott Shapiro. Oxford: Oxford University Press.

Bull, Hedley. 1977. *The Anarchical Society*. New York: Columbia University Press.

Caney, Simon. 2005. *Justice beyond Borders: A Global Political Theory*. Oxford: Oxford University Press.

Chayes, Abram, and Antonia F. Chayes. 1995. *The New Sovereignty: Compliance with International Regulatory Agreements*. Cambridge, MA: Harvard University Press.

Chesterman, Simon. 2002. *Just War or Just Peace? Humanitarian Intervention and International Law*. Oxford: Oxford University Press.

Clark, Ian. 1988. *Waging War: A Philosophical Introduction*. Oxford: Oxford University Press.

Clausewitz, Carl von. 1976. *On War.* Edited by Michael Howard and Peter Paret. Princeton, NJ: Princeton University Press.

Coady, C. A. J. 2008. *Morality and Political Violence.* Cambridge: Cambridge University Press.

Coates, A. J. 1997. *The Ethics of War.* Manchester, UK: Manchester University Press.

Coleman, Jules, and Scott Shapiro, eds. 2002. *The Oxford Handbook of Jurisprudence and Philosophy of Law.* Oxford: Oxford University Press.

Coyne, Christopher. 2007. *After War: The Political Economy of Exporting Democracy.* Stanford: Stanford University Press.

Craig, Gordon. 1978. *Germany 1866–1945.* Oxford: Oxford University Press.

Cronin, Bruce. 2003. *Institutions for the Common Good.* Cambridge: Cambridge University Press.

Decosse, David. E., ed. 1992. *But Was It Just? Reflections on the Morality of the Persian Gulf War.* New York: Doubleday.

Detter, Ingrid. 2000. *The Law of War,* 2nd ed. Cambridge: Cambridge University Press.

Dinstein, Yoram. 2004. "Comments on War." *Harvard Journal of Law & Public Policy* 27, no. 3: 877–92.

Doyle, Michael W. 1993. "Liberalism and International Relations." In *Kant and Political Philosophy: The Contemporary Legacy,* edited by Ronald Beiner and W. J. Booth, 173–204. New Haven, CT: Yale University Press.

Doyle, Michael W., and Nicholas Sambanis. 2006. *Making War and Building Peace: United Nations Peace Operations.* Princeton, NJ: Princeton University Press.

Durant, W., and A. Durant. 1968. *The Lessons of History.* New York: Simon and Schuster.

Elshtain, Jean Bethke. 2004. *Just War against Terrorism: The Burden of American Power in a Violent World.* New York: Basic Books.

Etzioni, Amitai. 1995. *Rights and the Common Good: The Communitarian Perspective.* New York: St. Martin's Press.

———. 2004. *The Common Good.* Cambridge: Polity Press.

Evans, Mark, ed. 2005. *Just War: A Reappraisal.* Edinburgh: Edinburgh University Press.

Fabre, Cécile. 2012. *Cosmopolitan War.* Oxford: Oxford University Press.

Feinberg, Joel. 1984. *Harm to Others.* Oxford: Oxford University Press.

Finnis, John. 1980. *Natural Law and Natural Rights.* Oxford: Oxford University Press.

———. 1998. *Aquinas: Moral, Political, and Legal Theory.* Oxford: Oxford University Press.

Fisher, David. 2007. "Humanitarian Intervention." In *The Price of Peace: Just War in the Twenty-first Century,* edited by Charles Reed and David Ryall, 101–17. Cambridge: Cambridge University Press.

Foot, Philippa. 2001. *Natural Goodness.* Oxford: Oxford University Press.

Fotion, Nick, and Bruno Coppieters, eds. 2002. *Moral Constraints on War: Principles and Causes*. Lanham, MD: Lexington Press.

Franck, Thomas M. 2002. *Recourse to Force*. Cambridge: Cambridge University Press.

Frey, R. G., and C. W. Morris, eds. 1991. *Liability and Responsibility*. Cambridge: Cambridge University Press.

Fuller, Lon. 1969. *The Morality of Law*, 2nd ed. New Haven, CT: Yale University Press.

Gaddis, John Lewis. 2005. *The Cold War: A New History*. New York: Penguin.

Gilbert, Paul. 2003. *New Terror, New Wars*. Edinburgh: Edinburgh University Press.

Girard, René. 1977. *Violence and the Sacred*. Baltimore: Johns Hopkins University Press.

Gray, Christine. 2008. *International Law and the Use of Force*, 3rd ed. Oxford: Oxford University Press.

Gray, Colin S. 1999. *Modern Strategy*. Oxford: Oxford University Press.

Greenspan, Alan. 2007. *The Age of Turbulence*. New York: Penguin.

Habermas, Jürgen. 2000. "Bestialität und Humanität: Ein Krieg an der Grenze zwischen Recht und Moral." In *Der Kosovo-Krieg und das Völkerrecht*, edited by Reinhard Merkel. Frankfurt: Suhrkamp.

———. 2004. *Der gespaltene Westen*. Frankfurt am Main: Suhrkamp Verlag. Translated as *The Divided West* (Cambridge: Polity Press, 2006).

Halberstam, David. 2002. *The Best and the Brightest*. New York: Random House.

Haldane, John. 2004. "Natural Law and Ethical Pluralism." In *Faithful Reason*. London: Routledge.

Hampton, Jean. 1991. "A New Theory of Retribution." In *Liability and Responsibility: Essays in Law and Morals*, edited by R. G. Frey and C. W. Morris, 377–414. Cambridge: Cambridge University Press.

Hehir, J. Bryan. 1998. "Military Intervention and National Sovereignty." In *Hard Choices: Moral Dilemmas in Humanitarian Intervention*, edited by Jonathan Moore. Lanham, MD: Rowman and Littlefield.

Hobbes, Thomas. 1994. *Leviathan*. Edited by Edwin Curley. Indianapolis: Hackett.

Hoffmann, Stanley. 2008. "Foreword: Intervention, Sovereignty, and Human Rights." In *Justifying War?*, edited by Gilles Andréani and Pierre Hassner. New York: Palgrave Macmillan.

Holmes, Robert L. 1989. *On War and Morality*. Princeton, NJ: Princeton University Press.

Honderich, Ted. 2003. *After the Terror*. Edinburgh: Edinburgh University Press.

Howard, Michael. 1978. *War and the Liberal Conscience*. Oxford: Oxford University Press.

———. 1983. *The Causes of Wars*. London: Unwin.

———. 2000. *The Invention of Peace: Reflections on War and International Order*. New Haven, CT: Yale University Press.

————. 2001. *War in European History*. Oxford: Oxford University Press.

Hurka, Thomas. 2005. "Proportionality in the Morality of War." *Philosophy and Public Policy* 33, no. 1: 34–66.

————. 2008. "Proportionality and Necessity." In *War: Essays in Political Philosophy*, edited by Larry May, 127–44. Cambridge: Cambridge University Press.

ICISS (International Commission on Intervention and State Sovereignty). 2001. *The Responsibility to Protect*. Ottawa: International Development Research Centre.

Ignatieff, Michael. 2005. *The Lesser Evil: Political Ethics in an Age of Terror*. Edinburgh: Edinburgh University Press.

Jacobs, Francis G. 2007. *The Sovereignty of Law: The European Way*. Cambridge: Cambridge University Press.

Johnson, James T. 1973. "Toward Reconstructing the *Jus ad Bellum*." *Monist* 57, no. 4: 461–88.

————. 1975. *Ideology, Reason, and the Limitation of War*. Princeton, NJ: Princeton University Press.

————. 1981. *Just War and the Restraint of War*. Princeton, NJ: Princeton University Press.

————. 1984. *Can Modern War Be Just?* New Haven, CT: Yale University Press.

————. 1999. *Morality and Contemporary Warfare*. New Haven, CT: Yale University Press.

————. 2005a. "Just War, as It Was and Is." *First Things* 149:14–24.

————. 2005b. *The War to Oust Saddam Hussein: Just War and the New Face of Conflict*. Lanham, MD: Rowman and Littlefield.

Kagan, Donald 1995. *On the Origins of War and the Preservation of Peace*. New York: Doubleday.

Kagan, Robert. 2008. *The Return of History and the End of Dreams*. New York: Alfred Knopf.

Kaldor, Mary. 2007a. *Human Security: Reflections on Globalization and Intervention*. Cambridge: Polity Press.

————. 2007b. *New and Old Wars: Organized Violence in a Global Era*, 2nd ed. Stanford, CA: Stanford University Press.

Kant, Immanuel. 1983a. "Idea for a Universal History from a Cosmopolitan Point of View." In *Perpetual Peace and Other Essays*, translated by Ted Humphrey. Indianapolis: Hackett.

————. 1983b. "To Perpetual Peace: A Philosophical Sketch." In *Perpetual Peace and Other Essays*, translated by Ted Humphrey. Indianapolis: Hackett.

————. 1991. *The Metaphysic of Morals: The Doctrine of Right*. Translated by Mary Gregor. Cambridge: Cambridge University Press.

Kaufmann, Walter, ed. 1982. *The Portable Nietzsche*. New York: Penguin.

Keen, David J. 2007. *Complex Emergencies*. Cambridge: Polity Press.

Kennan, George. 1951. *American Diplomacy 1900–1950*. Chicago: University of Chicago Press.

Kennedy, David. 2006. *Of War and Law*. Princeton, NJ: Princeton University Press.

Kleiderer, John, Paula Minaert, and Mark Mossa, eds. 2006. *Just War, Lasting Peace: What Christian Traditions Can Teach Us*. New York: Orbis Books.

Koskenniemi, Martti. 2002. "Iraq and the Bush Doctrine of the Pre-Emptive Self-Defence." *Crimes of War Project*. Accessed October 28, 2008. www.crimesof war.org/expert/bush-koskenniemi.html.

———. 2004. *The Gentle Civilizer of Nations: The Rise and Fall of International Law 1870–1960*. Cambridge: Cambridge University Press.

Larkin, Maurice. 1988. *France since the Popular Front*. Oxford: Oxford University Press.

Lee, Steven P. 2012. *Ethics and War: An Introduction*. Cambridge: Cambridge University Press.

Luban, David. 1980. "Just War and Human Rights." *Philosophy and Public Affairs* 9, no. 2: 160–81.

———. 1994. *Legal Modernism*. Ann Arbor: University of Michigan Press.

———. 2004. "Preventive War." *Philosophy and Public Affairs* 32, no. 3: 207–48.

———. 2007. "Preventive War and Human Rights." In *Preemption: Military Action and Moral Justification*, edited by Henry Shue and David Rodin, 171–201. Oxford: Oxford University Press.

May, Larry. 2007. *War Crimes and Just War*. Cambridge: Cambridge University Press.

———, ed. 2008. *War: Essays in Political Philosophy*. Cambridge: Cambridge University Press.

McMahan, Jeff. 2006. "Preventive War and the Killing of the Innocent." In *The Ethics of War*, edited by Richard Sorabji and David Rodin, 169–90. Aldershot, UK: Ashgate.

———. 2010. "Laws of War." In *The Philosophy of International Law*, edited by Samantha Besson and John Tasioulas, 493–510. Oxford: Oxford University Press.

Merkel, Reinhard, ed. 2000. *Der Kosovo-Krieg und das Völkerrecht*. Frankfurt: Suhrkamp.

Merleau-Ponty, Maurice. 1964. "The War Has Taken Place." In *Sense and Non-Sense*, translated by Hubert Dreyfus and Patricia Allen Dreyfus. Evanston, IL: Northwestern University Press.

Moore, Jonathan, ed. 1998. *Hard Choices: Moral Dilemmas in Humanitarian Intervention*. Lanham, MD: Rowman and Littlefield.

Moseley, Alex. 2009. "Just War Theory." *Internet Encyclopedia of Philosophy*. www .iep.utm.edu/justwar/.

Murphy, Séamus. 1997. "Notes on Proportionality." *Milltown Studies* 39:78–95.

Neff, Stephen C. 2005. *War and the Law of Nations: A General History*. Cambridge: Cambridge University Press.

O'Brien, William V. 1981. *The Conduct of a Just and Limited War*. New York: Praeger.

O'Donovan, Oliver. 1989. *Peace and Certainty*. Oxford: Clarendon Press.

———. 1996. *The Desire of the Nations*. Cambridge: Cambridge University Press.

————. 2003. *The Just War Revisited.* Cambridge: Cambridge University Press.

————. 2005. *The Ways of Judgment.* Cambridge: Eerdmans.

Orend, Brian. 2006. *The Morality of War.* Ontario: Broadview Press.

————. 2008. "War." *The Stanford Encyclopedia of Philosophy* (Fall ed.), edited by Edward N. Zalta. http://plato.stanford.edu/archives/fall2008/entries/war/.

Pasquino, Pasquale. 1993. "Political Theory of Peace and War: Foucault and the History of Modern Political Theory." *Economy and Society* 22, no. 1 (February).

Paulus, Andreas. 2010. "International Adjudication." In *The Philosophy of International Law*, edited by Samantha Besson and John Tasioulas, 207–24. Oxford: Oxford University Press.

Plato. 1970. *Laws.* Translated by Trevor Saunders. Middlesex, UK: Penguin.

Prins, Gwyn. 2007. "Conditions for *Jus in Pace* in the Face of the Future." In *The Price of Peace: Just War in the Twenty-first Century*, edited by Charles Reed and David Ryall, 236–54. Cambridge: Cambridge University Press.

Quinlan, Michael. 1997. *Thinking about Nuclear Weapons.* London: RUSI Whitehall Paper.

Ramsey, Paul. 1961. *War and the Christian Conscience: How Shall Modern War Be Conducted Justly?* Durham, NC: Duke University Press.

————. 1968. *The Just War: Force and Political Responsibility.* New York: Charles Scribner's Sons.

Rawls, John. 1971. *A Theory of Justice.* Oxford: Oxford University Press.

————. 1993. *Political Liberalism.* New York: Columbia University Press.

————. 1999. *The Law of Peoples.* Cambridge, MA: Harvard University Press.

Reed, Charles, and David Ryall, eds. 2007. *The Price of Peace: Just War in the Twenty-first Century.* Cambridge: Cambridge University Press.

Reichberg, Gregory M., Henrik Syse, and Endre Begby, eds. 2006. *The Ethics of War: Classic and Contemporary Readings.* Oxford: Blackwell.

Riordan, Patrick. 1996. *A Politics of the Common Good.* Dublin: Institute of Public Administration.

————. 2008. *A Grammar of the Common Good.* London: Continuum.

Rodin, David. 2002. *War and Self-Defence.* Oxford: Clarendon Press.

————. 2006. "The Ethics of Asymmetric War." In *The Ethics of War*, edited by Richard Sorabji and David Rodin, 153–68. Aldershot, UK: Ashgate.

Schelling, Thomas C. 1980. *The Strategy of Conflict*, 2nd ed. Cambridge: Harvard University Press.

Seybolt, Taylor B. 2007. *Humanitarian Military Intervention: The Conditions for Success and Failure.* Stockholm International Peace Research Institute. Oxford: Oxford University Press.

Shaw, George Bernard. 1983. *Major Barbara.* London: Penguin.

Sheridan, Richard Brinsley. N.d. *The Complete Plays.* London: Collins.

Shue, Henry, and David Rodin, eds. 2007. *Preemption: Military Action and Moral Justification.* Oxford: Oxford University Press.

Sidgwick, Henry. 1891. *The Elements of Politics.* London: Macmillan.

Slaughter, Anne-Marie. 2005. *A New World Order*. Princeton, NJ: Princeton University Press.

Smith, Matthew Noah. 2008. "Rethinking Sovereignty, Rethinking Revolution." *Philosophy and Public Affairs* 36, no. 4: 405–40.

Smith, Rupert. 2006. *The Utility of Force: The Art of War in the Modern World*. London: Penguin.

Sosa, Ernest. 2007. *A Virtue Epistemology*. Oxford: Oxford University Press.

Sorabji, Richard, and David Rodin, eds. 2006. *The Ethics of War*. Aldershot, UK: Ashgate.

Southey, Robert. 1860. *The Complete Poetical Works of Robert Southey*. New York: Appleton.

Spaemann, Robert. 2006. *Persons*. Oxford: Oxford University Press.

Statman, Daniel. 2008. "On the Success Condition for Legitimate Self-Defense." *Ethics* 118:659–86.

Steinhoff, Uwe. 2007. *On the Ethics of War and Terrorism*. Oxford: Oxford University Press.

Stewart, Rory, and Gerald Knaus. 2011. *Can Intervention Work?* New York: W. W. Norton.

Taylor, Charles. 1995. "Irreducibly Social Goods." In *Philosophical Arguments*. Cambridge: Harvard University Press.

Tennyson, Alfred. 1969. *The Poems of Tennyson*. Edited by Christopher Ricks. Harlow: Longmans.

Tesón, Fernando. 1992. "The Kantian Theory of International Law." *Columbia Law Review* 92:53–102.

Thucydides. 1998. *The Peloponnesian War*. Translated by Steven Lattimore. Indianapolis: Hackett.

Trachtenberg, Marc. 2007. "Preventive War and US Foreign Policy." In *Preemption: Military Action and Moral Justification*, edited by Henry Shue and David Rodin, 40–68. Oxford: Oxford University Press.

Tuck, Richard. 1999. *The Rights of War and Peace: Political Thought and the International Order from Grotius to Kant*. Oxford: Oxford University Press.

Uniacke, Suzanne. 2007. "On Getting One's Retaliation in First." In *Preemption: Military Action and Moral Justification*, edited by Henry Shue and David Rodin, 69–88. Oxford: Oxford University Press.

United Nations. 1945. *United Nations Charter*. www.un.org/en/documents/charter/index.shtml.

US Bishops 1983. *The Challenge of Peace*. Washington, DC: National Conference of Catholic Bishops.

Vasquez, John A. 1993. *The War Puzzle*. Cambridge: Cambridge University Press.

Väyrynen, Raimo, ed. 2005. *The Waning of Major War*. New York: Routledge.

Walt, Stephen M. 1987. *Origin of Alliances*. Ithaca, NY: Cornell University Press.

Walzer, Michael. 1977. *Just and Unjust Wars*. New York: Basic Books.

———. 2004. *Arguing about War*. New Haven, CT: Yale University Press.

Wedgwood, Ralph. 2007. *The Nature of Normativity*. Oxford: Clarendon Press.

Weigel, George. 1987. *Tranquillitatis Ordinis: Present Failure and Future Promise of American Catholic Thought on War and Peace*. Oxford: Oxford University Press.

———. 2003. "Moral Clarity in Time of War." *First Things* (January).

———. 2008. *Against the Grain: Christianity and Democracy, War and Peace*. New York: Crossroad Publishing.

Weinberger, Caspar. 1984. "The Uses of Military Power." Remarks Prepared for Delivery by the Hon. Caspar W. Weinberger, Secretary of Defense, to the National Press Club, Washington, DC, November 28. Accessed January 10, 2010, www.pbs.org/wgbh/pages/frontline/shows/military/force/weinberger.html.

Wheeler, Nicholas J. 2000. *Saving Strangers: Humanitarian Intervention in International Society*. Oxford: Oxford University Press.

Wittes, Benjamin. 2008. *Law and the Long War: The Future of Justice in an Age of Terror*. New York: Penguin.

Yeats, William Butler. 1983. *The Collected Poems of W. B. Yeats*. Edited by Richard J. Finneran. New York: Macmillan.

Index

223